Workbook for Wheelock's Latin

Paul T. Comeau
New Mexico State University

Revised by
Richard A. LaFleur
University of Georgia

3rd Edition, Revised

COLLINS
REFERENCE

A paperback edition of this book was published in 2000 by HarperResource.

COVER PHOTO
Vergil between two Muses, early 3rd century A.D., Musée National du Bardo, Tunis, Tunisia—Giraudon/Art Resource, NY

Wheelock's ™ is a trademark of Martha Wheelock and Deborah Wheelock Taylor

The *Answer Key to the Workbook for Wheelock's Latin,* is available online, only to teachers, professors, and persons studying Latin independently, at www.HarperAcademic.com; the site is password-protected and students enrolled in courses in which *Workbook* assignments are graded will not be issued a password or authorized to use the *Key.*

First Collins edition published 2005.

ISBN-10: 0-006-095642-9

ISBN-13: 978-0-06-095642-4

14 15   GCI/RRD   40 39 38 37 36 35

The WHEELOCK'S LATIN Series

WHEELOCK'S LATIN
Frederick M. Wheelock, revised by Richard A. LaFleur

WORKBOOK FOR WHEELOCK'S LATIN
Paul Comeau, revised by Richard A. LaFleur

WHEELOCK'S LATIN READER:
SELECTIONS FROM LATIN LITERATURE
Frederick M. Wheelock, revised by Richard A. LaFleur

Contents

Editor's Note

When *Wheelock's Latin* was first published in 1956, the book was heralded for its thoroughness, organization, and concision; one reviewer even went so far as to predict that it "might well become the standard text" for introducing mature students to elementary Latin. Now, 40 years later, that prediction has certainly proven accurate. Professor Frederic Wheelock continued to modify and further improve the text himself until his death in 1987, each new edition meeting with additional plaudits. Then in 1995 I had the distinct privilege of editing a major substantive revision of the text, the book's fifth edition, which was intended not to alter the basic concept of the work but rather to enhance it and make it perhaps even more useful to a new generation of students.

With the success of "Wheelock's Fifth," it has become my further good fortune to follow in the steps of Professor Paul Comeau by authoring this comprehensive revision of his *Workbook for Wheelock's Latin,* published in its first edition in 1980. A brief history of the *Workbook*'s conception and first two editions is presented by Professor Comeau in the Preface following these remarks. What he does not say there is how remarkably well received his work was throughout its 15 years in print, right up until the re-design of *Wheelock's Latin* in 1995 necessitated its replacement. From its initial publication, Comeau's *Workbook* provided the ideal companion to Wheelock for students at the college level, mature high-school students, and adults seeking to learn Latin independently. My hope for this new edition of the *Workbook* is precisely as it was for the Wheelock text itself: to enhance the usefulness of an already classic volume for another generation of students eager (as the Latin verb *studeō* so happily implies) to learn, enjoy, and reap the multiple benefits of Latin, the basic language.

Let me briefly survey the contents of this latest edition and point to some of its new features. As just one means of encouraging a more active use of the language in the classroom, the old "Objectives," "Grammar," "Drill," and "Practice Sentences" sections have been retitled *Intellegenda, Grammatica, Exercitātiōnēs,* and *Lēctiōnēs,* and a new section, *Vīs Verbōrum* ("The Power of Words"), has been added. Each chapter begins with a detailed set of objectives, now written as "learner outcomes" and designed to focus the student's attention immediately on the most important new material presented in that chapter. While you should not attempt to complete the workbook's exercises until you have thoroughly studied the corresponding chapter in the text itself, you will find that a preliminary look at the workbook lesson will help direct your attention very specifically to what you are expected to master in the chapter. These *Intellegenda* are immediately followed by a brief Latin greeting (again, modestly intended to encourage a more active use of the language and as a reminder that Latin, like any other language, was first and foremost for its native speakers a tool for communication) and some good advice on the value of memorizing new vocabulary and paradigms by repeating them aloud. Exploit always all of your language acquisition skills—listening and speaking, as well as reading and writing— in your study of Latin, just as you would in learning a modern language.

The *Grammatica* section presents a series of questions, in a variety of formats, designed to focus attention directly upon the newly introduced grammar. Several items on the Roman alphabet and pronunciation, covering material presented in the Introduction to *Wheelock's Latin,* have been included in the first lesson, again to underscore the importance of oral/aural activities in learning the language. The *Exercitātiōnēs* which follow include transformation drills, word and phrase translations, English-to-Latin sentences, and other exercises designed to sharpen your skills in actively manipulating new and recently introduced material.

The *Vīs Verbōrum* section presents exercises with synonyms, antonyms, analogies, and etymologies for the chapter's new vocabulary items, all designed to increase your "Word Power," both in Latin and in English. The final section of each lesson, the *Lēctiōnēs* ("Readings"), includes two types of activities. The Latin sentences provide translation practice and systematic reinforcement of vocabulary from the current and immediately preceding chapters; the reading comprehension questions, most of them written in Latin and many requiring responses in Latin, aim to test your understanding of the reading passages that follow the *Sententiae Antīquae* in *Wheelock's Latin,* while at the same time providing experience in both reading and writing Latin without resorting to English translation. Finally, each chapter concludes with a memorable quotation or motto, a little something to tuck into your chest of Latin treasures.

If you find anything of use or of pleasure in this modest companion to *Wheelock's Latin,* gentle reader, there are many to be thanked: Professor

Paul Comeau, most obviously, both for the original idea and masterful execution of the two earlier, highly successful editions of his *Workbook,* and for the very generous support he has given me with this revision; Professor Wheelock, for giving us all "the classic Latin text," a *sine quā nōn* to countless thousands of Latin students and their teachers and professors over the past four decades; Martha Wheelock and Deborah Wheelock Taylor, Professor Wheelock's daughters, for their tolerance of my editorial meddling and machinations, indeed for their unflagging support of my work with both their father's text and Professor Comeau's companion; my editor at Harper-Collins, Patricia Leasure, and her assistant Rob Amell, for their expert guidance and keen enthusiasm for both the text and workbook projects; my graduate assistants, Lakechia Payne-Davis and Joseph Stanfiel, for laboring in a variety of vineyards essential to this particular harvest; our Classics Department staff, JoAnn Pulliam, Mary Ricks, and Connie Russell, who always pay the price, in one way or another, for my "little projects"; my dean, Dr. Wyatt Anderson, who has firmly encouraged all our Classics Department's endeavors and been a steadfast personal friend; and, lastly, my dear wife Laura, and our children, Jean-Paul, Caroline, and Kimberley (all three of whom still pop into the house now and then), who, taking precedence over our five cats and even my trusty IBM computer, are the very lights of my life.

Richard A. LaFleur
University of Georgia
Summer, 1996

He studied Latin like the violin, because he liked it.
Robert Frost, "Death of the Hired Man"

Preface

This workbook was first published in 1980 as part of the College Outline Series and was intended as a companion to the highly respected *Wheelock's Latin,* by then in its third edition after its initial publication in 1956. The book should not perhaps have been the brainchild of a French teacher with no real credentials in classical languages; and though the venture has enjoyed a modicum of success over more than 15 years and, I believe, been well received in the classical teaching community, I have always felt a certain inadequacy as the author, though always enthusiastic about the endeavor and fully captivated by it.

My initial contact with Latin, as with many of my generation, came through the pre-Vatican II Catholic liturgy in a French-speaking parish as a youngster in the late 1930s. Still vivid are my memories of innumerable Holy Mass or Vesper services recited or sung in Gregorian chant, with much of the text not fully understood. My true introduction to classical Latin and Greek, however, took place on the benches of a typical Quebec boarding school at Joliette, near Montreal, in the early 1940s, where endless hours were spent for more than four years (even on Sundays) translating the ancient languages to and from French, using four-inch thick dictionaries. It was a true "immersion experience"—although, in today's language-teaching community, that term usually applies more to listening and speaking skills than to the reading and writing skills that were so paramount in those days to the teaching of Latin. When I left Canada in December, 1944, and was drafted into the U.S. Army only a few weeks later, I truly felt that my exposure to the classical world had ended.

Little did I know at the time that fate would lead me to earn graduate degrees in French at Princeton University, to spend six years on the faculty at the U.S. Air Force Academy, and, upon my retirement from the Air Force in 1975, to qualify for the position of Head of the Foreign Languages Department at New Mexico State University. One of the first requests made by my new Dean of Arts and Sciences, just a few days before the beginning of classes for the 1975–76 academic year, was that I establish a Latin program. Needless to say, I was not at all sure that I was up to the task. Nevertheless, my first action was to obtain and consult all the available bibliographies for Latin textbooks, and then to select several and quickly order examination copies. After a perusal of the four or five best options, it immediately became evident that none matched the thorough coverage, the efficient and logical organization, and the clear and concise explanations of Professor Frederic Wheelock's text, and so "Wheelock's Latin," as everyone called it in those days, literally became part of my life.

Not only did I have to stay ahead of the students, trying to revive grammatical principles which had lain dormant for years in my subconscious, but I also had to accustom myself to comparing Latin words to English, rather than to French. It was truly amazing, however, that paradigms of declensions and conjugations drilled into my memory some 35 years earlier could be successfully recalled. Thus began a new phase of my academic life with Latin, which lasted from the late 1970s through the 1980s. Within a few months of beginning my first course, I felt a strong need for some device to force my students to commit to learning the grammatical elements by illustrating their newly-acquired knowledge in an ordered, concise format, complete with practical exercises. Out of that need, the workbook project was born.

As I look back, I am delighted that so many students of Latin have diligently used and, I hope, benefitted from the first two editions of this *Workbook for Wheelock's Latin.* I wish to reiterate my debt of gratitude to my wife Ruby, to my editors, first at Barnes and Noble and then at HarperCollins, to my many Latin students who patiently suffered through the loose-leaf phase of the project from 1976 to 1979, to my colleagues who worked with the preliminary version in their classrooms at the University of Texas at El Paso and at New Mexico State University, and finally to the staff members who typed and proofread the manuscript. I am especially grateful and indebted to Professor Wheelock, who, though initially reluctant, later agreed to let his outstanding book be "accompanied." My wife and I had the unique privilege of spending a few hours at his lovely country home in New Hampshire as luncheon guests one summer day in 1981, and I often fondly recall the experience to this day.

I firmly believe that the workbook's existence is now at a crossroads. Professor Richard A. LaFleur, a scholar of stature and Head of the Department of Classics at the University of Georgia, has assumed the task of producing this revised and much improved third edition. It will serve as a fit companion for the recently published fifth edition of *Wheelock's Latin,* also revised by Professor LaFleur and the subject of extremely favorable reviews in the classical language teaching community.

When I retired from active teaching as Professor Emeritus of French, I felt that my professional life was, for all intents and purposes, at an end, and that the list of my publications—mainly in French literature and literary history—would stand undisturbed. I am deeply grateful to Patricia Leasure, Executive Editor at HarperCollins, and her assistant Rob Amell for promoting and pursuing this new edition and especially for persuading Professor LaFleur to accept the role of revision editor. The primary objective was to make the subject matter of each workbook chapter agree with the new, fifth edition of *Wheelock's Latin,* and to integrate its new vocabulary into the workbook exercises. Professor LaFleur has done so much more, however, that what had been an adequate work has now become an outstanding one. The *Workbook*'s new editor has been creative and innovative, improving nearly every feature, from the new Latin titles for the sections of each chapter to the redefined objectives (the *Intellegenda*), the recast grammar questions (*Grammatica*), the varied types of drills (*Exercitātiōnēs*), the more challenging practice sentences and reading comprehension items (*Lēctiōnēs*), and the exciting "Word Power" items of the new *Vīs Verbōrum* sections.

This revised workbook is so improved that it should appeal to the harshest critics, should play a capital role in imparting the knowledge of Latin to today's students, and should convince its teachers to consider *Wheelock's Latin* an attractive, indispensable textbook/workbook package. I consider it a privilege to have had the opportunity to collaborate with Professor LaFleur on this new edition, though my personal contribution has been decidedly meager, and I look forward to the continued resurgence of interest in Latin among American students that the new *Wheelock's Latin* is certain to inspire.

Paul T. Comeau
Las Cruces, New Mexico
Summer, 1996

Preface to the Third Edition, Revised

The third edition of the *Workbook* has been slightly revised to correct a few errata in the previous printing (thanks in particular to John McChesney-Young and Joseph Riegsecker for their assistance in identifying these) and especially to accommodate the new sixth edition of *Wheelock's Latin.* For the considerable success of both books, *maximās grātiās, lēctōrēs!*

Paul Comeau and Richard LaFleur

Workbook for Wheelock's Latin

1

The Alphabet and Pronunciation; Verbs; First and Second Conjugations: Present Infinitive, Indicative, and Imperative Active; Translating

INTELLEGENDA ("Objectives")

Upon completion of this lesson you should be able to

1. Discuss the Roman alphabet and the essentials of Latin pronunciation.

2. Define the five principal characteristics of a verb.

3. Explain the difference between the factors which mark the person and number of an English verb and those which mark a Latin verb.

4. Identify the active voice personal endings of a Latin verb.

5. Form the present stem of a first or second conjugation verb.

6. Recognize, form, and translate the present active infinitive, indicative, and imperative of a first or second conjugation verb.

7. Discuss and apply basic rules of word order and translation of simple Latin sentences.

Salvē, discipula or **discipule!** Whenever you turn to the exercises in this workbook, you should have already thoroughly studied the corresponding chapter of your text, *Wheelock's Latin,* especially the new grammar and vocabulary and even the **Latīna Est Gaudium** section; for this first workbook chapter you should also review carefully the pages on "The Alphabet and Pronunciation" in the text's Introduction. And remember always to memorize new paradigms (model conjugations and declensions) as well as vocabulary *by repeating the words aloud.* **Bonam fortūnam!** (*Good luck!*)

GRAMMATICA ("Grammar")

1. The Roman alphabet was like ours except that it lacked the letters ___ and ___, and the letter ___ originally stood for both the vowel **u** and the consonant **w.**

2. Long vowels were generally pronounced about _____ as long as short vowels.

3. Long **a** was pronounced as in (circle the correct answer)
    a. date   b. hat   c. father   d. Dinah

4. Long **e** was pronounced as in
    a. they   b. knee   c. pet   d. enough

5. Long **i** was pronounced as in
    a. ice   b. machine   c. pin   d. Latin

6. Long **o** was pronounced as in
    a. off   b. mother   c. women   d. over

7. Short **u** was pronounced as in
    a. put   b. unite   c. rude   d. rough

8. Which word does *not* contain a diphthong?
    a. saepe   b. poena   c. patria   d. nauta

9. Which word does *not* contain a diphthong?
    a. huius   b. fuit   c. cui   d. huic

10. **B** had the sound of ___ before **s** and **t.**

11. In the phrase "ice cream," the word _____ illustrates the sound of Latin **c.**

12. In the phrase "green gemstone," the word _____ illustrates the sound of Latin **g.**

13. When used before a vowel at the beginning of a word Latin **i** had the
sound of English ____.

14. Latin **qu** was pronounced as in "antique" or "quick"? _____

15. **S** was always pronounced as in
a. sight   b. easy   c. aisle   d. rise

16. Which illustrates the sound of Latin **t**?
a. nation   b. fraction   c. time   d. through

17. The consonant **v** had the sound of English ____.

18. **Ph** was pronounced as in "philology" or "uphill"? _____

19. A Latin word has as many syllables as it has _____
and _____.

20. Syllabify the following words, underline the long syllables, and mark
the accent (e.g., **c͞on-sér-vat**).

a. amō _____   b. salvēre _____

c. sententiae _____   d. philosophiā _____

e. antīqua _____   f. iuvāte _____

21. The person and number of an English verb are determined by
its _____.

22. The person and number of a Latin verb are determined by
its _____.

23. Write the personal endings for the active voice of a Latin verb and
give the English pronoun equivalent to each.

| **Singular** | | **Plural** | |
Latin Ending	**English Pronoun(s)**	**Latin Ending**	**English Pronoun(s)**
1. ___ or ___ = _____		1. _____ = _____	
2. _____ = _____		2. _____ = _____	
3. _____ = _____		3. _____ = _____	

Name: _____   Section: _____   Date: _____

24. The present active infinitive of the Latin verb which means *to praise* is _____. (It will serve as the model verb for the first conjugation throughout the course.)

25. The present active infinitive of the Latin verb which means *to advise* is _____. (It will serve as the model for the second conjugation throughout the course.)

26. The following forms are _____ of Latin verbs. Identify the conjugation to which they belong and their English meaning.

	Conjugation	Meaning(s)
a. vidēre	_____	_____
b. dare	_____	_____
c. valēre	_____	_____
d. cōgitāre	_____	_____
e. dēbēre	_____	_____
f. amāre	_____	_____

27. The present stem is formed by dropping _____ from the _____.

28. Conjugate **amō** in the present indicative active and provide the three English translations for each form.

Latin	English Translation 1	English Translation 2	English Translation 3
Singular			
1. _____	_____	_____	_____
2. _____	_____	_____	_____
3. _____	_____	_____	_____
Plural			
1. _____	_____	_____	_____
2. _____	_____	_____	_____
3. _____	_____	_____	_____

29. Conjugate **dēbeō** in the present indicative active and provide the three English translations for each form.

Latin	English Translation 1	English Translation 2	English Translation 3
Singular			
1. _____	_____	_____	_____
2. _____	_____	_____	_____
3. _____	_____	_____	_____
Plural			
1. _____	_____	_____	_____
2. _____	_____	_____	_____
3. _____	_____	_____	_____

30. The model, pattern, or example forms for the words of an inflected language are called _____.

31. Vowels that are normally long are usually shortened when they occur before another _____ or before the consonants ___, ___, or ___ at the end of a word, or before ___ or ___ in any position.

32. The singular imperative of a first or second conjugation verb is identical to the verb's _____ _____; for the plural imperative, simply add to this form the ending ___.

33. Provide the infinitive, the present stem, and the singular and plural imperatives for the following verbs.

	Infinitive	Stem	Imperatives Singular	Plural
a. errō	_____	_____	_____	_____
b. salveō	_____	_____	_____	_____
c. servō	_____	_____	_____	_____
d. terreō	_____	_____	_____	_____
e. valeō	_____	_____	_____	_____
f. vocō	_____	_____	_____	_____

34. Before attempting to translate a Latin sentence, you should always read it _____ from beginning to end.

35. The mnemonic device SOV reminds you that the _____ often appears last in a Latin sentence.

EXERCITĀTIŌNĒS ("Exercises")

A. Fill in the following blanks with the information requested.

	Person	Number	Tense	Mood	Voice	Translation
1. vidēte	_____	_____	_____	_____	_____	_____
2. dā	_____	_____	_____	_____	_____	_____
3. cōgitāte	_____	_____	_____	_____	_____	_____
4. vidē	_____	_____	_____	_____	_____	_____

B. Fill in the blanks for each verb.

	Person	Number	Tense	Mood	Voice	Translation
1. vocat	_____	_____	_____	_____	_____	_____
2. cōgitāmus	_____	_____	_____	_____	_____	_____
3. amant	_____	_____	_____	_____	_____	_____
4. dēbēs	_____	_____	_____	_____	_____	_____
5. videt	_____	_____	_____	_____	_____	_____
6. vident	_____	_____	_____	_____	_____	_____
7. dēbēmus	_____	_____	_____	_____	_____	_____
8. datis	_____	_____	_____	_____	_____	_____

C. Make the single transformation indicated and translate the new form (e.g., **amat** to plural: answer, **amant,** *they love*).

	Transformation	Translation
1. amāmus, to sg.	_____	_____
2. vocant, to 1st pers.	_____	_____
3. vidētis, to sg.	_____	_____
4. cōgitō, to 3rd pers.	_____	_____
5. terret, to pl.	_____	_____

6. cōnservā, to plural _____ _____

7. vidēte, to singular _____ _____

D. Supply the correct present active indicative form of the verb in parentheses, and translate.

1. Saepe _____ (errāre; 2nd pers. pl.).

_____

2. Nihil _____ (vidēre; 1st pers. pl.).

_____

3. _____ mē (amāre; 3rd pers. sg.).

_____

4. Quid _____ (vidēre; 2nd pers. pl.)?

_____

5. Vocā mē sī _____ (errāre; 3rd pers. pl.).

_____

6. _____ nihil (dare; 2nd pers. pl.).

_____

7. Quid _____ (servāre; 1st pers. pl.)?

_____

8. Mē saepe _____ (terrēre; 3rd pers. sg.).

_____

9. Mē nōn _____ (amāre; 3rd pers. pl.).

_____

10. Monē mē sī nihil _____ (vidēre; 2nd pers. sg.).

_____

E. Translate into Latin; remember to employ the standard word order learned thus far and to include all macrons.

1. Nothing frightens me.

_____

2. They are saving nothing.

_____

Name: _____ Section: _____ Date: _____

3. What must we preserve?

_____

4. Advise (sg. imper.) me often, please.

_____

VĪS VERBŌRUM ("Word Power")

A. Complete each statement with an English word that demonstrates your knowledge of the Latin etymology (e.g., "A 'laudatory' speech is full of praise").

1. To "annihilate" something is essentially to turn it into _____.

2. An "amatory" poem deals with _____.

3. Enter in the "debit" column the amount you _____.

4. To "admonish" someone is to give him a stern _____.

5. A "valid" argument has the _____ to persuade.

B. Which English word is *not* related to the Latin verb? (Use a good English dictionary, if necessary, to answer these.)

1. terreō: a. territory b. terrify c. terrible d. terrorize

2. valeō: a. prevail b. valiant c. veil d. invalid

3. amō: a. amiable b. aimless c. amateur d. amorous

4. errō: a. erratic b. erroneous c. errant d. erudite

LĒCTIŌNĒS ("Readings")

A. First read each sentence aloud twice, and then translate as literally as possible within the limits of sound English idiom.

1. Mē monent, sī errō. _____

2. Mē monet, sī errant. _____

3. Monēte mē, sī errat. _____

4. Dēbēs monēre mē. _____

5. Mē terrēre nōn dēbētis. _____

6. Nōn dēbent laudāre mē. _____

7. "Quid dat?" "Nihil saepe dat." _____

8. Mē saepe vocant et monent. _____

9. Nihil videō. Quid vidēs? _____

10. Mē laudā, sī nōn errō, amābō tē. _____

11. Sī valētis, valēmus. _____

12. Sī valet, valeō. _____

13. Sī mē amat, mē laudāre dēbet. _____

14. Nōn dēbēs errāre. _____

15. Quid dēbēmus laudāre? _____

16. Salvēte, discipulī! _____

B. Answer these questions on "The Poet Horace Contemplates an Invitation."

1. The author's mood is best described as
    a. confident   b. frightened   c. unsure   d. angry

2. Which verb has the most negative connotations?
    a. vocant   b. monent   c. culpant   d. laudant

Cōgitō ergō sum: *I think, therefore I exist*
Descartes

Name: _____ Section: _____ Date: _____

2

Nouns and Cases; First Declension; Agreement of Adjectives; Syntax

INTELLEGENDA ("Objectives")

Upon completion of this lesson you should be able to

1. Name the cases of a Latin noun and identify the basic uses or grammatical functions of each case in a sentence.

2. Form the base of any noun.

3. Recognize, form, and translate first declension nouns and adjectives.

4. Explain what is meant by noun and adjective gender.

5. State the rules for adjective/noun agreement and verb/subject agreement.

6. Describe the usual positioning of an adjective.

7. Define the terms "declension" and "syntax."

Salvēte, discipulae et discipulī! Remember: whenever you turn to the exercises in this workbook, you should have already thoroughly studied the corresponding chapter of your text, *Wheelock's Latin,* especially the new grammar and vocabulary and even the **Latīna Est Gaudium** section. And remember always to memorize new paradigms (model declensions and conjugations) and vocabulary by repeating the words *aloud.* **Bonam fortūnam!** (*Good luck!*)

GRAMMATICA ("Grammar")

1. The several inflected forms of a Latin noun or adjective are called _____.

2. Name the Latin cases used for the following grammatical functions.

   a. Direct object of a verb   _____

   b. Possession   _____

   c. Subject of a verb   _____

   d. Means   _____

   e. Direct address   _____

   f. Agent   _____

   g. Indirect object of a verb   _____

   h. Manner   _____

   i. Accompaniment   _____

   j. Place   _____

   k. Time   _____

   l. Object of a preposition (two cases) _____ and _____

3. While the listing of all the forms of a verb is called a "conjugation," the listing of a noun's cases is called a _____.

4. A noun is declined by adding the case endings to the _____, which is found by dropping the ending of the _____ case provided in the vocabulary list.

5. Give the base of the following nouns from this chapter's vocabulary.

   a. fāma, fāmae _____   b. fortūna, fortūnae _____

   c. patria, patriae _____   d. īra, īrae   _____

6. Equivalents of the articles "a," "an," and "the" do not exist in Latin and so must be supplied when translating into English.
   TRUE/FALSE (underline one).

7. Provide the information requested for each first declension ending.

	Case	Number	Function	English Preposition(s) (if any)
a. -ās	_____	_____	_____	_____
b. -a	voc. _____	_____	_____	_____
c. -am	_____	_____	_____	_____
d. -ae	dat. _____	_____	_____	_____
e. -a	nom. _____	_____	_____	_____
f. -ā	_____	_____	_____	_____
g. -īs	abl. _____	_____	_____	_____
h. -ae	gen. _____	_____	_____	_____
i. -ae	nom. _____	_____	_____	_____
j. -īs	dat. _____	_____	_____	_____
k. -ārum	_____	_____	_____	_____
l. -ae	voc. _____	_____	_____	_____

8. The gender of most first declension nouns is _____.

9. Which noun is feminine gender?
    a. agricola   b. nauta   c. poēta   d. patria

10. Identify the base of **vīta, vītae,** and decline it fully, spelling out the case names, and providing the English meanings appropriate to each case.

    base: _____

Case	Singular Latin	English
_____	vīta	life
_____	vītae	_____
_____	_____	_____
_____	_____	_____
_____	_____	_____
_____	_____	_____

Case	Plural Latin	English
_____	_____	_____
_____	_____	_____
_____	_____	_____
_____	_____	_____
_____	_____	_____
_____	_____	_____

11. Fill in the following blanks with the information requested for each noun.

	Translation	Use
a. fōrmam	_____	_____
b. fāma (nom. sg.)	_____	_____
c. fortūnās	_____	_____
d. īrae (nom. pl.)	_____	_____
e. philosophiae (dat. sg.)	_____	_____
f. puellīs (abl. pl.)	_____	_____
g. vītae (gen. sg.)	_____	_____
h. poenārum	_____	_____
i. patriīs (dat. pl.)	_____	_____

12. An adjective must agree with the noun it modifies in _____, _____, and _____; a verb must agree with its subject in _____ and _____.

13. The term for the grammatical function and interconnection of the words in a sentence is _____.

EXERCITĀTIŌNĒS ("Exercises")

A.   Supply the correct form of the words shown in parentheses in the nominative case, and translate.

1.   _____ (poēta) nōn cōgitat.

_____

2.   Date nautae _____ (pecūnia).

_____

3.   Sine _____ (īra) monet.

_____

4.   _____ (nauta) _____ (poena; pl.) dant.

_____

5.   Amātis _____ (vīta; sg.) et _____ (fāma).

6.   Est sine _____ _____ (multa pecūnia; sg.).

_____

7.   _____ (fortūna) saepe vocat.

_____

8.   _____ _____ (philosophia antīqua; sg.) laudō.

_____

9.   Cōnservant philosophiam tuam _____ (vīta; gen.).

_____

10. Fōrma _____ (porta; gen. pl.) est antīqua.

_____

11. _____ _____ (puella mea; pl.) rosās dare dēbētis.

_____

B. Transform from singular to plural or plural to singular and translate the new phrase.

	Transformation	Translation
1. multa philosophia	_____	_____
2. sententiīs meīs (abl.)	_____	_____
3. Nauta errat.	_____	_____
4. Puella nautam servat.	_____	_____
5. patriārum antīquārum	_____	_____

C. Transform one of the nominative nouns to genitive to create a meaningful phrase, and then translate (e.g., **puella fortūna** > **fortūna puellae**, *the girl's fortune*).

	Transformation	Translation
1. fāma patria	_____	_____
2. rosa fōrma	_____	_____
3. sententia puella	_____	_____
4. īra poēta	_____	_____
5. nauta pecūnia	_____	_____

D. Translate into Latin; remember to employ the standard word order learned thus far and to include all macrons.

1. Without philosophy the country often errs and is not strong.

   _____

2. Your country is great.

   _____

3. The sailors are saving much money.

   _____

4. The girl is giving the poet's rose to the sailor.

   _____

VĪS VERBŌRUM ("Word Power")

A.   Answer these questions on the chapter's vocabulary list.

1.   **Fāma** gives us English "fame"; list four other first declension words from the chapter's vocabulary list that also have English derivatives in which the Latin **-a** has become English "-e":

_____, _____, _____, _____

2.   The suffix **-ōsa,** meaning *full of* or *characterized by,* gives us, from **fāma,** the Latin adjective **fāmōsa,** which means *famous;* similarly, from **fōrma,** *beauty,* we have the Latin adjective _____, which essentially means _____.

B.   Complete each statement with an English word that demonstrates your knowledge of the Latin etymology (e.g., "A 'laudatory' speech is full of praise").

1.   An "irascible" person is prone to _____.

2.   A _____ is expert in "nautical" matters.

3.   If you are "impecunious" you have no _____.

4.   Something that is "vital" is literally essential to _____.

5.   An "expatriate" lives outside his or her _____.

LĒCTIŌNĒS ("Readings")

A.   First read each sentence aloud twice; then translate as literally as possible within the limits of sound English idiom.

1.   Valē, patria mea.

_____

2.   Fortūna puellae est magna.

_____

3.   Puella fortūnam patriae tuae laudat.

_____

4.   Ō puella, patriam tuam servā, amābō tē!

_____

5. Salvēte, nautae!

_____

6. Puellae nihil datis.

_____

7. Rosās puellae videt.

_____

8. Pecūniam puellārum nōn vidēs.

_____

9. Monēre nautās dēbēmus.

_____

10. Vīta multīs puellīs fortūnam dat.

_____

11. Vītam meam pecūniā tuā cōnservās.

_____

12. Fāma est nihil sine fortūnā.

_____

13. Sine fāmā et fortūnā patria nōn valet.

_____

14. Īram puellārum laudāre nōn dēbēs.

_____

15. Vītam sine poenīs amāmus.

_____

16. Sine philosophiā nōn valēmus.

_____

17. Quid est vīta sine philosophiā?

_____

18. Vīta nōn valet, sī saepe errās.

_____

Name: _____ Section: _____ Date: _____

19. Īra sententiae tuae mē terret.

B.   Answer these questions on "Catullus Bids His Girlfriend Farewell."

1.   What does the poet suggest he will do at the girl's departure?
a. be tough   b. love her   c. praise her beauty   d. send flowers

2.   The emotional shift from the beginning of the passage to the end
is from
a. happy to sad   b. joyful to unhappy
c. angry to calm   d. firm to wavering

Fortēs fortūna iuvat: *Fortune helps the brave*
Terence

3

Second Declension: Masculine Nouns and Adjectives; Apposition; Word Order

INTELLEGENDA ("Objectives")

Upon completion of this lesson you should be able to

1. Recognize, form, and translate second declension masculine nouns and adjectives.

2. Define the term "apposition" and state the rule for agreement of two words in apposition.

3. Discuss and apply basic rules of Latin word order.

Salvēte, amīcae et amīcī! Remember: whenever you turn to the exercises in this workbook, you should have already thoroughly studied the corresponding chapter of *Wheelock's Latin,* especially the new grammar and vocabulary and even the **Latīna Est Gaudium** section. And remember always to memorize new paradigms (model declensions and conjugations) and vocabulary by repeating the words *aloud.* **Bonam fortūnam!**

Name: _____ Section: _____ Date: _____

GRAMMATICA ("Grammar")

1. The gender of second declension nouns is either _____
    or _____, and the genitive singular always ends with the
    letter ____.

2. Besides **vir,** the nominative singular of all second declension mascu-
    lines ends with the two letters ____ or ____.

3. Give the base of the following **-er** nouns and a derivative whose spell-
    ing reflects the base.

	Base	Derivative
a. ager	_____	_____
b. puer	_____	_____

4. Only the _____ and _____ plural endings of the
    second declension are identical to those of the first.

5. Give the indicated information for each of the following second
    declension masculine case endings.

	Case	Number	Function	English Preposition(s) (if any)
a. -ō	abl. ____	____	____	____
b. -um	____	____	____	____
c. -ō	dat. ____	____	____	____
d. -ī	voc. ____	____	____	____
e. -ōrum	____	____	____	____
f. -us	____	____	____	____
g. -ōs	____	____	____	____
h. -ī (sg.)	____	____	____	____
i. -e	____	____	____	____
j. -īs	abl. ____	____	____	____
k. -ī	nom. ____	____	____	____
l. -īs	dat. ____	____	____	____

6. Identify the base of **numerus, numerī,** and decline it fully, spelling out the case names, and providing the English meanings appropriate to each case.

base: _____

Case	Singular Latin	English
_____	numerus	the number
_____	numerī	_____
_____	_____	_____
_____	_____	_____
_____	_____	_____
_____	_____	_____

Case	Plural Latin	English
_____	_____	_____
_____	_____	_____
_____	_____	_____
_____	_____	_____
_____	_____	_____
_____	_____	_____

7. Nouns in apposition always agree in
   a. number   b. gender   c. case   d. all three

8. Word order is crucial to meaning in
   a. English   b. Latin   c. neither   d. both

9. Assign numbers 1–5 to the following to show the typical order of words in a simple Latin sentence or clause.

   _____ Subject and its modifiers

   _____ Verb

   _____ Adverbial words or phrases

   _____ Direct object

   _____ Indirect object

10. The typical order listed above reflects the Roman fondness for a style indicating
    a. suspense   b. variety   c. confusion   d. all three

11. Give the indicated information for each of the following.

	Case	Function	Translation
a. fīliōrum meōrum			
b. fīliābus meīs	abl.		
c. populī Rōmānī	gen.		
d. populō Rōmānō	dat.		
e. virīs Rōmānīs	abl.		
f. virī magnī	nom.		
g. amīcōrum paucōrum			
h. amīcīs meīs	dat.		
i. amīcī Rōmānī	voc.		
j. magnum virum			
k. puer meus			
l. multōs agrōs			
m. magnī numerī (sg.)			
n. amīce magne			

EXERCITĀTIŌNĒS ("Exercises")

A. Supply the correct form of the words shown in parentheses in the nominative case, and translate.

1. _____ _____ (multa sapientia) semper habēmus.

   _____

2. Numerus _____ _____ (amīcus tuus; pl.) est magnus.

   _____

3. Agricola _____ _____ (fīlius meus; pl.) sapientiam dat.

_____

4. Paucī puerī _____ _____ (numerus magnus; sg.)
_____ _____ (vir magnus; gen. pl.) vident.

_____

5. Vocāte _____ (vir; pl.) _____ _____
(magna sapientia; gen. sg.).

_____

B. Translate into Latin; remember to employ standard word order and to include all macrons.

1. The reputation of the men and women is great, my friend.

_____

2. The people give much money to the sons of Romans.

_____

3. My friend's son sees the girl.

_____

4. We often praise the boy's friends.

_____

5. Many men today do not love the wisdom of ancient philosophy.

_____

_____

C. Transform from singular to plural or plural to singular and translate the new phrase.

	Transformation	Translation
1. Ō, meī amīcī	_____	_____
2. in agrīs	_____	_____
3. sine puerō	_____	_____
4. Puer rosam videt.	_____	_____
5. virōrum avārōrum	_____	_____

Name: _____ *Section:* _____ *Date:* _____

D. Transform one of the nominative nouns to genitive to create a meaning-ful phrase, and then translate (e.g., **puer amīcus** > **amīcus puerī,** *the boy's friend*).

	Transformation	Translation
1. vir patria	_____	_____
2. poena amīcus	_____	_____
3. sententia populus	_____	_____
4. agricola ager	_____	_____
5. fīlia fortūna	_____	_____

VĪS VERBŌRUM ("Word Power")

A. Answer these questions on the chapter's vocabulary list.

1. Since the Latin root **col-** means *to cultivate,* an **agricola** is literally a person who _____ _____.

2. If "innumerable" means "not able to be numbered or counted," then "insatiable" means "not able to be _____."

B. Complete each statement with an English word that demonstrates your knowledge of the Latin etymology (e.g., "A 'laudatory' speech is full of praise").

1. An "amicable" person easily attracts _____.

2. "Filial" devotion is that of a _____ or _____ to a parent.

3. The man's "puerile" behavior made him look like a _____.

4. His "paucity" of resources meant that he had _____ things to work with.

LĒCTIŌNĒS ("Readings")

A. First read each sentence aloud twice, and then translate as literally as possible within the limits of sound English idiom.

1. Valē, mī amīce.

   _____

2. Ō vir magne, populum Rōmānum servā!

   _____

3. Sī nihil mē satiat, saepe errō.

   _____

4. Nautae fīliābus meīs nihil dant.

   _____

5. Agricolās in agrō videō.

   _____

6. Amīcum fīliī meī hodiē vidēs.

   _____

7. Puellae et puerī fōrmam rosārum amant.

   _____

8. Nōn dēbēs fīliās et fīliōs tuōs terrēre.

   _____

9. Dēbent amīcam tuam laudāre.

   _____

10. Vīta paucīs virīs fāmam dat, mī fīlī.

    _____

11. Virī magnī paucōs amīcōs saepe habent.

    _____

12. Amīcus meus dē philosophiā semper cōgitat.

    _____

13. Fīlius magnī virī nōn semper est magnus vir.

_____

14. Quid vir avārus dē pecūniā cōgitat?

_____

15. Philosophiam, sapientiam magnōrum virōrum, laudāre dēbētis.

_____

_____

B.   Answer these questions on "The Grass Is Always Greener."

1.   Quid agricola laudat? (**Respondē Latīnē,** _Respond in Latin,_ i.e., with a complete Latin sentence.)

_____

2.   Quid nautae saepe laudant? (**Respondē Latīnē.**)

_____

3.   Quid virī avārī habent? _____ _____

4.   What one vice does Horace suggest causes men to envy others? _____

Dux fēmina factī: _A woman (was) leader of the enterprise_
Vergil

4

Second Declension Neuters; Adjectives; Present Indicative of Sum; Predicate Nouns and Adjectives; Substantive Adjectives

INTELLEGENDA

Upon completion of this lesson you should be able to

1. Recognize, form, and translate second declension neuter nouns and adjectives.

*2. Recognize, conjugate, and translate the irregular verb **sum** in the present indicative.*

3. Define the terms "predicate noun" and "predicate adjective" and state the rule for agreement of a predicate adjective with the subject.

4. Define the term "substantive adjective" and recognize and translate such an adjective in a Latin sentence.

Salvēte, amīcae et amīcī! Whenever you turn to the exercises in this workbook, you should have already thoroughly studied the corresponding chapter of *Wheelock's Latin,* especially the new grammar and vocabulary and even the **Latīna Est Gaudium** section. And remember always to memorize new paradigms and vocabulary by repeating the words *aloud.* **Bonam for-tūnam!**

GRAMMATICA

1. The gender of second declension nouns is either _____ or _____, and the genitive singular always ends with the letter ____.

2. The nominative singular of all second declension neuters ends with the two letters ____.

3. Give the base of the following nouns and adjectives.

   a. cōnsilium _____   b. cūra _____

   c. magister _____   d. perīculum _____

   e. bonus, -a, -um _____   f. vērus, -a, -um _____

4. Which of the following nouns is feminine?
   a. bāsia   b. dōna   c. mora   d. all three

5. For all neuter nouns and adjectives, the _____, _____, and _____ cases are identical to one another.

6. Fill in the following blanks with the information requested for each second declension neuter ending.

	Case	Number	Function	English Preposition(s) (if any)
a. -ōrum	_____	_____	_____	_____
b. -ī	_____	_____	_____	_____
c. -um	acc.	_____	_____	_____
d. -īs	abl.	_____	_____	_____
e. -ō	abl.	_____	_____	_____
f. -um	nom.	_____	_____	_____
g. -a	acc.	_____	_____	_____
h. -īs	dat.	_____	_____	_____

i. -ō   <u>dat.</u>   _____   _____   _____

j. -a   <u>nom.</u>   _____   _____   _____

7. Identify the base of **officium bonum,** *good service,* decline it fully, and provide the English meanings appropriate to each case.

base: _____ _____

Singular

	Latin		English
Nom.	officium	bonum	the good service
Gen.			
Dat.			
Acc.			
Abl.			
Voc.			

Plural

	Latin		English
Nom.			
Gen.			
Dat.			
Acc.			
Abl.			
Voc.			

8. Fill in the following blanks with the information requested for each noun.

	Translation	Function
a. dōnōrum		
b. cōnsiliī		
c. ōtiō		
d. perīculīs		
e. bella		

9. Choose the correct form of the adjective and then translate the entire phrase.

	Adjective	Translation
a. ager (small)	_____	_____
b. exitiī (much)	_____	_____
c. bellōrum (evil)	_____	_____
d. remedia (few)	_____	_____
e. oculōs (pretty)	_____	_____

10. The important irregular verb **sum** is
    a. transitive   b. linking   c. active   d. passive

11. The personal endings of **esse** in the present indicative, when compared with the standard active voice personal endings in Latin, are
    a. identical   b. different   c. irregular   d. none of these

12. As an intransitive linking verb, **sum** connects its subject with a
    a. direct object   b. indirect object
    c. predicate noun or adjective d. possessive

13. Translate the following.

    a. sumus _____   b. estis _____

    c. sunt _____   d. est _____

    e. sum _____   f. es _____

14. A predicate adjective agrees with its subject in
    a. number   b. gender   c. case   d. all these

15. When employed as a substantive, an adjective is used in place of a
    a. subject   b. noun   c. adverb   d. direct object

16. Identify the number, gender, case, and grammatical use of these nouns in this chapter's Practice and Review sentences (e.g., **Ōtium** [sentence 1], singular, neuter, nominative, subject).

	Number	Gender	Case	Use
a. Bella (2)	_____	_____	_____	_____
b. perīcula (2)	_____	_____	_____	_____
c. ōtiō (3)	_____	_____	_____	_____
d. poēta (7)	_____	_____	_____	_____
e. amīcī (7)	_____	_____	_____	_____

EXERCITĀTIŌNĒS

A. Translate each of the following into Latin or English; remember to include all macrons.

1. real danger (subject) _____

2. ōtium magnum _____

3. bella mala _____

4. dōna bella _____

5. of a foolish plan _____

6. remediī vērī _____

7. for great leisure _____

8. an evil war (direct object) _____

9. by beautiful gifts _____

10. multa bāsia _____

11. of small services _____

12. multō exitiō _____

B. Supply the correct forms of the words shown in parentheses in the nominative case and translate.

1. _____ (perīculum) hodiē sunt _____
   (vērus, -a, -um).

   _____

2. Perīculum _____ (bellum; gen.) _____
   (parvus, -a, -um) est.

   _____

3. Puer et puella nōn sunt _____ (avārus, -a, -um).

   _____

4. Officium et ōtium saepe sunt _____ (bonus, -a, -um).

   _____

5. Multī dē _____ (exitium) patriae cōgitant.

   _____

Name: _____ *Section:* _____ *Date:* _____

C. Translate into Latin; remember to employ the standard word order learned thus far and to include all macrons.

1. War is often foolish and not humane.

   _____

2. Peace is not always good.

   _____

3. The teacher loves the old gifts.

   _____

4. Your eyes are pretty.

   _____

5. The danger of delay is real.

   _____

D. Make the single transformation indicated and translate the new form (e.g., **dōnōrum** to ablative: answer, **dōnīs,** *by/with/from the gifts*).

	Transformation	Translation
1. poētās, to singular	_____	_____
2. populum, to nominative	_____	_____
3. agricolae, to singular	_____	_____
4. cōnsilia, to dative	_____	_____
5. exitia, to singular	_____	_____

E. Transform from singular to plural or plural to singular and translate the new phrase.

	Transformation	Translation
1. puerōrum Rōmānōrum	_____	_____
2. parvīs dōnīs (abl.)	_____	_____
3. oculum tuum	_____	_____
4. officium meum	_____	_____
5. fēmina bona	_____	_____

F. Transform one of the nominative nouns to genitive to create a meaning-ful phrase, and then translate (e.g., **puella fortūna** > **fortūna puellae,** *the girl's fortune*).

	Transformation	Translation
1. amīca cōnsilium	_____	_____
2. magistra cūra	_____	_____
3. officium magister	_____	_____
4. fāma vir	_____	_____
5. fīlius sententia	_____	_____

VĪS VERBŌRUM

A. Answer these questions on the chapter's vocabulary list.

1. Since the Latin prefix **neg-** means *the absence of,* the noun **negōtium,** *business,* is literally *the _____ of _____.*

2. If **fōrmōsus, -a, -um,** from **fōrma,** *beauty,* means *full of or charac-terized by beauty,* then the Latin adjective _____, from **perīculum,** means *full of or characterized by _____.*

B. Complete each statement with an English word that demonstrates your knowledge of the Latin etymology (e.g., "A 'laudatory' speech is full of praise").

1. A museum "curator" literally takes _____ of its collection.

2. To "embellish" a decoration is to make it even more _____.

3. A "stultifying" experience makes one feel _____.

4. An "adjutant's" role is to provide _____.

C. Which English word is *not* related to the Latin noun or adjective? (Use a good English dictionary, if necessary, to answer these.)

1. bellus, -a, -um: a. belle b. bellicose c. beauty d. belladonna

2. oculus: a. monocle b. binoculars c. oculist d. occult

3. perīculum: a. puerile b. perilous c. imperil d. peril

LĒCTIŌNĒS

A. First read each sentence aloud twice, and then translate as literally as possible within the limits of sound English idiom.

1. Mora saepe est remedium bellī, Ō Rōmānī!

    _____

2. Paucī vērum ōtium hodiē habent.

    _____

3. Dā parvum bāsium fīliae bellae tuae, mī amīce!

    _____

4. Quid dē mē et exitiō patriae meae cōgitās?

    _____

5. Porta antīqua nōn est magna sed bella est.

    _____

6. Oculī puellae sunt bellī.

    _____

7. Et fōrma et numerus rosārum fēminam satiant.

    _____

8. Multa bella ōtium nōn cōnservant.

    _____

9. Et ōtium perīcula saepe habet.

    _____

10. Stultus vir mala bellī laudat.

    _____

11. Officiō cūram sine morā dare dēbēmus.

    _____

12. Sī cōnsilium bonum nōn habēs, in magnō perīculō sumus.

    _____

13. Vītae magnōrum nōn sunt sine multīs perīculīs.

_____

14. Officia magistrae sunt multa et magna.

_____

15. Vir parvī ōtiī es.

_____

B. Answer these questions on "The Rarity of Friendship."

1. Quid paucī habent?
   a. pecūniam   b. vērōs amīcōs   c. dignī   d. stultī

2. Sī _____ habēmus, valēre possumus.
   a. pecūniam   b. omnia   c. nihil   d. amīcitiam

3. Translate into English the title of Cicero's essay from which this reading passage has been adapted: _____ _____.

Perīculum in morā: *(There is) danger in delay*
Livy

5

First and Second Conjugations: Future and Imperfect; Adjectives in -er

INTELLEGENDA

Upon completion of this lesson you should be able to

1. Identify the future and imperfect tense signs for first and second conjugation verbs.

2. Recognize, form, and translate the future and imperfect active indicative of a first or second conjugation verb.

3. Recognize and form first/second declension adjectives with masculine nominatives in -er.

Salvēte, amīcae et amīcī! Whenever you turn to the exercises in this workbook, you should have already thoroughly studied the corresponding chapter of *Wheelock's Latin,* especially the new grammar and vocabulary and even the **Latīna Est Gaudium** section. And remember always to memorize paradigms and vocabulary by repeating the words *aloud.* **Habēte animōs magnōs!**

GRAMMATICA

1. The present stem of a first or second conjugation verb is found by dropping _____ from the _____ principal part.

2. In most forms of the future active indicative of first and second conjugation verbs, the future tense sign is _____; the tense sign for the imperfect is _____.

3. The personal endings (plus tense signs) for the present, future, and imperfect active indicative are:

Present		**Future**	
Singular	**Plural**	**Singular**	**Plural**
1. _____	_____	_____	_____
2. _____	_____	_____	_____
3. _____	_____	_____	_____

Imperfect	
Singular	**Plural**
1. _____	_____
2. _____	_____
3. _____	_____

4. Both the future and imperfect tenses are composed of three elements in the following order: _____ _____, _____ _____, and _____ _____.

5. Conjugate **amō, amāre,** in the present, future, and imperfect active indicative.

Present		**Future**	
Singular	**Plural**	**Singular**	**Plural**
1. _____	_____	_____	_____
2. _____	_____	_____	_____
3. _____	_____	_____	_____

Imperfect

Singular	Plural
1. _____	_____
2. _____	_____
3. _____	_____

6. Translate the preceding future and imperfect active indicative forms of **amō, amāre,** *to love.*

Future		Imperfect	
Singular	Plural	Singular	Plural
1. _____	_____	_____	_____
2. _____	_____	_____	_____
3. _____	_____	_____	_____

7. The imperfect tense can indicate an action in the past that was
   a. continuous   b. repeated   c. habitual   d. all these

8. To identify the base of an **-er** adjective, you should memorize the
   a. masculine nominative   b. feminine or neuter nominative
   c. case endings   d. all these

9. Decline the following adjectives.

Singular

Nom.	līber	lībera	līberum	noster	nostra	nostrum
Gen.	_____	_____	_____	_____	_____	_____
Dat.	_____	_____	_____	_____	_____	_____
Acc.	_____	_____	_____	_____	_____	_____
Abl.	_____	_____	_____	_____	_____	_____

Plural

Nom.	_____	_____	_____	_____	_____	_____
Gen.	_____	_____	_____	_____	_____	_____
Dat.	_____	_____	_____	_____	_____	_____
Acc.	_____	_____	_____	_____	_____	_____
Abl.	_____	_____	_____	_____	_____	_____

10. Identify the base of **caelum pulchrum,** *beautiful sky,* decline it fully, and provide the English meanings appropriate to each case.

base: _____ _____

	Singular **Latin**		**English**
Nom.	caelum	pulchrum	the beautiful sky
Gen.	_____	_____	_____
Dat.	_____	_____	_____
Acc.	_____	_____	_____
Abl.	_____	_____	_____
Voc.	_____	_____	_____

	Plural **Latin**		**English**
Nom.	_____	_____	_____
Gen.	_____	_____	_____
Dat.	_____	_____	_____
Acc.	_____	_____	_____
Abl.	_____	_____	_____
Voc.	_____	_____	_____

11. Choose the correct form of the adjective and then translate the entire phrase.

	Adjective	**Translation**
a. adulēscentiam (healthy)	_____	_____
b. animum (free)	_____	_____
c. culpārum (our)	_____	_____

EXERCITĀTIŌNĒS

A. Translate the following into English or Latin.

1. culpābimus _____

2. remanēbat _____

3. vidēbunt _____

4. superābimus _____

5. cēnābam _____

6. I shall help _____

7. you (pl.) will have _____

8. she used to err _____

9. we shall give _____

10. they were satisfying _____

B. Supply the correct forms of the words shown in parentheses and translate.

1. Semper _____ (superāre; 1st pers. pl. impf.) perīcula.

   _____

2. Sapientia satis _____ (valēre; fut.).

   _____

3. Saepe _____ (dare; 2nd pers. pl. impf.) glōriam amīcō.

   _____

4. Tum culpa nostra nōn _____ (remanēre; fut.).

   _____

5. Puella et puer crās _____ (errāre; fut.).

   _____

6. Magistrōs herī _____ (vidēre; 1st pers. sg. impf.).

   _____

7. Quandō _____ (cōgitāre; 2nd pers. sg. fut.) dē philosophiā?

   _____

8. Propter bellum, igitur, tē _____ (superāre; 1st pers. sg. impf.).

   _____

C. Make the transformation(s) indicated and translate the new form (e.g., **rosam amat,** to plural: answer, **rosās amant,** *they love roses*).

	Transformation	Translation
1. amīcī nostrī, to sg.	_____	_____
2. ager pulcher, to acc.	_____	_____
3. agricolam monet, to pl.	_____	_____
4. mē laudat, to impf.	_____	_____
5. verba mala, to abl.	_____	_____

D. Identify the verb tense and translate.

	Tense	Translation
1. cōnservābit	_____	_____
2. terrēbās	_____	_____
3. dēbent	_____	_____
4. vocābātis	_____	_____
5. sumus	_____	_____

E. Translate into Latin; remember to employ the standard word order learned thus far and to include all macrons.

1. Therefore, the Roman people used to praise our good plans.

   _____

2. Then they will save few free men in our country.

   _____

3. The farmer's roses are often small but always beautiful.

   _____

4. The sailor kept giving many gifts and kisses to the woman.

   _____

VĪS VERBŌRUM

A. Answer these questions on the chapter's vocabulary list.

1. Which adjective does not have a related meaning?
    a. meus   b. noster   c. stultus   d. tuus

2. Which adverb does not have a related meaning?
    a. hodiē   b. satis   c. semper   d. tum

3. Which noun is nearly synonymous with **glōria**?
    a. animus   b. culpa   c. fāma   d. remedium

4. Which verb is an antonym of **culpō**?
    a. cēnō   b. laudō   c. maneō   d. sum

5. Which is not interrogative?
    a. -ne   b. quandō   c. quid   d. propter

B. Complete each statement with an English word that demonstrates your knowledge of the Latin etymology (e.g., "A 'laudatory' speech is full of praise").

1. An "animated" cheerleader has a lot of school _____.

2. To "exculpate" a defendant is to free him from _____.

3. If an "insatiable" appetite is one that cannot be satisfied, then an "insuperable" difficulty is one that _____ _____ _____.

4. To "procrastinate" is to move some action forward to _____.

LĒCTIŌNĒS

A. First read each sentence aloud twice, and then translate as literally as possible within the limits of sound English idiom.

1. Laudābuntne, igitur, fāmam fīliārum et fīliōrum nostrōrum?

    _____

2. Līberī magnum numerum officiōrum semper habēbunt.

    _____

3.   Sī oculī tuī hodiē sunt sānī, bellōs agrōs meōs sine morā vidēre dēbēs.

_____

_____

4.   Multī in pulchrā patriā nostrā magnum ōtium et paucās cūrās habēbant.

_____

_____

5.   Propter exitium patriae, poenam avārōrum tum laudābant.

_____

6.   Salvē, amīca mea! Quandō cēnābimus?

_____

7.   Magistra nostra mē laudat et tē saepe laudābit.

_____

8.   Multās culpās hūmānās habēmus et semper habēbimus.

_____

9.   Sī īram tuam superābis, tē superābis.

_____

10.   Habetne animus tuus satis sapientiae?

_____

B.   Answer these questions on "His Only Guest" and "Thermopylae."

1.   If the boar is, so to speak, Caecilianus' dinner-guest, then who is the real pig?
a. Titus   b. Caecilianus   c. Martial   d. none of these

2.   Quid Lacedaemoniī in caelō vidēbunt?
a. exercitus   b. Persicus   c. sagittae   d. all these

3.   Quandō Lacedaemoniī fortasse cēnābunt?
a. cum animīs   b. hodiē   c. saepe   d. apud umbrās

4.   The humorous point depends on the two very different meanings
     of which one word?
     a. videō   b. caelum   c. umbra   d. animus

Mēns sāna in corpore sānō: *A healthy mind in a healthy body*
Juvenal

6

Sum: Future and Imperfect Indicative; Possum: Present, Future, and Imperfect Indicative; Complementary Infinitive

INTELLEGENDA

Upon completion of this lesson you should be able to

1. Recognize and translate **sum, esse,** *in the future and imperfect indicative.*

2. Recognize and translate **possum, posse,** *in the present, future, and imperfect indicative.*

3. Define, recognize, and translate a "complementary infinitive."

Salvēte, discipulae discipulīque! Whenever you turn to the exercises in this workbook, you should have already thoroughly studied the corresponding chapter of *Wheelock's Latin,* especially the new grammar and vocabulary and even the **Latīna Est Gaudium** section. And remember always to memorize paradigms and vocabulary by repeating the words *aloud.* **Sī Latīnam semper amābitis, multam fortūnam bonam habēre poteritis!**

GRAMMATICA

1. The personal endings for the present, future, and imperfect tenses of both **sum** and **possum** are the same as those already learned for regular verbs.   T/F

2. The stem of **sum** in the future and imperfect tenses is _____.

3. The Latin verb meaning *to be able* or *can* is a compound of the stem _____, meaning *able, capable,* and the irregular verb _____.

4. In conjugating the verb **possum, pot-** becomes **pos-** before forms of **sum, esse,** beginning with the letter _____.

5. A complementary infinitive is so called because it _____ the meaning of another verb.

6. Which cannot take a complementary infinitive?
    a. cēnō   b. possum   c. dēbeō   d. none of these

7. A complementary infinitive has a subject separate from that of the verb whose meaning it completes.   T/F

8. List, giving the sentence number, all the complementary infinitives in the Latin Practice and Review sentences of Chapter 6.

    _____ _____ _____ _____ _____

9. Conjugate **esse** in the active indicative tenses indicated.

Present		**Future**		**Imperfect**	
Latin	**English**	**Latin**	**English**	**Latin**	**English**
Singular					
1. _____	_____	_____	_____	_____	_____
2. _____	_____	_____	_____	_____	_____
3. _____	_____	_____	_____	_____	_____
Plural					
1. _____	_____	_____	_____	_____	_____
2. _____	_____	_____	_____	_____	_____
3. _____	_____	_____	_____	_____	_____

10. Conjugate **posse** in the active tenses indicated.

Present		Future		Imperfect	
Latin	**English**	**Latin**	**English**	**Latin**	**English**

Singular

1. _____ _____ _____ _____ _____ _____

2. _____ _____ _____ _____ _____ _____

3. _____ _____ _____ _____ _____ _____

Plural

1. _____ _____ _____ _____ _____ _____

2. _____ _____ _____ _____ _____ _____

3. _____ _____ _____ _____ _____ _____

EXERCITĀTIŌNĒS

A. Translate the following into English or Latin.

1. erat _____   2. we shall be able to _____

3. poterit _____   4. I can _____

5. poterāmus _____   6. you were able to _____

7. erō _____   8. he will be _____

9. poterunt _____   10. we were _____

B. Supply the correct forms of the words shown in parentheses and translate.

1. Multī librī Graecōrum _____ (esse; impf.) perpetuī.

_____

2. Liber vester _____ (esse; fut.) magnus.

_____

3. Librī nostrī _____ (esse; pres.) vērī.

_____

4. Nōn _____ (posse; 1st pers. pl. pres.) tolerāre vitia tyrannōrum.

_____

5. Nōn _____ (posse; 1st pers. pl. fut.) tolerāre librōs malōs.

_____

6. Nōn _____ (dēbēre; 1st pers. pl. pres.) tolerāre vestrās culpās.

_____

7. Ubi _____ (posse; 2nd pers. sg. impf.) superāre tyrannōs? Ibi.

_____

C. Make only the transformations indicated and translate the new form (e.g., **amābit,** to 2nd person plural: answer, **amābitis,** *you will love*).

	Transformation	Translation
1. potest, to pl. impf.	_____	_____
2. erunt, to 1st pers. sg.	_____	_____
3. poterāmus, to pres. sg.	_____	_____
4. es, to pl. fut.	_____	_____

D. Change the verb to a complementary infinitive with a form of **possum** in the same tense as the original verb, and then translate the new sentence (e.g., **Perīculum superābat:** answer, **Perīculum superāre poterat,** *He was able to overcome the danger*).

1. Tyrannum avārum nunc nōn tolerat.

Transformation: _____

Translation: _____

2. Discipulae vestrae, igitur, crās ibi remanēbunt.

Transformation: _____

Translation: _____

3. Vidēsne librōs discipulōrum bonōrum?

Transformation: _____

Translation: _____

4. Īnsidiās vitiaque tyrannī tum superābāmus.

   Transformation: _____

   Translation: _____

E. Translate into Latin; remember to employ the standard word order learned thus far and to include all macrons.

   1. The glory of the Greek and (use **-que**) Roman gods was perpetual.

   _____

   2. Teachers, are your students able to be safe now?

   _____

VĪS VERBŌRUM

A. Answer these questions on the chapter's vocabulary list.

   1. The suffix **-ōsus, -a, -um,** meaning *full of* or *characterized by,* gives us the Latin adjective **fāmōsus, -a, -um,** which is formed on the base of **fāma** and means *famous* (which also happens to be an English derivative); similarly, from **vitium,** *vice,* we have the Latin adjective _____, which essentially means *full of/characterized by* _____ and gives us the derivative _____, and from **īnsidiae,** *treachery,* comes the Latin adjective _____, meaning *full of/characterized by* _____ and giving us the derivative _____.

   2. Which adjective does not have a related meaning?
      a. meus   b. secundus   c. tuus   d. vester

   3. Which adverb does not have a related meaning?
      a. hodiē   b. ibi   c. nunc   d. tum

   4. Which noun is nearly synonymous with **vitium**?
      a. adulēscentia   b. animus   c. caelum   d. culpa

   5. Which is not interrogative?
      a. -ne   b. quandō   c. -que   d. ubi

   6. Which is not a conjunction?
      a. igitur   b. propter   c. -que   d. ubi

Name: _____ *Section:* _____ *Date:* _____

B. Complete each statement with an English word that demonstrates your knowledge of the Latin etymology (e.g., "A 'laudatory' speech is full of praise").

1. To "perpetuate" the memory of an event is to make it _____.

2. A "plenipotentiary" is, literally, a person _____ of _____.

LĒCTIŌNĒS

A. First read each sentence aloud twice, and then translate as literally as possible within the limits of sound English idiom.

1. Patria vestra semper erit lībera; quārē, discipulī meī, ibi remanēte!

   _____

2. Sī nunc cēnābitis, satis habēre poteritis.

   _____

3. Nōn dēbēmus culpāre verba sāna magistrae nostrae, amīca mea.

   _____

4. Poterāsne, igitur, in pulchrā patriā tuā manēre?

   _____

5. Ubi tyrannus est, virī nōn possunt esse līberī.

   _____

6. Tyrannī multa vitia semper habēbunt.

   _____

7. Poterātis perīcula bellī vidēre.

   _____

   Īnsidiās nautae herī nōn tolerābās.

   _____

9. Dēbēs virōs stultōs dē īnsidiīs monēre.

   _____

10. Librī bonī vērīque poterant patriam Graecōrum cōnservāre.

    _____

B. Answer these questions on "Dr. Fell" and "The Decline of Roman Morals."

1. Amatne poēta Sabidium? (**Respondē Latīnē,** *Respond in Latin,* i.e., with a complete Latin sentence.)

   _____

2. Potestne poēta dīcere quārē? (**Respondē Latīnē.**)

   _____

3. Quid poēta Sabidiō dīcere potest? (**Latīnē.**)

   _____

4. What is unusual in the arrangement of the poem's four clauses (look at the order of the four verbs)?

   _____

5. How is this arrangement especially appropriate to the point Martial is making in the poem?

   _____

6. The Livy passage employs contrast to make its point. What two phrases are contrasted in the first sentence?
   _____ _____ and _____ _____
   What two words are contrasted in the last sentence?
   _____ and _____.

7. The overall tone of the passage is
   a. joyful   b. optimistic   c. patriotic   d. pessimistic

Sīc semper tyrannīs: *Thus always to tyrants*
Motto of the state of Virginia

7

Third Declension Nouns

INTELLEGENDA

Upon completion of this lesson you should be able to

1. Identify the case endings for third declension nouns (other than i-stems, which are introduced in Chapter 14) of all three genders.

2. Recognize, form, and translate third declension nouns (other than i-stems) of all genders.

Salvēte, discipulae discipulīque! Whenever you turn to the exercises in this workbook, you should have already thoroughly studied the corresponding chapter of *Wheelock's Latin*, especially the new grammar and vocabulary and even the **Latīna Est Gaudium** section. And remember always to memorize paradigms and vocabulary by repeating the words *aloud*. **Bonam fortūnam!**

GRAMMATICA

1. The gender of third declension nouns may be
    a. masculine   b. feminine   c. neuter   d. any of these

2. Which case ending firmly identifies the declension to which a noun belongs?
    a. nominative   b. genitive   c. dative   d. accusative

3. With the exception of the singular of **-us/-ius** words of the second declension, the vocative of all nouns and adjectives of all declensions is identical to the
   a. nominative   b. genitive   c. dative   d. accusative

4. The gender of third declension nouns denoting human beings is usually _____ or _____, according to sense; otherwise, the best rule for third declension nouns is to _____ the gender when first encountered in a chapter's vocabulary list.

5. An adjective's ending must agree with that of the noun it modifies in all but which one of the following?
   a. number   b. gender   c. case   d. spelling

6. Give the information requested below for each of the third declension endings listed.

	Case(s)	Number	Gender(s)
a. -um	_____	_____	_____
b. -ibus	_____	_____	_____
c. -a	_____	_____	_____
d. -ēs	_____	_____	_____
e. -is	_____	_____	_____
f. -em	_____	_____	_____
g. -e	_____	_____	_____
h. -ī	_____	_____	_____

7. Choose the correct form of the adjective and then translate the entire phrase.

	Adjective	Translation
a. cīvitātem (Greek)	_____	_____
b. temporī (second)	_____	_____
c. rēgēs (safe)	_____	_____
d. amōris (perpetual)	_____	_____
e. corporum (healthy)	_____	_____

8. Identify the base and gender of **labor vester,** *your labor,* decline it
    fully, and provide the English meanings appropriate to each case.

    base: _____ _____   gender: _____

	Singular **Latin**		**English**
Nom.	labor	vester	your labor
Gen.	_____	_____	_____
Dat.	_____	_____	_____
Acc.	_____	_____	_____
Abl.	_____	_____	_____

	Plural **Latin**		**English**
Nom.	_____	_____	_____
Gen.	_____	_____	_____
Dat.	_____	_____	_____
Acc.	_____	_____	_____
Abl.	_____	_____	_____

9. Identify the base and gender of **carmen novum,** *new song,* decline it
    fully, and provide the English meanings appropriate to each case.

    base: _____ _____   gender: _____

	Singular **Latin**		**English**
Nom.	carmen	novum	new song
Gen.	_____	_____	_____
Dat.	_____	_____	_____
Acc.	_____	_____	_____
Abl.	_____	_____	_____

	Plural Latin		English
Nom.	_____	_____	_____
Gen.	_____	_____	_____
Dat.	_____	_____	_____
Acc.	_____	_____	_____
Abl.	_____	_____	_____

10. Identify the number, gender, case, and grammatical use of these nouns in the chapter's Practice and Review sentences (e.g., **magistrī** [sentence 1], singular, masculine, genitive, possession).

	Number	Gender	Case	Use
a. cīvitātem (2)	_____	_____	_____	_____
b. Mōrēs (4)	_____	_____	_____	_____
c. mōrēs (7)	_____	_____	_____	_____
d. temporum (8)	_____	_____	_____	_____
e. pāce (9)	_____	_____	_____	_____

EXERCITĀTIŌNĒS

A. Transform from singular to plural or plural to singular and translate the new phrase.

	Transformation	Translation
1. hominum līberōrum	_____	_____
2. nōmina nostra	_____	_____
3. virgine Rōmānā	_____	_____
4. carminī pulchrō	_____	_____

Name: _____ Section: _____ Date: _____

B. Transform one of the nominative nouns to genitive to create a meaning-ful phrase, and then translate (e.g., **puella fortūna** > **fortūna puellae,** *the girl's fortune*).

	Transformation	Translation
1. rēgīna glōria	glōria rēgīnae ✓	glory of the queen
2. liber uxor	liber uxōris	the book of the wife
3. tyrannus terra	terra tyrannī	the earth's tyranny ✗

the land of the tyrant

C. Supply the correct forms of the words shown in parentheses and translate.

1. Audēbimus, igitur, servāre ___pācis___ (pāx).   *listen* *pacem* *save*

    We will ~~hear~~, therefore to (serve) peace

2. ___Mōres___ (mōs) ___hominum___ (homō; gen. pl.) hodiē sunt malī.

    Today the customs of men are ~~evil~~ ✓   *bad*

3. Propter ___virtū__x_ (virtūs), herī audēbās ibi remanēre.

    Because of virtue, you (listened) ~~yesterday~~ to ~~remain here~~

4. In ___labore___ (labor) saepe est vēra ___virtūs___ (virtūs).

    In work, there is often true virtue.

5. Sunt multa ___carmen__x_ *carmina* (carmen) dē ___amōris___ (amor)
    in ~~litterīs~~ (littera) poētārum antīquōrum.

    There are many songs ~~about~~ love in the
    letters of ancient poets.

D. Translate into Latin; employ standard word order and include all ma-crons.

1. The students then could not tolerate the tyrant's vices and bad character.

    _____

    _____

2. Will you, therefore, now dare to overcome and murder the state's new king?

    _____

    _____

[left margin handwritten notes:]
audiēbās = you heard
semi-deponent
(2) audeō audēre, ausus sum
? (dare)
litterīs
labore = in tabl = in/on
(laborem in + acc = into/on to)

3. The Greeks used to praise the goddess in beautiful literature.

_____

_____

VĪS VERBŌRUM

A. Answer these questions on the chapter's vocabulary list.

1. Which Latin word does not have an English derivative with identical spelling (except for macrons)?
   a. audeō   b. labor   c. mōrēs   d. post

2. What adjective learned in a previous chapter is related in form and meaning to **homō**? _____ What noun learned previously is related to **virtūs**? _____

3. List three words learned previously that are related to the noun **amor.** _____ _____ _____

4. Which preposition cannot take the accusative?
   a. dē   b. post   c. propter   d. sub

5. Which noun is least closely related in meaning?
   a. homō   b. rēgīna   c. uxor   d. virgō

6. Which noun is least closely related in meaning?
   a. carmen   b. labor   c. liber   d. littera

7. Which noun is an antonym of **labor**?
   a. cīvitās   b. mōs   c. pāx   d. ōtium

B. Complete each statement with an English word that demonstrates your knowledge of the Latin etymology (e.g., "A 'laudatory' speech is full of praise").

1. To "collaborate" is to _____ closely together.

2. An "audacious" person is ready to _____ anything.

3. An "uxorious" husband is especially submissive to his _____.

4. A "subterranean" animal lives _____ the _____.

Name: _____   Section: _____   Date: _____

LĒCTIŌNĒS

A. First read each sentence aloud twice, and then translate as literally as possible within the limits of sound English idiom.

1. Litterae Graecae erant plēnae multōrum carminum dē amōre virginum puerōrumque.

_____

_____

2. Dabuntne crās litterās rēgīnae rēgīque?

_____

3. Propter multum labōrem, corpora virōrum vestrōrum erant satis sāna.

_____

_____

4. Quārē, post tempora mala et propter īnsidiās, paucōs magnae virtūtis ibi habēbāmus.

_____

_____

5. Ubi nōmina stultōrum vidēbimus?

_____

6. Pecūnia est nihil sine mōribus bonīs.

_____

7. Mōrēs hominis bonī erunt bonī.

_____

8. In multīs cīvitātibus terrīsque pāx nōn poterat valēre.

_____

9. Hominēs avārī tyrannōs nunc superāre et necāre audēbunt.

_____

10. Amor patriae in cīvitāte nostrā semper valēbat.

_____

B. Answer these questions on "Lucretia" and "Catullus."

1. Quārē Lucrētia sē necāvit? (**Respondē Latīnē,** *Respond in Latin,* i.e., with a complete Latin sentence.)

   _____

2. Quid Lucrētia amābat? (**Respondē Latīnē.**)

   _____

3. Quid poēta Cornēliō dabat? (**Latīnē.**)

   _____

4. Cornēlius erat _____ Catullī.
   a. liber   b. vir   c. amīcus   d. doctus

5. Quid erat in librō novō Catullī?
   a. carmina   b. poēta   c. perpetua   d. magister

Amor magnus doctor est: *Love is a powerful teacher*
St. Augustine

8

Third Conjugation: Present Infinitive, Present, Future, and Imperfect Indicative, Imperative

INTELLEGENDA

Upon completion of this lesson you should be able to

1. Recognize, form, and translate the present infinitive, the present, future, and imperfect indicative, and the present imperative of third conjugation verbs in the active voice.

2. Recognize, form, and translate the four irregular third conjugation singular imperatives.

Salvē, discipule! When you turn to these exercises, you should have already thoroughly studied the corresponding chapter of *Wheelock's Latin*, especially the new grammar and vocabulary and even the **Latīna Est Gaudium** section. And always memorize paradigms and vocabulary by repeating the words *aloud*. **Sī Latīnam discis, age grātiās magistrō tuō!**

GRAMMATICA

1. Which of the four Latin verb conjugations is characterized by a short stem vowel?
   a. first   b. second   c. third   d. fourth

2. Which two verbs in the chapter's vocabulary are not third conjugation?
   _____ _____

3. The third conjugation stem vowel **-e-** is replaced by what three vowels in the present tense? _____ _____ _____

4. The vowel alternation in the present tense of third conjugation verbs is comparable to that seen in what tense of first and second conjugation verbs?
   a. present   b. future   c. imperfect   d. all these

5. Which vowel is not seen in the future tense endings of third conjugation verbs?
   a. a   b. e   c. ē   d. ō

6. The imperfect tense is formed just as in the first and second conjugations, except that the stem vowel is changed to
   a. ā   b. ē   c. ī   d. ō

7. Write out the irregular singular imperatives of **dīco, dūcō, faciō,** and **ferō.**
   _____ _____ _____ _____

8. Give the information requested for each of the following third conjugation endings.

	Tense	Number	Person
a. -imus	_____	_____	_____
b. -ēs	_____	_____	_____
c. -unt	_____	_____	_____
d. -itis	_____	_____	_____
e. -ēmus	_____	_____	_____
f. -ō	_____	_____	_____
g. -ent	_____	_____	_____
h. -it	_____	_____	_____

    i. -ētis   _____   _____   _____

    j. -am   _____   _____   _____

9. Conjugate **gerō, gerere,** in the present, future, and imperfect active indicative, and give the two imperatives.

Present		**Future**	
Singular	**Plural**	**Singular**	**Plural**
1. _____	_____	_____	_____
2. _____	_____	_____	_____
3. _____	_____	_____	_____

Imperfect	
Singular	**Plural**
1. _____	_____
2. _____	_____
3. _____	_____

Imperatives: _____ (singular)   _____ (plural)

10. List in order the third conjugation verbs in Practice and Review sentences 1–8, and identify the person, number, and tense of each.

Verb	**Person**	**Number**	**Tense**
a. _____	_____	_____	_____
b. _____	_____	_____	_____
c. _____	_____	_____	_____
d. _____	_____	_____	_____
e. _____	_____	_____	_____
f. _____	_____	_____	_____
g. _____	_____	_____	_____
h. _____	_____	_____	_____

EXERCITĀTIŌNĒS

A. Transform from singular to plural or plural to singular and translate the new phrase.

1. Dūcite hominēs.

   Transformation: _____

   Translation: _____

2. Frātrem doceō.

   Transformation: _____

   Translation: _____

3. Dē lībertātibus scrībunt.

   Transformation: _____

   Translation: _____

4. Bella gerēbant.

   Transformation: _____

   Translation: _____

5. Dēmōnstrābis ratiōnem.

   Transformation: _____

   Translation: _____

6. Tyrannōs necābunt.

   Transformation: _____

   Translation: _____

7. Graecum vincēbam.

   Transformation: _____

   Translation: _____

8. Discipulī crās discent.

   Transformation: _____

   Translation: _____

Name: _____ *Section:* _____ *Date:* _____

9. Corpus trahēbat.

   Transformation: _____

   Translation: _____

10. Virgō herī erat salva.

   Transformation: _____

   Translation: _____

B. Transform one of the nominative nouns to genitive to create a meaningful phrase, and then translate (e.g., **poēta liber** > **liber poētae,** _the poet's book_).

	Transformation	Translation
1. laus scrīptor	_____	_____
2. victōriae rēx	_____	_____
3. sorōrēs virtūtēs	_____	_____
4. carmen discipula	_____	_____
5. rēgīna mōrēs	_____	_____

C. Supply the correct forms of the words shown in parentheses and translate.

1. Ratiō hominēs nunc ex vitiīs ad virtūtem _____ (agere; pres.).

   _____

2. _____ (scrībere; 2nd pers. sg. imper.) nihil dē cōpiīs.

   _____

3. Dea amōris multōs _____ (vincere; pres.).

   _____

4. Amor laudis victōriaeque hominēs semper _____ (trahere; fut.).

   _____

D. Translate into Latin; employ standard word order and include all macrons.

1. He will lead the troops to perpetual glory there.

   _____

2. The state will never thank the Greek tyrant.

   _____

3. Your (sg.) new friend was writing a letter to my sister.

   _____

4. Because of your work, you will have an abundance of praise.

   _____

VĪS VERBŌRUM

A. Answer these questions on the chapter's vocabulary list.

1. "Victorious" derives from the Latin adjective _____,
   which is formed from the noun **victōria.**

2. Which verb does not have a related meaning?
   a. agō   b. discō   c. dūcō   d. trahō

3. Which noun does not have a related meaning?
   a. frāter   b. scrīptor   c. soror   d. uxor

4. Which noun does not have a related meaning?
   a. fāma   b. glōria   c. laus   d. lībertās

5. Which adverb is an antonym of **numquam**?
   a. ibi   b. nunc   c. semper   d. tamen

6. Many Latin verbs form masculine third declension nouns by
   replacing **-um** of the verb's fourth principal part with **-or;** such
   nouns typically denote a person who performs whatever action is
   indicated by the verb stem. E.g., **agō** gives us **āctor, āctōris,** m.,
   meaning literally *a person who acts, an actor.* Identify the nouns,
   and their meanings, that are similarly derived from the following
   Latin verbs.

	Latin Noun	**Translation**
a. doceō	_____	_____
b. scrībō	_____	_____
c. vincō	_____	_____
d. dēmōnstrō	_____	_____

B. Complete each statement with an English word that demonstrates your knowledge of the Latin etymology (e.g., "A 'laudatory' speech is full of praise").

1. An "expatriate" lives _____ of his _____.

2. To "inscribe" a document is literally to _____ _____ it.

3. A "docile" animal is easily _____.

4. A "p.s." or "postscript" is _____ _____ the main part of a letter or other document.

5. One who is "invincible" can _____ be _____.

LĒCTIŌNĒS

A. First read each sentence aloud twice, and then translate as literally as possible within the limits of sound English idiom.

1. Quārē scrīptor litterās dē īnsidiīs scrībere nōn tum audēbat?

     _____

2. Propter tempora secunda pācem vēram habēre poterimus.

     _____

3. Agricola uxorque in terrā sub caelō pulchrō saepe cēnābant.

     _____

4. Ubi hominēs rēgem malum nunc tolerāre possunt?

     _____

5. Dūc Graecum ad mē, et deābus grātiās agam.

     _____

6. Dum tyrannus cōpiās dūcit, possumus nihil agere.

     _____

7. Novī, igitur, cīvitātī nostrae grātiās agēbant.

     _____

8. Tyrannus magnās cōpiās ex cīvitāte nostrā dūcet et bellum geret.

     _____

9. Magna cōpia pecūniae, tamen, hominēs ad sapientiam nōn dūcit.

    _____

10. Ratiō hominēs ex culpīs ad bonam vītam saepe dūcere potest.

    _____

B. Answer these questions on "The Ethics of Waging War."

1. Cīvitās _____ bellum gerere dēbet.
    a. sine causā bonā   b. sine īrā
    c. sine officiō   d. sine clēmentiā

2. Bellum erit necessārium, sī patriam lībertātemque sine bellō
    _____ dēfendere poterimus.
    a. nōn   b. tum   c. tamen   d. autem

3. The attitude toward waging war expressed by Cicero in this
    passage is
    a. belligerent   b. pacifist   c. pragmatic   d. incendiary

Amor vincit omnia: *Love conquers all*
Vergil

9

Demonstratives Hic, Ille, Iste; Special -īus Adjectives

INTELLEGENDA

Upon completion of this lesson you should be able to

1. Recognize, decline, and translate the "demonstratives" **hic, ille,** *and* **iste**.

2. Distinguish between these demonstratives, in both usage and translation, as either adjectives or pronouns.

3. Recognize, decline, and translate the nine common irregular first/second declension adjectives that have a genitive singular ending in **-īus** *and a dative singular in* **-ī.**

Salvēte, discipulae discipulīque! Whenever you turn to the exercises in this workbook, you should have already thoroughly studied the corresponding chapter of *Wheelock's Latin*, especially the new grammar and vocabulary and even the **Latīna Est Gaudium** section. And remember always to memorize paradigms and vocabulary by repeating the words *aloud.* **Semper amāte Latīnam!**

GRAMMATICA

1. Demonstratives are used to _____ _____ particular persons or things.

2. In general **hic** indicates a person or thing near the _____, **iste** indicates a person or thing near the _____, and **ille** indicates a person or thing distant from _____.

3. The declension of demonstratives generally follows that of **magnus, -a, -um;** the principal irregularities occur in the _____, _____, and _____ singular cases.

4. Which is not a possible translation for the forms of **hic, haec, hoc**?
   a. this   b. these   c. those   d. the latter

5. Which is not a possible translation for the forms of **ille, illa, illud**?
   a. that   b. those   c. the famous   d. the latter

6. Which of the three demonstratives can have a contemptuous or disparaging sense?
   a. hic   b. ille   c. iste   d. all these

7. The nine irregular first/second declension adjectives introduced in this chapter are declined like **magnus, -a, -um;** the principal exceptions are in the _____ and _____ singular cases.

8. Which of the following is not a special **-īus/-ī** adjective?
   a. alius   b. nūllus   c. secundus   d. ūnus

9. Decline the phrase **ille locus** (*that place*) in the singular only, with the English meanings.

	Latin		**English**
Nom.	ille	locus	that place
Gen.	_____	_____	_____
Dat.	_____	_____	_____
Acc.	_____	_____	_____
Abl.	_____	_____	_____

10. Decline the phrase **hoc studium** (*this study*) in the plural only, with English meanings.

	Latin		**English**
Nom.	_____	_____	_____
Gen.	_____	_____	_____
Dat.	_____	_____	_____
Acc.	_____	_____	_____
Abl.	_____	_____	_____

11. Identify in order the five demonstratives used as adjectives in Practice and Review sentences 1–8.

    _____ _____ _____ _____ _____

12. Identify in order the four demonstratives used as pronouns in **Sententiae Antīquae** 1–7.

    _____ _____ _____ _____

13. Choose the correct form of the adjective and then translate the entire phrase.

	Adjective	Translation
a. studiī (neither)	_____	_____
b. morbō (dat., one)	_____	_____
c. scrīptōris (another)	_____	_____
d. laudī (alone)	_____	_____
e. frātris (either)	_____	_____

14. Give the information requested for each demonstrative.

	Case(s)	Number(s)	Gender(s)	Translation(s)
a. istī	_____	_____	_____	_____
b. istīs	_____	_____	_____	_____
c. istīus	_____	_____	_____	_____
d. istō	_____	_____	_____	_____
e. illī	_____	_____	_____	_____
f. illum	_____	_____	_____	_____
g. haec	_____	_____	_____	_____
h. hoc	_____	_____	_____	_____
i. huic	_____	_____	_____	_____
j. illae	_____	_____	_____	_____

15. Give the information requested for each irregular adjective.

	Case(s)	Number(s)	Gender(s)	Translation(s)
a. nūllīus	_____	_____	_____	_____
b. ūllō	_____	_____	_____	_____

c. tōtī   _____ _____ _____ _____

d. sōlum   _____ _____ _____ _____

e. ūnīus   _____ _____ _____ _____

f. aliī   _____ _____ _____ _____

g. aliud   _____ _____ _____ _____

h. alterī   _____ _____ _____ _____

i. utrīus   _____ _____ _____ _____

j. neutrum   _____ _____ _____ _____

EXERCITĀTIŌNĒS

A. Translate the following into English or Latin.

1. haec carmina _____

2. illa cōpia _____

3. huic temporī _____

4. huius virginis _____

5. illī rēgīnae _____

6. nūllī morbō _____

7. huic cīvitātī sōlī _____

8. tōtīus corporis _____

9. nūllīus ratiōnis _____

10. huius nōminis sōlīus _____

11. no love (acc.) _____

12. to/for the whole country _____

13. to/for one place _____

14. no brothers (acc.) _____

15. by another book _____

16. to/for that king alone _____

Name: _____   Section: _____   Date: _____

17. those customs (acc.) _____

18. that study (nom.) _____

19. of that sister alone _____

20. to/for one wife _____

B. Supply the correct form of the words shown in parentheses, and translate.

1. Habētis enim _____ (nūllus, -a, -um) virtūtēs.

   _____

2. Crās vidēbimus tamen _____ (alius, -a, -ud) nova loca.

   _____

3. Fāma _____ (ille, -a, -ud) victōriae remanet.

   _____

4. Multī locī _____ (hic, haec, hoc) librī sunt plēnī sapientiae.

   _____

5. Propter istum labōrem, pācem lībertātemque in _____ (tōtus, -a, -um) terrā habēbāmus.

   _____

   _____

C. Translate into Latin; employ standard word order and include all macrons.

1. They were never able to teach those studies of yours.

   _____

2. No passage of either letter is true.

   _____

3. Another friend will thank my daughters.

   _____

4. We often dared to lead our troops into that other region.

   _____

5. Without any reason, they were waging a new war.

   _____

D. Transform from singular to plural or plural to singular and translate the new phrase.

	Transformation	**Translation**
1. ad aliam cīvitātem	_____	_____
2. ex illīs terrīs	_____	_____
3. post hās sorōrēs	_____	_____
4. sub portīs alterīs	_____	_____
5. in aliud studium	_____	_____

VĪS VERBŌRUM

A. Answer these questions on the chapter's vocabulary list.

1. The adjective **studiōsus, -a, -um** means literally _____ *of* _____, and gives us the English derivative _____.

2. Which adjective is an antonym of **morbōsus, -a, -um**?
   a. novus   b. sānus   c. secundus   d. vester

3. Which English word is not related to **ūnus, -a, -um**?
   a. unit   b. unite   c. untie   d. onion

B. Complete each statement with an English word that demonstrates your knowledge of the Latin etymology (e.g., "A 'laudatory' speech is full of praise").

1. Persons who are "unanimous" are of _____ _____.

2. A "student" approaches his or her work with _____.

3. A "neutral" party takes _____ side in a dispute.

4. An "annulled" contract has _____ legal force.

LĒCTIŌNĒS

A. First read each sentence aloud twice, and then translate as literally as possible within the limits of sound English idiom.

1. Dum istī bellum nimis malum gerēbant, hī cīvitātem ex bellō ad pācem dūcere audēbant.

   _____

   _____

2. Ex hīs aliīs studiīs novīs multam sapientiam virtūtemque tra-hēmus.

   _____

   _____

3. Vincetne illum avārum amor pecūniae?

   _____

4. In illō librō multa dē hōc homine dēmōnstrābit.

   _____

5. Ūnus vir istās cōpiās in hanc terram tum dūcēbat.

   _____

6. Tōta patria huic deae sōlī grātiās hodiē aget.

   _____

7. Hic sōlus, igitur, mē dē amōre carminum litterārumque docēre poterat.

   _____

   _____

8. Illī sōlī stultī nūlla perīcula in hōc cōnsiliō vident.

   _____

9. Nōn sōlum mōrēs sed etiam īnsidiās illīus laudāre nunc audēs.

   _____

10. Propter victōriam enim ūnīus hominis haec cīvitās valēbat.

    _____

B.   Answer these questions on "When I Have Enough."

1.   Āfricānus est
     a. avārus   b. bonus   c. sānus   d. vir magnae sapientiae

2.   Quid nōn habet Āfricānus?
     a. mīliēns   b. multa pecūnia   c. satis pecūniae   d. amor pecūniae

3.   Quandō vir avārus satis pecūniae habēbit?
     a. hodiē   b. numquam   c. nunc   d. semper

4.   Quid dēbet avārus discere?
     a. nihil   b. amor pecūniae   c. philosophia   d. excūsātiōnēs bonae

Haec studia adulēscentiam alunt: *These studies nourish the young*
Cicero

10

Fourth Conjugation and -iō Verbs of the Third

INTELLEGENDA

Upon completion of this lesson you should be able to

1. Recognize, form, and translate the present active infinitive and imperative and the present, future, and imperfect active indicative of fourth conjugation verbs.

2. Recognize, form, and translate the present active infinitive and imperative and the present, future, and imperfect active indicative of -iō verbs of the third conjugation.

Salvēte, discipulae discipulīque! Whenever you turn to the exercises in this workbook, you should have already thoroughly studied the corresponding chapter of *Wheelock's Latin*. And remember always to memorize paradigms and vocabulary by repeating the words *aloud.* **Vīvite et valēte!**

GRAMMATICA

1. The fourth conjugation is characterized by the stem vowel _____.

2. The stem vowel is long in all conjugations except the
    a. first   b. second   c. third   d. fourth

3. Certain third conjugation verbs are formed in the present, future, and imperfect active indicative in exactly the same way as fourth conjugation verbs, except that the stem vowel is always
   a. long   b. short   c. dropped   d. changed to **-e-**

4. Third **-iō** and fourth conjugation verbs retain the **-i-** throughout all forms of the present, future, and imperfect active indicative.   T/F

5. The imperfect tense sign **-bā-** is preceded in third **-iō** and fourth conjugation verbs by
   a. **-ā-**   b. **-ē-**   c. **-i-**   d. **-iē-**

6. The future tense sign for the fourth conjugation is the same as for the
   a. first   b. second   c. third   d. none of these

7. Identify the conjugation, give the singular and plural imperatives, and translate the following verbs.

	Conjugation	Sg. Imper.	Pl. Imper.	Translation
a. discō, discere	_____	_____	_____	_____
b. doceō, docēre	_____	_____	_____	_____
c. fugiō, fugere	_____	_____	_____	_____
d. veniō, venīre	_____	_____	_____	_____
e. tolerō, tolerāre	_____	_____	_____	_____
f. faciō, facere	_____	_____	_____	_____
g. inveniō, invenīre	_____	_____	_____	_____
h. dīcō, dīcere	_____	_____	_____	_____
i. maneō, manēre	_____	_____	_____	_____
j. trahō, trahere	_____	_____	_____	_____

8. Conjugate **veniō, venīre,** in the present, future, and imperfect active indicative.

Present		Future	
Singular	**Plural**	**Singular**	**Plural**
1. _____	_____	_____	_____
2. _____	_____	_____	_____
3. _____	_____	_____	_____

Imperfect

Singular	Plural
1. _____	_____
2. _____	_____
3. _____	_____

9. Conjugate **faciō, facere,** in the present, future, and imperfect active indicative.

Present

Singular	Plural	**Future** Singular	Plural
1. _____	_____	_____	_____
2. _____	_____	_____	_____
3. _____	_____	_____	_____

Imperfect

Singular	Plural
1. _____	_____
2. _____	_____
3. _____	_____

EXERCITĀTIŌNĒS

A. Transform the indicative sentence into an imperative sentence that would result in the action indicated, and then translate into English (e.g., **Discipulus Latīnam discit** > **Discipule, disce Latīnam,** *Student, learn Latin!*).

1. Sorōrēs viam inveniunt.

   Transformation: _____

   Translation: _____

2. Frāter officium facit.

   Transformation: _____

   Translation: _____

3. Cōpiae timōrem fugiunt.

   Transformation: _____

   Translation: _____

4. Scrīptor vēritātem dīcit.

   Transformation: _____

   Translation: _____

5. Amīcus meus ratiōnem audit.

   Transformation: _____

   Translation: _____

B. Make the single transformation indicated and translate the new form (e.g., **dīcit,** to imperfect: answer, **dīcēbat,** *he was speaking*).

	Transformation	**Translation**
1. hōra fugit, to fut.	_____	_____
2. dūcite nautās, to sg.	_____	_____
3. Graecōs capis, to impf.	_____	_____
4. ibi vīvent, to pres.	_____	_____
5. ex viā veniēbam, to pl.	_____	_____

C. Supply the correct form of the words shown in parentheses and translate.

1. In illō locō numquam _____ (vīvere; 1st pers. pl. impf.).

   _____

2. Hī frātrēs beātī voluptātem amīcitiae in senectūte _____ (invenīre; fut.).

   _____

3. _____ (fugere; imper.) cupiditātem laudis, mī amīce!

   _____

4. Victōria sōla enim lībertātem nōn semper _____ (facere; pres.).

   _____

D. Translate into Latin; employ standard word order and include all macrons.

1. The other sister finds pleasure in the study of nature.

_____

2. While we speak, the hours are fleeing.

_____

3. The sailors were coming to the troops on another road.

_____

VĪS VERBŌRUM

A. Answer these questions on the chapter's vocabulary list.

1. Many third declension nouns with nominatives in **-tās** give us English derivatives in -ty. Identify the English words that are formed in this way from the following nouns.
cupiditās _____ **lībertās** _____ **vēritās** _____

2. The Latin adjective _____ is based on the noun **timor,** gives us the English derivative _____, and literally means _fearful_.

3. Many Latin verbs form feminine third declension nouns by replacing **-um** of the verb's fourth principal part with **-iō,** genitive **-iōnis;** such nouns typically produce English derivatives in -ion and denote performance of the action indicated by the verb stem. E.g., **cōnservō** gives us Latin **cōnservātiō, cōnservātiōnis,** f., and English "conservation," both meaning literally (_the act of_) _saving, preserving._ Identify the Latin and English nouns, and their meanings, that are similarly derived from the following Latin verbs.

	Latin Noun	**Eng. Noun**	**Translation**
a. audiō	_____	_____	_____
b. dīcō	_____	_____	_____
c. inveniō	_____	_____	_____

B. Complete each statement with an English word that demonstrates your knowledge of the Latin etymology (e.g., "A 'laudatory' speech is full of praise").

1. A "viaduct" is a type of bridge that literally _____ or supports a _____.

2. A "voluptuary's" chief goal in life is _____.

3. A "convention" is an event where people _____ _____ to conduct business.

LĒCTIŌNĒS

A. First read each sentence aloud twice, and then translate as literally as possible within the limits of sound English idiom.

1. Neuter scrīptor dē remediō ūllō istīus morbī dīcēbat.

   _____

2. Istī hominēs propter cupiditātem pecūniae erunt nimis stultī.

   _____

3. Ille poēta ūnus multa carmina dē frātre beātō scrībēbat.

   _____

4. Tyrannus hanc tōtam cīvitātem capere numquam poterit.

   _____

5. Tempus fugit; hōrae fugiunt; senectūs venit, sed mē nōn vincet.

   _____

6. In patriam vestram cum sorōribus frātribusque meīs veniēbant.

   _____

7. Fīliam tuam in cīvitāte utrā nōn inveniēs.

   _____

8. Quoniam iste bellum semper facit, nūllam pācem habēbimus.

   _____

Name: _____ Section: _____ Date: _____

B.   Answer these questions on "The Incomparable Value of Friendship."

1.   Quis (*Who*) erat scrīptor huius locī? (**Respondē in tōtā sententiā Latīnā,** *Respond in a complete Latin sentence.*)

   _____

2.   Quid Cicerō cum amīcitiā comparāre potest? _____

3.   Amīcitia ex _____ nōn venit.
     a. fortūnā   b. sapientiā   c. amōre   d. virtūte

4.   Vīta tyrannī nōn est beāta, quoniam iste habet _____ _____.
     a. vērōs amīcos   b. mōrēs bonōs
     c. nūllam amīcitiam   d. magnam fortūnam

Vīve hodiē: *Live today*
Martial

11

Personal Pronouns Ego, Tū, and Is; Demonstratives Is and Īdem

INTELLEGENDA

Upon completion of this lesson you should be able to

1. Define the term "personal pronoun."

2. Recognize, decline, and translate the first, second, and third person pronouns.

3. Explain the limited uses of personal pronouns.

4. Distinguish, in usage and translation, the differences between is, ea, id as personal pronoun and as demonstrative.

5. Recognize, decline, and translate the demonstrative īdem, eadem, idem.

6. Identify the four first and second person possessive adjectives.

Salvēte, discipulae discipulīque! Before you begin these exercises, be sure you have already thoroughly studied Chapter 11 of *Wheelock's Latin,* especially the new grammar and vocabulary and even the **Latīna Est Gaudium** section. And remember, as always, to memorize the new paradigms and vocabulary by repeating them *aloud.* **Ego Latīnam amō—amātisne Latīnam etiam vōs?**

GRAMMATICA

1. A personal pronoun is employed in place of a _____ to indicate a particular _____ from the point of view of the _____.

2. Which is not a personal pronoun?
   a. ego   b. is   c. iste   d. tū

3. Decline the first and second person pronouns and give translations.

	1st Person Latin	English	2nd Person Latin	English
Singular				
Nom.	_____	_____	_____	_____
Gen.	_____	_____	_____	_____
	_____	_____		
Dat.	_____	_____	_____	_____
Acc.	_____	_____	_____	_____
Abl.	_____	_____	_____	_____
Plural				
Nom.	_____	_____	_____	_____
Gen.	_____	_____	_____	_____
Dat.	_____	_____	_____	_____
Acc.	_____	_____	_____	_____
Abl.	_____	_____	_____	_____

4. Decline the third person pronoun **is, ea, id,** and give the translations.

	Masculine Latin	English	Feminine Latin	English	Neuter Latin	English
Singular						
Nom.	_____	_____	_____	_____	_____	_____
Gen.	_____	_____	_____	_____	_____	_____
Dat.	_____	_____	_____	_____	_____	_____
Acc.	_____	_____	_____	_____	_____	_____
Abl.	_____	_____	_____	_____	_____	_____

Plural

Nom.   _____ _____ _____ _____ _____ _____

Gen.   _____ _____ _____ _____ _____ _____

Dat.   _____ _____ _____ _____ _____ _____

Acc.   _____ _____ _____ _____ _____ _____

Abl.   _____ _____ _____ _____ _____ _____

5. Decline fully in Latin the demonstrative **īdem, eadem, idem.**

	Masculine	**Feminine**	**Neuter**
Singular			
Nom.	_____	_____	_____
Gen.	_____	_____	_____
Dat.	_____	_____	_____
Acc.	_____	_____	_____
Abl.	_____	_____	_____
Plural			
Nom.	_____	_____	_____
Gen.	_____	_____	_____
Dat.	_____	_____	_____
Acc.	_____	_____	_____
Abl.	_____	_____	_____

6. When preceding and modifying a noun in the same gender, number, and case, forms of **is, ea, id** function as

a. personal pronouns   b. demonstratives

c. possessive adjectives   d. all these

7. List, giving the sentence number, the three instances of **is, ea, id** as a demonstrative in the Latin Practice and Review sentences of Chapter 11.

(___) _____   (___) _____   (___) _____

8. The nominatives of the Latin personal pronouns were most commonly used for
   a. subjects   b. predicate nominatives   c. emphasis   d. all these

9. The genitives of the first and second personal pronouns were most commonly used to indicate possession.   T/F

10. Which was/were used to show possession?
    a. tuus   b. eius   c. eōrum   d. all these

11. Identify the number, case, and grammatical use of these personal pronouns in the chapter's Practice and Review sentences (e.g., **eum** [sentence 1], singular, accusative, direct object).

	Number	Case	Use
a. eam (1)	_____	_____	_____
b. Tū (2)	_____	_____	_____
c. eius (2)	_____	_____	_____
d. ego (3)	_____	_____	_____
e. mē (5)	_____	_____	_____
f. eī (6)	_____	_____	_____
g. nōbīs (9)	_____	_____	_____
h. eōrum (12)	_____	_____	_____

EXERCITĀTIŌNĒS

A. Translate the following into English or Latin.

1. nōbīs (abl.) _____   2. it _____

3. idem _____   4. vestrī _____

5. mihi _____   6. for you (pl.) _____

7. eius (f.) _____   8. by her _____

9. nostrum _____   10. the same man (acc.) _____

B.   Transform from singular to plural or plural to singular and translate the new phrase.

	Transformation	**Translation**
1. eīdem cōnsulī	_____	_____
2. caput eius	_____	_____
3. Mē intelleget.	_____	_____
4. Eam mittēbam.	_____	_____
5. Tū es cāra.	_____	_____

C.   Supply the correct personal pronoun in the second clause to refer to the underlined word in the first clause, and then translate (e.g., **Puella est bona;** _____ **laudō.** > **Puella est bona; eam laudō,** *The girl is good; I praise her*).

1.   Alter <u>cōnsul</u> in hanc patriam venit, ubi _____ vidēbō.

_____

2.   Quoniam iste <u>vir</u> est avārus, _____ nūllam pecūniam dabimus.

_____

3.   <u>Nōs</u> sōlī sumus sānī; _____ sōlōs, igitur, audīte!

_____

4.   Quod <u>tē</u> nimium amō, sine _____ vīvere numquam poterō.

_____

D.   Supply the correct form of the word shown in parentheses and translate.

1.   Nēmō ad _____ (is) cōpiās mittet.

_____

2.   Dīc _____ (ego) vēritātem.

_____

3.   Fīlia beāta tua _____ (tū) bene intellegēbat.

_____

4.   Mittō nēminem ad _____ (is) cōnsulem.

_____

E. Translate into Latin; employ standard word order and include all macrons.

1. The same friendly girl will send their books to us.

_____

2. Her dear daughter was fleeing with one friend into another place.

_____

3. Give him your friendship.

_____

4. You will not find it without care.

_____

VĪS VERBŌRUM

A. Answer these questions on the chapter's vocabulary list.

1. Which verb does not have a related meaning?
    a. cōgitō   b. intellegō   c. mittō   d. sentiō

2. Which adverb does not have a related meaning?
    a. hodiē   b. satis   c. semper   d. tum

3. Which conjunction is nearly synonymous with **quoniam**?
    a. autem   b. enim   c. neque   d. quod

4. Which conjunction is not postpositive?
    a. autem   b. enim   c. igitur   d. quod

5. Which is not negative?
    a. -ne   b. nec   c. nōn   d. numquam

6. Complete the analogy **caput:oculus::liber:**_____.
    a. cupiditās   b. hōra   c. morbus   d. verbum

B. Complete each statement with an English word that demonstrates your knowledge of the Latin etymology (e.g., "A 'laudatory' speech is full of praise").

1. We "cherish" persons who are _____ to us.

2. To "emit" signals is literally to _____ them _____.

3. A "benefactor" _____ things _____ for others (who regard him as a "beneficent" person); and in a "benediction" a minister speaks briefly at the end of a service, blessing his congregation and wishing them _____.

LĒCTIŌNĒS

A. First read each sentence aloud twice, and then translate as literally as possible within the limits of sound English idiom.

1. Vidēsne eam fēminam? Amāsne eam? Dabisne eī id dōnum?

   _____

2. Nec eum nec eam, autem, ad mē mittent.

   _____

3. Quid tū dē nātūrā senectūtis intellegis?

   _____

4. Mitte, Ō mī frāter, ūllam cupiditātem pecūniae et studium voluptātis.

   _____

   _____

5. Is morbus etiam mē terrēbat; quid tū, soror cāra, dē eō sentīs?

   _____

6. Uter amīcus tibi id hodiē dabit.

   _____

7. Fugiēsne mēcum in eā viā, amīca mea?

   _____

8. Cōpiae eōrum illam tōtam cīvitātem numquam capient.

   _____

9. Vōs mēcum ad amīcum cārum eius mittunt.

   _____

10. Nōs tēcum in terram eōrum nunc mittit.

   _____

Name: _____   *Section:* _____   *Date:* _____

B.   Answer these questions on "Cicero Denounces Catiline in the Senate."

1.   Quis (*Who*) in eō locō dīcit? (**Respondē in tōtā sententiā Latīnā.**)

_____

2.   Quid Catilīna agere audet?
     a. in senātum venīre   b. īnsidiās facere
     c. cōnsilia mala agere   d. all these

3.   Quārē senātus cōnsulque errant?

     a. quod dē Catilīnā et īnsidiīs eius nōn intellegunt
     b. quoniam Catilīnam amīcōsque eius nimis amant
     c. quod cōnsilium habent sed tamen nōn agunt
     d. all these

4.   Quid Catilīna agere dēbet?
     a. ex patriā fugere   b. in cīvitāte remanēre
     c. cōnsulem ad mortem dūcere   d. all these

Nēmō sōlus satis sapit: *No one by himself is sufficiently wise*

Plautus

12

Perfect Active System of All Verbs

INTELLEGENDA

Upon completion of this lesson you should be able to
1. *Identify the forms of the four principal parts of regular Latin verbs.*
2. *Define and explain the temporal sense of the three "perfect system" tenses.*
3. *Identify the perfect active stem of any verb.*
4. *Recognize, form, and translate verbs of all four conjugations in the three tenses of the perfect active system.*

Salvēte, amīcī! Have you already studied Chapter 12 of *Wheelock's Latin*? Be sure to do so before attempting these exercises, and remember to memorize the paradigms and vocabulary by repeating the words *aloud*. Do a thorough job with this chapter and you, like Caesar, will be able to exclaim, **Vēnī, vīdī, vīcī!**

GRAMMATICA

1. Which tense does not belong to the perfect system?
   a. future perfect   b. imperfect   c. perfect   d. pluperfect

2. All perfect active system forms are constructed on the stem found in the _____ principal part.
    a. first   b. second   c. third   d. fourth

3. The four principal parts of a regular Latin verb are the
    a. first person singular of the _____ _____ _____
    b. _____ _____ _____
    c. first person singular of the _____ _____ _____
    d. _____ _____ _____

4. Supply the indicated principal parts for these verbs from recent chapters, and translate each literally.

    Principal Parts: creō   _____ _____ _____

    Translation: I create   _____ _____ _____

    Principal Parts: _____ facere   _____ _____

    Translation: _____ to make   _____ _____

    Principal Parts: _____ _____ mīsī   _____

    Translation: _____ _____ I have sent   _____

    Principal Parts: _____ _____ _____ inventum

    Translation: _____ _____ _____ having been found

5. The perfect active stem of any verb is found by dropping _____ from the third principal part.

6. Identify the perfect active stem of the following verbs from recent chapters.

    a. āmittō _____   b. audiō _____   c. capiō _____

    d. dīcō _____   e. fugiō _____   f. intellegō _____

    g. sentiō _____   h. veniō _____   i. vīvō _____

7. The _____ tense of **esse** provides the endings of the active indicative _____ tense; and the _____ tense of **esse** (except for the 3rd person plural) provides the endings of the active indicative _____ _____ tense in all conjugations.

8. Conjugate these Latin verbs from the current chapter in the indicated tenses.

Perfect
(āmittō, *to lose***)**

Singular	Plural		
1. _____	_____		
2. _____	_____		
3. _____	_____		

Fut. Perf.
(cadō, *to fall***)**

Singular	Plural
1. _____	_____
2. _____	_____
3. _____	_____

Pluperfect
(creō, *to create***)**

Singular	Plural
1. _____	_____
2. _____	_____
3. _____	_____

9. Translate the preceding verbs into English.

Perfect
(āmittō, *to lose***)**

Singular	Plural
1. _____	_____
2. _____	_____
3. _____	_____

Fut. Perf.
(cadō, *to fall***)**

Singular	Plural
1. _____	_____
2. _____	_____
3. _____	_____

Pluperfect
(creō, *to create***)**

Singular	Plural
1. _____	_____
2. _____	_____
3. _____	_____

10. Which is not a correct translation of **cecidī**?
    a. I fell   b. I have fallen
    c. I was falling   d. none of these

11. Which is not a correct translation of **creābās**?
    a. you kept creating   b. you have created
    c. you were creating   d. you used to create

12. Complete the analogy, the _____ tense : photograph : : the _____ tense : video.

13. In the perfect system we look at events of the past, present, or future, and consider the impact of previously _____ actions upon those events.

EXERCITĀTIŌNĒS

A. Translate the following into English or Latin.

1. dīxeram _____   2. they will have created _____

3. mīserimus _____   4. we shall have lost _____

5. vēnistī _____   6. she had fallen _____

7. vīcerant _____   8. you have seen (pl.) _____

9. vocāvērunt _____   10. I had thought _____

B. Supply the correct form of the words in parentheses and translate.

1. In Asiā diū _____ (remanēre; 3rd pers. sg. perf.).

   _____

2. Dī ad caelum eam _____ (mittere; fut. perf.).

   _____

3. Caesar rēgī lībertātem nūper _____ (dare; plupf.).

   _____

4. Dē nātūrā amīcitiae litterās _____ (scrībere; 1st pers. pl. perf.).

   _____

C. Transform from singular to plural or plural to singular and translate the new phrase.

1. Adulēscēns cecidit.

   Transformation: _____

   Translation: _____

2. Patrēs timōrēs āmīserant.

   Transformation: _____

   Translation: _____

3. Vōs viās invēneritis.

   Transformation: _____

   Translation: _____

4. Mātrēs eōrum herī vēnērunt.

   Transformation: _____

   Translation: _____

5. Medicus diū vīxerat.

   Transformation: _____

   Translation: _____

D. Translate into Latin; employ standard word order and include all macrons.

1. Even after many years no one had learned the whole truth.

   _____

2. Your mother and father have taught you well, my dear friend.

   _____

3. You had said (pl.) nothing about that consul's plans.

   _____

4. We shall have conquered neither our desires nor our fears.

   _____

VĪS VERBŌRUM

A. Answer these questions on the chapter's vocabulary list.

1. Complete the analogy **magnus:parvus::pater:**_____.
   a. adulēscēns   b. fīlius   c. prīncipium   d. puer

2. Which noun does not have a related meaning?
   a. annus   b. hōra   c. medicus   d. tempus

3. Which adverb is an antonym of the others?
   a. diū   b. numquam   c. saepe   d. semper

4. Which verb is an antonym of **āmittō**?
   a. cadō   b. creō   c. intellegō   d. inveniō

5. Give the third declension **-or** and **-iō** nouns derived from the
   fourth principal part of **creō,** their literal meanings, and their
   direct English derivatives.

	Meaning	**Derivative**
a. **-or:** _____	_____	_____
b. **-iō:** _____	_____	_____

B. Complete each statement with an English word that demonstrates your
   knowledge of the Latin etymology (e.g., "A 'laudatory' speech is full
   of praise").

   1. A "pro forma" action is undertaken _____ appearances
      only.

   2. An "acerbic" letter has a _____ tone.

   3. The leaves of a "deciduous" tree _____ _____ in
      winter.

   4. A "matrilineal" society traces descent or inheritance through
      the _____ side of a family.

LĒCTIŌNĒS

A. First read each sentence aloud twice, and then translate as literally as
   possible within the limits of sound English idiom.

   1. Īdem cōnsul, autem, tum fuit vērum caput patriae nostrae.

      _____

   2. Ea medica dē morbīs senectūtis et remediīs eōrum scrīpserat.

      _____

3. Quoniam hī acerbī diū remanēbant, illī beātī ad Asiam numquam vēnērunt.

_____

_____

4. Studium litterārum nōbīs multās voluptātēs dedit.

_____

5. Nimis multī adulēscentēs prō patriā cecidērunt et vītās āmīsērunt.

_____

_____

6. Quod magister amīcus eōrum discipulōs ā prīncipiō cum patientiā docēbit, multa post parvum tempus didicerint.

_____

_____

7. Is poēta cārus carmina magnā cum cūrā semper creābat.

_____

8. Caesar eadem dē prīncipiō illīus bellī dīxit.

_____

9. Etiam id bene fēcerās.

_____

10. Eum in eōdem locō post paucās hōrās invēnērunt.

_____

B. Answer these questions on "Pliny Writes to Marcellinus" and "Diaulus."

1. Quis hās litterās scrīpsit?
   a. Fundānus   b. fīlia Fundānī   c. Marcellīnus   d. Plīnius

2. Hic scrīptor dē puellā cārā dīcit; quis fuit pater eius? (**Respondē in tōtā sententiā.**)

_____

3. How old was the girl?
   a. 10 years   b. 11 years   c. 12 years   d. 13 years

4. Quid nātūra eī puellae dederat? _____ _____

5. Quid haec puella nōn habuit?
   a. amor patris mātrisque   b. magnī animī
   c. sapientia et patientia   d. remedium morbī

6. The ABBA arrangement known as "chiasmus," seen in **vespillō facit, fēcerat . . . medicus** in Martial's short poem about Diaulus, was often used by Roman writers to emphasize contrast. Explain briefly how the chiastic word order here not only demonstrates a then/now contrast, but also humorously emphasizes a consistency in Diaulus' activities from past to present.

   _____

   _____

   _____

In prīncipiō erat Verbum, et Verbum erat apud Deum, et Deus erat Verbum:
In the beginning was the Word, and the Word was with God,
and God was the Word
St. John 1.1

13

Reflexive Pronouns and Possessives; Intensive Pronoun

INTELLEGENDA

Upon completion of this lesson you should be able to
  1. Define, recognize, form, and translate "reflexive pronouns" and "reflexive possessive adjectives."
  2. Define, recognize, form, and translate the "intensive pronoun."

Salvēte, discipulae discipulīque! Be sure that you have thoroughly studied Chapter 13 of *Wheelock's Latin,* especially the new grammar and vocabulary, and memorized the new paradigms and vocabulary by repeating the words *aloud.* Remember: **Sī Latīnam dīligētis, semper eritis fortūnātī!**

GRAMMATICA

1. Since reflexive pronouns by definition _____ to the _____, they cannot serve as the _____ of finite verbs and therefore lack the _____ case.

2. The first and second person reflexive pronouns are identical to the personal pronouns (except in the one case indicated above).   T/F

3. The forms of the third person reflexive most resemble those of
   a. ego   b. tū   c. is   d. ipse

4. In English translation the third person reflexive pronoun must reflect
   both the _____ and the _____ of the subject.

5. In English, both the reflexive and the intensive pronouns end with
   the suffix _____.

6. The first and second person reflexive possessive adjectives are identical to the regular first and second person possessives already
   learned.   T/F

7. The third person reflexive possessive must agree with the noun it
   modifies in _____, _____, and _____, but in
   English translation must reflect the _____ and _____
   of the subject.

8. The intensive pronoun follows the declensional pattern of **magnus, -a,
   -um,** except in the singular _____ and _____ cases.

9. In English translation the intensive pronoun must reflect the empha-
   sized word's
   a. number   b. gender   c. person   d. all these

10. List in order and identify the number, case, and grammatical use of
    the three reflexive pronouns in this chapter's **Sententiae Antīquae** 5–8
    (e.g., **sē** [sentence 1], singular, accusative, object of the preposition
    ante).

    Reflexive (Sent. No.)   Number   Case   Use

    a. _____   _____   _____   _____

    b. _____   _____   _____   _____

    c. _____   _____   _____   _____

11. Give all the possible meanings, both personal and reflexive.

    a. mihi _____

    b. vōbīs _____

    c. sē _____

    d. tibi _____

    e. mē _____

    f. sibi _____

12. Decline the Latin intensive pronoun in the singular only.

	Masculine	**Feminine**	**Neuter**
Nom.	_____	_____	_____
Gen.	_____	_____	_____
Dat.	_____	_____	_____
Acc.	_____	_____	_____
Abl.	_____	_____	_____

EXERCITĀTIŌNĒS

A. Supply the correct form of the words in parentheses and translate.

1. Nam quisque patrem _____ (reflexive possessive) dīlēxit.

   _____

2. Caesar, autem, _____ (acc. reflexive) cum eōdem cōnsule nūper iūnxerat.

   _____

   _____

3. Ante bellum, cōpiae eōrum sē cum amīcīs _____ (his) in Asiā iūnxērunt.

   _____

   _____

4. Medica _____ (nom. intensive) dē prīncipiō morbī multum intellēxit.

   _____

   _____

B. Translate into Latin; employ standard word order and include all macrons.

1. The young man's mother sent him great riches, but saved nothing for herself.

   _____

   _____

2. Caesar himself was standing there for a long time before his own troops.

_____

_____

3. Nevertheless, the doctor said nothing about himself and his own deeds yesterday.

_____

_____

C. Transform from singular to plural or plural to singular and translate the new sentence.

1. Vir sē culpāvit.

   Transformation: _____

   Translation: _____

2. Mātrēs sē culpāverant.

   Transformation: _____

   Translation: _____

3. Ego mē servābō.

   Transformation: _____

   Translation: _____

4. Cōnsul ipse mē laudābat.

   Transformation: _____

   Translation: _____

5. Soror sibi dōnum dederat.

   Transformation: _____

   Translation: _____

6. Tū ipsa factum eius laudās.

   Transformation: _____

   Translation: _____

7. Fīlium suum docet.

   Transformation: _____

   Translation: _____

8. Patrēs signa sua vīdērunt.

   Transformation: _____

   Translation: _____

VĪS VERBŌRUM

A. Answer these questions on the chapter's vocabulary list.

1. Some Latin nouns produce English derivatives by simply dropping the nominative case ending; e.g., **verbum** > "verb." List two such English derivatives from this chapter's vocabulary list.

   _____ _____

2. Which adverb does not have a related meaning?
   a. ante   b. bene   c. nūper   d. ōlim

3. Which adjective is nearly synonymous with **fortūnātus**?
   a. acerbus   b. amīcus   c. beātus   d. doctus

4. Which conjunction has a meaning in common with **nam**?
   a. autem   b. enim   c. nec   d. -que

5. Which verb is similar in meaning to **dīligō**?
   a. agō   b. alō   c. amō   d. cadō

6. Complete the analogy **multus : nūllus :: doctus :** _____ .
   a. cārus   b. sānus   c. stultus   d. suus

B. Complete each statement with an English word that demonstrates your knowledge of the Latin etymology (e.g., "A 'laudatory' speech is full of praise").

1. An animal receives _____ through its "alimentary" canal.

2. A "conjunction" literally _____ one item _____ another.

3. An "antebellum" home was built _____ the _____ .

4. Something "permanent" _____ _____ many years.

LĒCTIŌNĒS

A. First read each sentence aloud twice, and then translate as literally as possible within the limits of sound English idiom.

1. In prīncipiō Deus hominēs in fōrmā suā creāvit.

_____

2. Quod dīvitiās āmīserat, pater ipse nec fīliās nec fīliōs suōs alere potuit.

_____

_____

3. Ea fēmina nūllum timōrem sēnsit sed, propter virtūtem, sē necāvit.

_____

_____

4. Etiam post multōs annōs nēmō patientiam eius laudat.

_____

5. Ille adulēscēns doctus multa per sē et labōrem suum didicerat.

_____

6. Prō patriā Caesarī ipsī multum dederāmus, sed nōbīs nihil dedimus.

_____

_____

7. Rēgīna ipsa ōlim erat caput patriae suae in Asiā.

_____

8. Ego tē dīligō, amīca mea, sed dīligisne tē ipsam?

_____

B. Answer these questions on "Alexander the Great" and "Authority of a Teacher's Opinion."

1. Complete the analogy, **Alexander : scrīptōrēs : : Achillēs :**_____.

2. Quid litterae magnae virō magnō dare possunt?
    a. multa facta   b. magna fortūna
    c. fāma perpetua   d. corpus sānum

3. Quandō magistrī doctī discipulīs sententiās suās dīcere dēbent?
    a. hodiē b. nōn semper c. saepe d. semper

4. Ubi vēritātem inveniēmus?
    a. in disputātiōnibus   b. in philosophiā
    c. in sententiā   d. in ratiōne

Labor ipse voluptās: *Work itself (is) a pleasure*
Manilius

14

I-Stem Nouns of the Third Declension; Ablatives of Means, Accompaniment, and Manner

INTELLEGENDA

Upon completion of this lesson you should be able to

1. Distinguish between "i-stem nouns" and "consonant-stem nouns" of the third declension.

2. Recognize, form, and translate third declension i-stem nouns, including the irregular noun vīs.

3. Define, distinguish among, and translate ablatives of "means," "accompaniment," and "manner."

Salvēte, discipulae discipulīque! Be sure you have thoroughly studied Chapter 14 of *Wheelock's Latin* before attempting these exercises. And remember to memorize paradigms and vocabulary by repeating the words *aloud*. **Semper discite cum studiō et voluptāte!**

GRAMMATICA

1. All third declension **i**-stems differ from consonant stems in the _____ plural case, which has the ending _____.

2. In addition, neuter **i**-stems differ from consonant stems in the _____ singular case, which ends with _____ instead of _____, and in the _____, _____, and _____ plural, which end with _____ instead of _____.

3. Which does not describe a category of **i**-stem nouns?
   a. neuters with nominatives ending in **-e, -al,** or **-ar**
   b. masculine and feminine nouns with nominatives in **-is** or **-ēs** and the same number of syllables in both the nominative and genitive singular
   c. neuters with monosyllabic nominatives in **-um** or **-us** and a base ending in two consonants
   d. masculine and feminine nouns with nominatives in **-s** or **-x** and a base ending in two consonants

4. Which two third declension nouns in the chapter's vocabulary list are not **i**-stems?

   _____ _____

5. Identify the base and gender of **urbs antīqua,** *the ancient city,* decline it fully, and provide the English meanings appropriate to each case.

   base: _____ _____   gender: _____

	Singular **Latin**		**English**
Nom.	urbs	antīqua	the ancient city
Gen.	_____	_____	_____
Dat.	_____	_____	_____
Acc.	_____	_____	_____
Abl.	_____	_____	_____

Plural

Nom.	_____	_____	_____
Gen.	_____	_____	_____
Dat.	_____	_____	_____
Acc.	_____	_____	_____
Abl.	_____	_____	_____

6. Decline **animal bellum,** *the beautiful animal,* and provide the English meanings.

Singular

	Latin	English	
Nom.	animal	bellum	the beautiful animal
Gen.	_____	_____	_____
Dat.	_____	_____	_____
Acc.	_____	_____	_____
Abl.	_____	_____	_____

Plural

Nom.	_____	_____	_____
Gen.	_____	_____	_____
Dat.	_____	_____	_____
Acc.	_____	_____	_____
Abl.	_____	_____	_____

7. Decline both **vir** and **vīs,** with English meanings.

Singular

	Latin	English	Latin	English
Nom.	vir	the man	vīs	force
Gen.	_____	_____	_____	_____
Dat.	_____	_____	_____	_____
Acc.	_____	_____	_____	_____
Abl.	_____	_____	_____	_____

Plural

Nom.	_____	_____	_____	_____
Gen.	_____	_____	_____	_____
Dat.	_____	_____	_____	_____
Acc.	_____	_____	_____	_____
Abl.	_____	_____	_____	_____

8. Match.
   He wrote the letter
   ____ with a pen   a. ablative of accompaniment
   ____ with a friend   b. ablative of manner
   ____ with care   c. ablative of means

9. Match.
   ____ with whom   a. ablative of accompaniment
   ____ with what   b. ablative of manner
   ____ how   c. ablative of means

10. Which ablative case usage never requires a preposition?
    a. accompaniment   b. manner   c. means   d. all these

11. Translate and indicate the type of ablative case usage.

	Translation	Type of Ablative
a. with a citizen	_____	_____
b. by death	_____	_____
c. with patience	_____	_____
d. with skill	_____	_____
e. by sea	_____	_____
f. iūre	_____	_____
g. cum cīvibus	_____	_____
h. auribus meīs	_____	_____
i. cum cūrā	_____	_____
j. cum medicīs	_____	_____

Name: _____ *Section:* _____ *Date:* _____

EXERCITĀTIŌNĒS

A. Transform from singular to plural or plural to singular and translate the new phrase.

	Transformation	Translation
1. cum cīvibus doctīs	_____	_____
2. factīs (abl.) eōrum	_____	_____
3. cum patre eius	_____	_____
4. eō signō (abl.)	_____	_____
5. parvae partis	_____	_____

B. Transform one of the nominative nouns to genitive to create a meaningful phrase, and then translate (e.g., **puella fortūna** > **fortūna puellae,** *the girl's fortune*).

	Transformation	Translation
1. vīs ars	_____	_____
2. partēs urbēs	_____	_____
3. Caesar mors	_____	_____
4. dīvitiae mātrēs	_____	_____
5. annus prīncipium	_____	_____

C. Supply the correct form of the words in parentheses and translate.

1. Cīvēs illārum _____ (urbs) bellum acerbum diū gerēbant.

    _____

2. Cum _____ (virtūs) et patientiā mortem tolerāvērunt.

    _____

3. Adulēscentēs ipsōs trāns _____ (mare; pl.) mīserat.

    _____

4. Nam tōtam urbem _____ (vīs; sg.) nūper tenēbant.

    _____

5. Agricola stultus _____ (animal) sua prō pecūniā necāvit.

    _____

D. Translate into Latin; employ standard word order and include all macrons.

1. The young men stood before Caesar with courage.

   _____

2. The boy and girl were running into the water with their friends.

   _____

3. The father can support himself and his daughter with his own money.

   _____

   _____

4. The force of the seas restrained them yesterday.

   _____

5. The mob dragged the tyrant across the street and through the city.

   _____

VĪS VERBŌRUM

A. Answer these questions on the chapter's vocabulary list.

1. Some Latin nouns produce English derivatives by simply dropping the genitive case ending; e.g., **virgō, virginis** > "virgin." List two such English derivatives from this chapter's vocabulary list. _____ _____

2. Which does not belong?
   a. auris b. bāsium c. oculus d. ōs

3. Which noun is an antonym of **mors**?
   a. animal b. caput c. vīs d. vīta

4. Which verb is an antonym of **teneō**?
   a. āmittō b. cadō c. creō d. habeō

5. Which English word is not related to the Latin word? (Use a good English dictionary, if necessary, to answer these.)
   a. mors: a. moratorium b. mortal c. mortify d. mortgage
   b. vīs: a. inviolate b. vim c. violent d. virile
   c. currō: a. cure b. current c. incur d. recur

B. Complete each statement with an English word that demonstrates your knowledge of the Latin etymology (e.g., "A 'laudatory' speech is full of praise").

1. A "subaqueous" creature lives _____ _____.

2. Something "inevitable" can _____ be _____, and something "immutable" can _____ be _____.

LĒCTIŌNĒS

A. First read each sentence aloud twice, and then translate as literally as possible within the limits of sound English idiom.

1. Medicus ipse tōtam vēritātem ōre suō dīxit, et ego verba eius auribus meīs audīvī.

   _____

   _____

2. Propter illās nūbēs et timōrem maris, nautae in Asiā remanēbant.

   _____

3. Rōmam antīquam semper appellābimus urbem magnam pulchramque.

   _____

   _____

4. Quisque mōrēs suōs mūtāverat et ista vitia tum vītābat.

   _____

5. Rēgēs Rōmam ōlim tenuērunt et eam cum aliīs urbibus iūnxērunt.

   _____

6. Quod cōnsulēs cīvitātem magnā cum sapientiā gessērunt, eōs dīlēximus.

   _____

   _____

B. Answer these questions on "Store Teeth" and "The Catilinarian Conspirators."

1. Quis (*Who*) dentēs ēmptōs habet?
   a. Thais   b. Laecania   c. Martial   d. all of them

2. Quārē sunt dentēs alterīus fēminae nigrī?
   a. suōs habet   b. ēmptōs habet   c. ea est bella   d. all these

3. What is peculiar in the word order of each of the two phrases **Thāis . . . nigrōs, niveōs Laecānia** and **Ēmptōs haec . . . illa suōs,** and what is the purpose of this arrangement?

   _____

   _____

4. Quid Cicerō agere dēbet?
   a. poenās dare   b. amīcōs Catilīnae ad mortem dūcere
   c. cōgitāre malōs esse cīvēs   d. istōs numquam morte multāre

5. Sī Cicerō amīcōs Catilīnae multābit, Rōma eī _____
   _____ dabit.

Ars artium omnium cōnservātrīx: *The art (that is) preserver of all arts*
Motto of the profession of printers

15

Numerals; Genitive of the Whole; Genitive and Ablative with Cardinal Numerals; Ablative of Time

INTELLEGENDA

Upon completion of this lesson you should be able to

1. Explain the difference between "cardinal" and "ordinal" numerals.

2. Recognize and translate the cardinal numerals from **ūnus** *through* **vīgintī quīnque**, *as well as* **centum** *and mīle.*

3. Decline **ūnus, duo, trēs,** *and* **mīl**

4. Recognize, decline, and translate the ordinal numerals from **prīmus** *through* **duodecimus**.

5. Define, recognize, and translate the "genitive of the whole" (or "partitive genitive") construction.

6. Define, recognize, and translate the "ablative with cardinal numerals" construction.

7. Define, recognize, and translate the "ablative of time when or within which" construction.

Salvēte, discipulae discipulīque! Be sure you have learned the numerals and new case constructions introduced in Chapter 15, before beginning these exercises; remember to memorize the numerals, declensions, and vocabulary by repeating the words *aloud.* **Parvō tempore Latīnam bene intellegētis!**

GRAMMATICA

1. The basic "counting" numbers (one, two, three, etc.) are called _____, while numerals used to indicate order of occurrence are, quite aptly, called _____.

2. Which does not belong?
    a. quattuor b. sextus c. novem d. ūndēvīgintī

3. Which does not belong?
    a. ūnus b. secundus c. quīntus d. ūndecimus

4. Which is not declinable?
    a. ūnus b. vīgintī c. dūcentī d. mīlia

5. Decline **duae nūbēs** and **tria animālia,** in the plural only.

Nom.	duae	nūbēs	tria	animālia
Gen.	_____	_____	_____	_____
Dat.	_____	_____	_____	_____
Acc.	_____	_____	_____	_____
Abl.	_____	_____	_____	_____

6. Which can not be used with a genitive of the whole?
    a. quīnque b. mīlia c. pars d. nihil

7. Which phrase does not contain a genitive of the whole?
    a. pars ōris b. dīvitiae urbis c. nēmō cīvium d. satis vīrium

8. Identify the three nouns used as genitives of the whole in Practice and Review sentences 1–10. _____ _____ _____

9. Identify the two nouns used as ablatives with cardinal numerals in Practice and Review 1–5. _____ _____

10. Which English preposition is not an option for translating the ablative of time construction?
    a. at b. for c. on d. within

11. Identify the three nouns used as ablatives of time in **Sententiae Antīquae** 1–9. _____ _____ _____

EXERCITĀTIŌNĒS

A. Translate into Latin and identify the case and usage (e.g., with a
    friend > **cum amīcō,** ablative of accompaniment).

	Translation	Case and Usage
1. with six animals	_____	_____
2. enough wealth	_____	_____
3. in the water	_____	_____
4. in two hours	_____	_____
5. ten of the citizens	_____	_____
6. much (of) art	_____	_____
7. within four years	_____	_____
8. the city's streets	_____	_____
9. with little care	_____	_____
10. with his own ears	_____	_____

B. Transform from singular to plural or plural to singular and translate
    the new phrase or sentence.

1. illīs temporibus

    Transformation: _____

    Translation: _____

2. Tempestātem herī exspectāvit.

    Transformation: _____

    Translation: _____

3. cum turbīs miserīs

    Transformation: _____

    Translation: _____

4. Mortēs timēbant.

    Transformation: _____

    Translation: _____

C. Supply the correct form of the words in parentheses and translate.

1. Nam illī miserī tempestātem _____ _____ (id tempus) timēbant.

   _____

   _____

2. Itaque Rōmam ipsam tribus ex _____ (cīvis) ōlim commīsērunt.

   _____

   _____

3. Propter facta eius, nēmō in Italiā satis _____ (iūs; pl.) tenuit.

   _____

4. Caesar cōpiās suās cum mīlibus _____ (nauta) trāns maria dūxerat.

   _____

   _____

D. Translate into Latin; employ standard word order and include all macrons.

1. Within a few hours those fortunate men had thrown the tyrant out of Italy.

   _____

   _____

2. You were entrusting part of the city to the two consuls.

   _____

3. Because of their deeds, we called six of those men friends.

   _____

4. They will at that time esteem thousands of these citizens.

   _____

VĪS VERBŌRUM

A. Answer these questions on the chapter's vocabulary list.

1. **Glōria** gives us English "glory"; what English derivatives are simi-
    larly derived from the first declension nouns in this chapter's vo-
    cabulary?

    _____ _____

2. Which word has a meaning similar to that of **itaque**?
    a. ante   b. igitur   c. ōlim   d. trāns

3. Which adjective is an antonym of **miser**?
    a. acerbus   b. doctus   c. fortūnātus   d. stultus

4. The third declension **-iō** noun _____ derives from the
    fourth principal part of **committō** and literally means
    _____ or _____.

5. Complete the analogy _____ : **centum :: decem : ūnus.**

6. Give the Latin numeral that indicates the total.
    a. ūnus + septem: _____   b. duo + quattuor: _____
    c. novem + ūndecim: _____   d. octō + decem: _____

7. Complete the series.
    quīntus _____ _____ octāvus nōnus
    decimus _____

8. The derivative of **iaciō** that literally means "downcast" is

    _____ .

B. Complete each statement with an English word that demonstrates your
    knowledge of the Latin etymology (e.g., "A 'laudatory' speech is full
    of praise").

1. An event's "quincentennial" is celebrated _____
    _____ _____ after it occurred.

2. A "projectile" is an object that has been _____
    _____ , something "ejected" has been _____
    _____ , and a "trajectory" is the path such an object has
    been _____ _____ .

3. A "timorous" person is _____ -ful.

LĒCTIŌNĒS

A. First read each sentence aloud twice, and then translate as literally as possible within the limits of sound English idiom.

1. Quisque sē memoriā factōrum bonōrum eius aluerat.

   _____

2. Ante signum per viās urbis cucurrērunt et sē cum aliīs cōpiīs iūnxērunt.

   _____

   _____

3. Quoniam nihil pecūniae tenuimus, cōnsilia mūtābāmus.

   _____

4. Centum ex adulēscentibus ante portam cum virtūte stetērunt, sed exitium urbis nōn vītāre potuērunt.

   _____

   _____

5. Hās magistrās doctās, quod multum sapientiae inter sē tenēbant, discipulae semper dīligēbant.

   _____

   _____

6. Paucīs annīs Rōmānī eam partem Italiae cēperant.

   _____

7. Vīdistīne eō tempore patrem nostrum inter illōs aliōs virōs, mī frāter?

   _____

   _____

8. Quod eum nōn amābat, fēmina dōnum librōsque poētae in viam iēcit.

   _____

   _____

B.   Answer these questions on "Cyrus' Dying Words" and "Fabian Tactics."

    1.   Quis dēbet esse miser?
        a. Cyrus   b. Cicerō   c. fīliī Cyrī   d. nēmō

    2.   Cyrus est beātus quod
        a. trēs fīliōs habet   b. animus suus erit perpetuus
        c. corpus semper remanēbit   d. fīliī facta intellegēbant

    3.   Fabius Maximus parvum virtūtis et nihil animōrum habuit.   T/F

    4.   Quid Fabius ante patriam ponēbat?
        a. rūmor   b. fāma   c. glōria   d. nihil

Vēra amīcitia est inter bonōs: *There is true friendship (only) among good men*
Cicero

16

Third Declension Adjectives

INTELLEGENDA

Upon completion of this lesson you should be able to
   1. Distinguish among third declension adjectives of "one ending," "two endings," and "three endings."
   2. Recognize, form, and translate third declension adjectives.
   3. Distinguish among adjectives used as "attributives," "objective complements," and "predicate nominatives."
   4. State the rule for adjective word order.

Salvēte, discipulae discipulīque! Whenever you turn to the exercises in this workbook, you should have already thoroughly studied the corresponding chapter of *Wheelock's Latin,* especially the new grammar and vocabulary and even the **Latīna Est Gaudium** section. And remember always to memorize paradigms and vocabulary by repeating the words *aloud.* **Sī Latīnam dīligētis, amīcī et amīcae, eritis omnipotentēs!**

GRAMMATICA

1. Most third declension adjectives are declined like **i**-stem nouns, except that the _____ case ends in the singular with _____ in all three genders.

2. Third declension adjectives of three endings are so called because
    they have different endings for each of the three genders in the
    _____ case.

3. The majority of third declension adjectives are those of
    a. one ending   b. two endings   c. three endings   d. none of these

4. The masculine and feminine forms of third declension adjectives of
    two or three endings differ from the neuter forms only in the
    _____, _____, and _____ cases, singular and
    plural.

5. Match.
    ____ cīvēs sunt beātī   a. attributive
    ____ sapientia fēcit cīvēs beātōs b. objective complement
    ____ cīvēs beātōs dīligimus   c. predicate nominative

6. Attributive adjectives are usually placed _____ the nouns they
    modify, except
    a. those denoting size or quantity   b. demonstratives
    c. for emphasis   d. all these

7. Third declension adjectives can modify nouns of the
    a. first declension   b. second declension
    c. third declension   d. all these

8. The base of any third declension adjective can be found by dropping
    the _____ case ending.

9. Identify the base and gender of **mēns potēns,** *a powerful mind,* decline
    in the singular only, and provide the English meanings appropriate to
    each case.

    base: _____ _____   gender: _____

	Latin		**English**
Nom.	mēns	potēns	_____
Gen.	_____	_____	_____
Dat.	_____	_____	_____
Acc.	_____	_____	_____
Abl.	_____	_____	_____

10. Identify the base and gender of **satura ācris,** *a harsh satire,* and
    decline in the plural only.

base: _____ _____   gender: _____

Nom. _____   _____

Gen. _____   _____

Dat. _____   _____

Acc. _____   _____

Abl. _____   _____

11. Identify the base and gender of **animal ingēns,** *a huge animal,* and decline fully.

base: _____ _____   gender: _____

	Singular		**Plural**	
Nom.	animal	ingēns	_____	_____
Gen.	_____	_____	_____	_____
Dat.	_____	_____	_____	_____
Acc.	_____	_____	_____	_____
Abl.	_____	_____	_____	_____

12. Choose the correct form of the third declension adjective and then translate the entire phrase.

	Adjective	**Translation**
a. aetāte (brief)	_____	_____
b. artium (difficult)	_____	_____
c. tempestātēs (powerful)	_____	_____
d. audītōrī (every)	_____	_____
e. aquārum (sweet)	_____	_____
f. clēmentiam (pleasant)	_____	_____
g. maria (fierce)	_____	_____
h. nūbium (swift)	_____	_____
i. urbī (brave)	_____	_____
j. carmina (easy)	_____	_____

Name: _____   *Section:* _____   *Date:* _____

EXERCITĀTIŌNĒS

A.   Translate the following.

1.   omnī marī _____

2.   omnium partium _____

3.   omnia nōmina _____

4.   Italiam potentem _____

5.   omnī arte _____

6.   omnium bellōrum _____

7.   Rōmā potentī _____

8.   mortis celeris _____

9.   aure ācrī _____

10.   omnia iūra _____

11.   omnī artī _____

12.   dulcī puellae _____

13.   vī celerī _____

14.   ōs omne _____

15.   omnium rēgum _____

16.   turbae ācris _____

B.   Supply the correct form of the words in parentheses and translate.

1.   Memoriae _____ (dulcis) senectūtem iuvant.

     _____

2.   Quam _____ (celer) sunt aetātēs nostrae!

     _____

3.   Senex duōs amīcōs _____ (miser) fīliōrum _____ (fortis) exspectābat.

     _____

4.   Itaque Rōmam semper appellābimus urbem _____ (potēns).

     _____

C. Transform from singular to plural or plural to singular and translate the new phrase.

1. Animal ācre tenuit.

   Transformation: _____

   Translation: _____

2. Aetātēs brevēs timēbātis.

   Transformation: _____

   Translation: _____

3. Trāns mare difficile herī fūgit.

   Transformation: _____

   Translation: _____

4. Mentibus celeribus regunt.

   Transformation: _____

   Translation: _____

5. Fortis crās nōn curret.

   Transformation: _____

   Translation: _____

D. Translate into Latin; employ standard word order and include all macrons.

1. We had many memories of a difficult life.

   _____

2. In a short period of time the fierce war had changed all the citizens.

   _____

3. Within three hours you expected all your friends.

   _____

4. They found strength in the pleasant woman's courage.

   _____

VĪS VERBŌRUM

A. Answer these questions on the chapter's vocabulary list.

1. Many Latin third declension adjectives form feminine abstract nouns by adding **-itās** (genitive **-itātis**) to the base; these Latin words in turn often produce English derivatives in "-ity" (e.g., **celer > celeritās, -tātis,** f., *speed, swiftness,* English "celerity"). Provide the indicated information for the following adjectives from this chapter's vocabulary.

	Latin Noun	**Meaning**	**Derivative**
a. brevis	_____	_____	_____
b. facilis	_____	_____	_____

2. The masculine noun from **regō** meaning *one who rules, directs* is
    a. rēctiō   b. rēctus   c. rēctor   d. regendus

3. An "acrimonious" person is
    a. bitter   b. guiltless   c. wealthy   d. protective

4. Which noun is nearly synonymous with **mēns**?
    a. animus   b. culpa   c. fāma   d. remedium

5. Using a third declension adjective, complete the analogy
    difficilis : facilis : : longus : _____.
    a. brevis   b. dulcis   c. ingēns   d. omnis

B. Complete each statement with an English word that demonstrates your knowledge of the Latin etymology (e.g., "A 'laudatory' speech is full of praise").

1. "Inclement" weather is literally _____ _____.

2. An "omnivorous" animal eats _____ things.

3. To "facilitate" a task is to make it _____.

4. An "omnipotent" force is _____-_____.

LĒCTIŌNĒS

A. First read each sentence aloud twice, and then translate as literally as possible within the limits of sound English idiom.

1. Aetās difficilis, autem, potest esse beāta.

   _____

2. Quam brevis erat dulcis vīta eius!

   _____

3. In omnī terrā virōs fēmināsque fortēs vidēbitis.

   _____

4. Perīcula ingentia paucīs hōrīs superāvimus.

   _____

5. Itaque audītōrēs ācrēs poētae potentī mentēs commīsērunt.

   _____

6. Inter amīcōs nihil est nimium difficile.

   _____

7. Ille vir fortis animālia ācria ex portā urbis iēcit.

   _____

8. Omnēs stultī labōrem prō vītā facilī vītābant.

   _____

B. Answer these questions on "Juvenal Explains His Impulse to Satire" and "On a Temperamental Friend."

1. Quid erit Iuvenālis (*Juvenal*)?
    a. audītor   b. poēta   c. satura   d. indignātiō

2. Quid Iuvenālis scrībet?
    a. carmina iūcunda   b. liber dē amōre
    c. saturae ācrēs   d. saturae dulcēs

3. Quid urbs Rōma habet?
    a. multī poētae   b. multa vitia   c. multī malī   d. omnia haec

4. The overall tone of Juvenal's introduction is
    a. optimistic   b. cynical   c. joyful   d. forgiving

Name: _____ *Section:* _____ *Date:* _____

5. Whom does Martial address in his epigram?
    a. a close friend   b. an enemy
    c. a casual acquaintance   d. a girlfriend

6. Which rhetorical or poetic device is exploited in the poem?
    a. metaphor   b. simile   c. antithesis   d. onomatopoeia

7. Potestne poēta sine amīcō suō esse beātus?
    a. potest   b. nōn potest   c. nōn dīcit   d. semper

Dulce et decōrum est prō patriā morī:
A sweet and decorous thing it is to die for one's country
Horace

17

The Relative Pronoun

INTELLEGENDA

Upon completion of this lesson you should be able to
 1. *Define and explain the function of a "relative pronoun."*
 2. *State the rule for the agreement of a relative pronoun and its "antecedent."*
 3. *Recognize, form, and translate a relative pronoun.*

Salvē, discipula aut discipule! Before attempting these exercises, be sure you have thoroughly studied Chapter 17 of *Wheelock's Latin* and memorized both the declension of **quī, quae, quod** and the new vocabulary by repeating them *aloud.* **Disce omnia quae sunt in hōc libellō, et eris beātus (aut beāta)!**

GRAMMATICA

1. A relative pronoun introduces a type of _____ clause known as a "relative clause" and refers back to a noun or pronoun (i.e., a person or thing) called its _____.

2. The relative clause itself functions
 a. adverbially   b. adjectivally   c. verbally   d. as a noun

3. The term "antecedent" means literally someone or something that has _____ _____.

4. A relative pronoun must agree with its antecedent in every respect except
   a. number   b. gender   c. case   d. none of these

5. The _____ of a relative pronoun is determined by its use in its own clause.

HW 6. Decline the relative pronoun in the masculine gender only and provide the English meanings (note that the genitive may be translated either *of whom* or *whose*).

	Singular Latin	English	**Plural** Latin	English
Nom.	quī	who	*quī*	*Who pl.*
Gen.	*cuius*	*vhose*	*quorum*	*Whose* "
Dat.	*cui*	*to whom*	*quibus*	*to whom* "
Acc.	*quem*	*who*	*quos*	*wh*
Abl.	*quo*	*for who*	*quibus*	*for who* "

7. Identify the gender, number, case, use, and antecedent of these five relative pronouns in **Sententiae Antīquae** 1–4.

	Gender	Number	Case	Use	Antecedent
a. cui (1)	_____	_____	_____	_____	_____
b. quō (2)	_____	_____	_____	_____	_____
c. quae (3, first occurrence)	_____	_____	_____	_____	_____
d. quae (3, second occurrence)	_____	_____	_____	_____	_____
e. quī (4)	_____	_____	_____	_____	_____

EXERCITĀTIŌNĒS

A. Translate the following into English or Latin.

HW 1. mēns celeris quam _The quick mind which_

2. libellōs quōs *by* _The books which_

3. Italia trāns quam _Across Italy which_

4. clēmentiā prō quā _Mercy for which_
5. audītōrum inter quōs _Among the listeners who_
6. illā aetāte post quam _That age after which_
7. saturās dē quibus _The satires about which_
8. Caesarem cui _Caesar to whom_
9. adulēscentī cuius _Of the young man whose_
10. aquās sub quibus _____
11. the state (subj.) which (dir. obj.) _____
12. the daughter (dir. obj.) whose _____
13. the seas (dir. obj.) across which _____
14. the little books (subj.) in which _____
15. the sister (subj.) to whom _____
16. the citizen (dir. obj.) who _____
17. the friends (dir. obj.) with whom _____
18. the memory (subj.) which (subj.) _____
19. the brothers (subj.) whom _____
20. the mothers (dir. obj.) who _____

B. Supply the correct form of the relative pronoun and translate.

1. Aetās dē ___quo___ dīxistī erat nimium difficilis.

   The age about whom you said was too difficult.

2. Ubi sunt omnēs audītōrēs ___quos___ tum exspectābās?

   Where are all the listeners who you were expecting then?

3. Timēbant decem saturās potentēs ___qui/quas___ ille fortis nūper scrīpserat.

   They feared the ten powerful satires which he that brave man wrote lately. / had bravely written recently.

4. Mātrem iūcundam, ___cuius___ quattuor fīliī miserī ex tempestāte ācrī fūgerant, ibi vīdī.

   I saw there the pleasant mother, whose four miserable sons had fled out of the fierce storm.

[margin notes: HW; acer, acris, acre]

5. Amīcus, _____ cui _____ fīliam dulcem commīserāmus, eam neg-
    legēbat.

    The friend, to whom we had entrusted our sweet
    daughter, neglected her

C. Transform from singular to plural or plural to singular and translate
    the new phrase.

    1. mare trāns quod navigās

        Transformation: _____

        Translation: _____

    2. saturās quās recitāvērunt

        Transformation: _____

        Translation: _____

    3. urbis quam dēlēverat

        Transformation: _____

        Translation: _____

    4. rosā quam iaciēbās

        Transformation: _____

        Translation: _____

D. Transform the two simple sentences into a single complex sentence by
    replacing the personal pronoun with a relative pronoun, and then
    translate the new sentence (e.g., **Caesar fuit cōnsul. Eum laudāvī.** >
    Caesar fuit cōnsul quem laudāvī, *Caesar was the consul whom I praised*).

    1. Italia est terra bella. Eam vidēre dēsīderō.

        Transformation: _____

        Translation: _____

    2. Illa septem carmina brevia quoque audīre cupīvī. Ea ille poēta
        scrīpserat.

        Transformation: _____

        Translation: _____

    3. Tyrannus cīvitātem regēbat. Ad eam navigāre coeperās.

        Transformation: _____

        Translation: _____

[handwritten top margin: tēcum vobiscum sēcum / mēcum nobiscum]

4. Magistra discipulōs nunc admittere incipit. Mātrēs eōrum dīligis.

   Transformation: _____

   Translation: _____

E. Translate into Latin; employ standard word order and include all macrons.

[handwritten: HW]

1. The tyrant whom we feared is evil.

   [handwritten answer: Tyrannus, quem timēbāmus, malus est]

2. You will quickly lead into Italy those troops with whom you came.

   [handwritten answer: Illās copiās quibuscum veniēbās, in Italiam celeriter dūcēs.]

3. He is beginning to destroy the sweet friendship which we have.

   [handwritten answer: Amīcitam dulcem, quem tenēmus, delēre incipit]

4. They neglected the two blind men whose deeds were great.

   [handwritten answer: caecos Virōs duos, quōrum rēs magnae erant, neglectabant.]

5. The new age which is now beginning will be happy.

   [handwritten answer: Aetās nova, quae nunc incipit felīx erit.]

VĪS VERBŌRUM

A. Answer these questions on the chapter's vocabulary list.

1. Identify the third declension **-iō** noun derived from the fourth principal part of the following verbs, and then give their direct English derivatives and their meanings.

	Latin Noun	Eng. Noun	Translation
a. dēleō	_____	_____	_____
b. incipiō	_____	_____	_____
c. navigō	_____	_____	_____
d. recitō	_____	_____	_____

2. What third declension noun formed from the fourth principal part of **navigō** means *one who sails*? _____

Name: _____   Section: _____ Date: _____

3. On the analogy of **brevis** > **brevitās** > "brevity," provide the
    indicated words.
    levis > _____ > _____

4. Which adjective is most closely related in meaning to **levis**?
    a. dulcis   b. facilis   c. ingēns   d. longus

5. Which verb is an antonym of **admittō**?
    a. committō   b. ēmittō   c. submittō   d. trānsmittō

B. Complete each statement with an English word that demonstrates your
    knowledge of the Latin etymology (e.g., "A 'laudatory' speech is full
    of praise").

1. To "alleviate" a burden is to make it _____.

2. An "indelible" memory can _____ be _____.

3. A list of "desiderata" itemizes things a person _____.

4. The Roman deity "Cupid" was god of _____.

LĒCTIŌNĒS

A. First read each sentence aloud twice, and then translate as literally as
    possible within the limits of sound English idiom.

1. Quam iūcundī sunt illī trēs libellī quōs mihi nūper mīsistī!

    _____

2. Itaque mīlia hārum cōpiārum, quibus Caesar clēmentiam dedit,
    aut officia neglegunt aut ea nōn intellegunt.

    _____

    _____

3. Centum ex virīs quibuscum trāns maria difficilia navigāverās ad
    urbem veniēbant.

    _____

    _____

4. Quod magister senex fuit caecus, dōna dulcia quae discipulī mīserant nōn bene vidēre poterat.

_____

_____

5. Levis est labor quem bene tolerāmus.

_____

6. Cīvem quoque laudāvērunt cuius fīlius fortis patriam cum virtūte servāverat.

_____

7. Tyrannus duās urbēs cito dēlēvit in quās cīvēs miserī fūgerant.

_____

8. Virō fortī cuius fīliam cāram amās vītam suam sine timōre commīsit.

_____

_____

B. Answer these questions on "The Pleasures of Love" and "It's All in the Delivery."

1. _____ est minor in senectūte.
   a. voluptās   b. cupiditās   c. amor   d. haec omnia

2. Quandō, in sententiā Cicerōnis, aetātem iūcundam habēmus?
   a. ubi sumus adulēscentēs   b. ubi sumus senēs
   c. ubi nimis dēsīderāmus   d. ubi multās cupiditātēs habēmus

3. Ubi Fīdentīnus carmina alterīus poētae male recitat, facit ea
   a. dulcia   b. iūcunda   c. eius   d. sua

4. What does this epigram imply about the importance of proper delivery when reciting poetry?

_____

Fortūna caeca est: *Fortune is blind*
Cicero

Name: _____ Section: _____ Date: _____

18

First and Second Conjugations: Passive Voice of the Present System; Ablative of Agent

INTELLEGENDA

Upon completion of this lesson you should be able to

1. Explain the difference between "active voice" and "passive voice."

2. Identify the personal endings for the passive voice of the three present system tenses.

3. Recognize, form, and translate the present system tenses, passive voice, of first and second conjugation verbs.

4. Define, recognize, and translate the "ablative of agent" construction.

Salvē amīce aut amīca! Before beginning these exercises, be sure you have thoroughly studied Chapter 18 of *Wheelock's Latin* and memorized both the verb paradigms and the new vocabulary by repeating them *aloud.* **Sī hoc caput cum cūrā legēs, ā magistrō aut magistrā in tempus perpetuum laudāberis!**

GRAMMATICA

1. In the active voice the subject _____ the _____; in the passive voice the subject _____ the _____.

2. Passive endings are substituted for active endings except in the _____ person singular of the _____ and _____ tenses, where the passive ending is _____ to the active ending.

3. The consonant _____ appears in five of the six passive endings.

4. Which of the following forms is an exception to the general rule for forming passives?
   a. dēlēbitur   b. dēsīderāberis   c. vidēbimur   d. movēbiminī

5. Give the active or passive equivalents.
   a. -tis _____   b. -bāmur _____   c. -buntur _____   d. -bō _____

6. Which form contains a macron error?
   a. miscet   b. miscent   c. miscētur   d. miscēntur

7. Conjugate **amō, amāre,** in the present, future, and imperfect passive indicative.

Present		**Future**	
Singular	**Plural**	**Singular**	**Plural**
1. _____	_____	_____	_____
2. _____	_____	_____	_____
3. _____	_____	_____	_____

Imperfect	
Singular	**Plural**
1. _____	_____
2. _____	_____
3. _____	_____

8. Translate the above conjugation of **amō, amāre,** in the present, future, and imperfect passive indicative.

Present		**Future**	
Singular	**Plural**	**Singular**	**Plural**
1. _____	_____	_____	_____
2. _____	_____	_____	_____
3. _____	_____	_____	_____

Imperfect	
Singular	**Plural**
1. _____	_____
2. _____	_____
3. _____	_____

9. Conjugate the indicated verbs in the present, future, and imperfect passive indicative.

Present		**Future**	
Singular	**Plural**	**Singular**	**Plural**
1. moveor	_____	vidēbor	_____
2. _____	_____	_____	_____
3. _____	_____	_____	_____

Imperfect	
Singular	**Plural**
1. dēlēbar	_____
2. _____	_____
3. _____	_____

10. Supply the missing active or passive equivalents and translate.

Active	**Translation**	**Passive**	**Translation**
a. recitāre	_____	_____	_____
b. _____	_____	dēlērī	_____
c. _____	_____	dēsīderārī	_____
d. miscēre	_____	_____	_____
e. movēre	_____	_____	_____

11. Identify, in order, the six passive verbs in Practice and Review sentences 1–6 and then give their active equivalents.

Passive	Active	Passive	Active
a. _____	_____	b. _____	_____
c. _____	_____	d. _____	_____
e. _____	_____	f. _____	_____

12. In general which type verb is found in the passive?
    a. transitive   b. intransitive   c. linking   d. all these

13. In passive sentence types the ablative of _____ indicates the person by whom an action is performed, while the ablative of _____ indicates the thing by which an action is performed.

14. In converting an active sentence construction to a passive one, the object becomes the _____, the subject becomes an ablative of _____ or _____, and the appropriate _____ verb form is substituted for the _____ form.

15. Transform the following active sentence to passive without altering the sense of the action, and then translate both active and passive versions.

	Active	Passive
Latin:	Hostis cōpiās movet.	_____
English:	_____	_____

16. Identify the two ablatives of agent in Practice and Review sentences 1–4. _____ _____

17. Provide the information indicated for the following ablative case uses.

	Latin preposition (if none, so indicate)	Used for people and/or things?
a. means/instrument	_____	_____
b. accompaniment	_____	_____
c. manner	_____	_____
d. time	_____	_____
e. cardinal numerals	_____	_____
f. personal agent	_____	_____

EXERCITĀTIŌNĒS

A.   Translate the following into Latin or English.

1. dēlēbitur

2. it was mixed

_____

_____

3. dēsīderābuntur

4. you (sg.) were moved

_____

_____

5. creantur

6. we will seem

_____

_____

7. exspectāminī

8. they are recited

_____

_____

9. satiābāmur

10. you (pl.) will be frightened

_____

_____

B.   Supply the correct passive form of the words in parentheses, and translate.

1.   In lūdō omnēs puellae hodiē _____ (docēre; pres.).

_____

2.   Duo puerī ā magistrō nōn crās _____ (movēre; fut.).

_____

3.   Quattuor ex urbibus ā cōpiīs ācribus _____ (dēlēre; impf.).

_____

4.   Brevis mora cōnsiliōrum ā nōbīs herī _____ (exspectāre; impf.).

_____

C.   Transform the following active sentences to passive without altering the sense of the action, and then translate.

1.   Discipulī carmina facilia cito recitābant.

Transformation: _____

Translation: _____

2. Magistra secunda probitātem tuam quoque laudābit.

   Transformation: _____

   Translation: _____

3. Deinde tria dōna ad alium locum movēbimus.

   Transformation: _____

   Translation: _____

D. Translate into Latin; employ standard word order and include all macrons.

1. The school will be changed quickly by this difficult plan.

   _____

2. We were not helped by that type of knowledge.

   _____

3. Why is he not affected even by his own brave old father?

   _____

4. You will not be feared either by your citizens or by your enemies.

   _____

VĪS VERBŌRUM

A. Answer these questions on the chapter's vocabulary list.

1. Many Latin first declension nouns in **-ntia** give us English derivatives in "-nce" (e.g., **patientia** > "patience"); what English word similarly derives from **scientia**? _____

2. On the analogy of **brevis** > **brevitās** > "brevity," provide the indicated words.
   mortālis > _____ > _____

3. Which adverb does not have a related meaning?
   a. crās   b. herī   c. hodiē   d. quam

4. Which adverb has a meaning similar to **cūr**?
   a. quam   b. quandō   c. quoque   d. quārē

5. Complete the analogy **probitās:vitium::**_____ : **hostis.**
   a. aetās   b. amīcus   c. clēmentia   d. cōpiae

6. Give the third declension **-or** and **-iō** nouns derived from the
   fourth principal part of **moveō**, their literal meanings, and their direct English derivatives.

	Meaning	**Derivative**
a. **-or:** _____	_____	_____
b. **-iō:** _____	_____	_____

B. Complete each statement with an English word that demonstrates your
   knowledge of the Latin etymology (e.g., "A 'laudatory' speech is full
   of <u>praise</u>").

   1. "Hostile" actions are generally exhibited by an _____.

   2. An "immiscible" compound is _____ able to be _____,
      and an "illegible" script is _____ _____
      to be _____.

   3. The "confluence" of two streams is the place at which they
      _____ _____.

   4. To "demote" someone is literally to _____ him _____
      in rank, and to "degenerate" is to move _____ from one's
      original _____.

LĒCTIŌNĒS

A. First read each sentence aloud twice, and then translate as literally as
   possible within the limits of sound English idiom.

   1. Librī huius generis puerīs ā magistrō dabantur sed paucī legē-
      bantur.

      _____

      _____

   2. Paucīs hōrīs illa flūmina celeria in mare ingēns fluere coeperant.

      _____

3. Mentēs omnium audītōrum tertiā saturā illīus poētae clārī movēbantur.

_____

_____

4. Quod discipulōs in lūdum nōn admīsit, ad aliam urbem aut cīvitātem movērī cupīvērunt.

_____

_____

5. Quoniam numquam laudābantur, etiam illa studia levia neglegere incipiēbant.

_____

_____

6. Fortūna caeca regit mentēs eōrum quī cum cūrā nōn docentur.

_____

7. Omnēs memoriā dulcī aetātum iūcundārum movēmur.

_____

8. Post tempus longum, hōs libellōs difficilēs legere poteris.

_____

B. Answer these questions on "Death and Metamorphosis."

1. Quid hominēs nimis timent? (**Respondē in tōtā sententiā.**)

_____

2. Quid omnia nōn faciunt?
   a. sē mūtant   b. fluunt   c. ad mortem veniunt   d. errant

3. Ubi est animus post mortem?
   a. in aliīs corporibus   b. in prīmō corpore
   c. in eādem fōrmā   d. in nūllō locō

4. Quid crās erimus?
   a. quod herī fuimus   b. quod hodiē sumus   c. nihil   d. nōn eīdem

Genus est mortis male vīvere: *To live wickedly is a kind of death*
Ovid

19

Perfect Passive System of All Verbs; Interrogative Pronouns and Adjectives

INTELLEGENDA

Upon completion of this lesson you should be able to

1. Recognize, form, and translate the three perfect system tenses, passive voice, of all verbs.

2. Define and explain the function of an "interrogative pronoun" and an "interrogative adjective."

3. Recognize, form, and translate the interrogative pronoun **quis, quid**, *and the interrogative adjective* **quī, quae, quod**.

Salvē, discipule docte aut discipula docta! Before beginning these exercises, be sure you have thoroughly studied Chapter 19 of *Wheelock's Latin* and memorized both the paradigms and the new vocabulary by repeating them *aloud.* **Quem librum hodiē legēs amābisque?—hunc librum!**

GRAMMATICA

1. The Latin perfect passive indicative is composed of the _____ _____ _____ and the _____ tense of **esse**.

2. The Latin future perfect passive indicative is composed of the
    _____ _____ _____ and the _____
    tense of **esse.**

3. The Latin pluperfect passive indicative is composed of the
    _____ _____ _____ and the _____
    tense of **esse.**

4. Conjugate **amō, amāre,** in the perfect, future perfect, and pluperfect
    passive indicative.

Perfect		Fut. Perf.	
Singular	Plural	Singular	Plural
1. _____	_____	_____	_____
2. _____	_____	_____	_____
3. _____	_____	_____	_____

Pluperfect	
Singular	Plural
1. _____	_____
2. _____	_____
3. _____	_____

5. Translate the above conjugation of **amō, amāre,** in the perfect, future
    perfect, and pluperfect passive indicative.

Perfect		Fut. Perf.	
Singular	Plural	Singular	Plural
1. _____	_____	_____	_____
2. _____	_____	_____	_____
3. _____	_____	_____	_____

Pluperfect	
Singular	Plural
1. _____	_____
2. _____	_____
3. _____	_____

6. Conjugate the indicated verbs in the perfect, future perfect, and pluperfect passive indicative.

Perfect, līberāre   **Fut. Perf., movēre**

Singular	**Plural**	**Singular**	**Plural**
1. _____	_____	_____	_____
2. _____	_____	_____	_____
3. _____	_____	_____	_____

Pluperfect, neglegere

Singular	**Plural**
1. _____	_____
2. _____	_____
3. _____	_____

7. Identify, in order, the three perfect system passive verbs in Practice and Review sentences 1–8 and then give their active equivalents.

Passive	**Active**
a. _____	_____
b. _____	_____
c. _____	_____

8. Transform the following active sentence to passive without altering the sense of the action, and then translate both active and passive versions.

	Active	**Passive**
Latin:	Iūdex argūmenta certa parāvit.	_____
English:	_____	_____

9. The interrogative pronoun asks for the general _____ of a _____ or _____.

10. The interrogative adjective asks for the _____ _____ of a _____ or _____.

11. A relative pronoun and its clause identify or provide further information about a _____ or _____.

12. Which is not identical to the others in the singular?
    a. relative pronoun　　　　　b. interrogative pronoun
    c. interrogative adjective　　d. none of these

13. Which is not identical to the others in the plural?
    a. relative pronoun　　　　　b. interrogative pronoun
    c. interrogative adjective　　d. none of these

14. Complete the chart, showing distinctions between the relative pronoun and the interrogative pronoun and adjective.

	Modifies noun (yes/no)	Expressed or implied antecedent (has/has not)	Introduces question (yes/no)	Sentence ends with question mark (yes/no)
a. relative pronoun	_____	_____	_____	_____
b. interrogative pron.	_____	_____	_____	_____
c. interrogative adj.	_____	_____	_____	_____

15. Identify the type (relative pronoun, interrogative pronoun, interrogative adjective), case, and grammatical use of the indicated words in the Practice and Review sentences (e.g., **Quis** [sent. 1], interrogative pronoun, nominative, subject).

	Type	Case	Use
a. Cuius (2)	_____	_____	_____
b. Quōs (3)	_____	_____	_____
c. quōs (4)	_____	_____	_____
d. quod (6)	_____	_____	_____
e. quā (8)	_____	_____	_____
f. Quī (10)	_____	_____	_____
g. quō (10)	_____	_____	_____
h. Quae (11, first occurrence)	_____	_____	_____
i. Quae (11, second occurrence)	_____	_____	_____

EXERCITĀTIŌNĒS

A. Translate the following into Latin or English.

1. Beneficia laudāta erunt.

_____

2. Familiae admissae sunt.

_____

3. Flūmen dēmōnstrātum erat.

_____

4. Libellus recitātus est.

_____

5. Hostis vīsus erit.

_____

6. The arguments have been prepared.

_____

7. The authors had been delighted.

_____

8. The city has been destroyed.

_____

9. The judgment will have been made.

_____

10. The poems had been read.

_____

B. Transform the following active sentences to passive without altering the sense of the action, and then translate.

1. Senēs id genus lūdōrum nōn dīlēxerant.

    Transformation: _____

    Translation: _____

2. Multī virī fortēs haec maria navigāvērunt.

   Transformation: _____

   Translation: _____

3. Auctor bonus multōs librōs lēgerit.

   Transformation: _____

   Translation: _____

C. Supply the correct form of the interrogative adjective and translate.

   Translation

   1. _____ probitātem   _____

   2. _____ scientiā   _____

   3. _____ scelerum   _____

   4. _____ iūdicī   _____

   5. _____ argūmentīs (abl.)   _____

D. Supply the correct form of the interrogative pronoun and translate.

   Translation

   1. _____ id cupīvit?   _____

   2. _____ (dat.) libellum dedistī? _____

   3. Ā _____ (sg.) līberātī sunt?   _____

   4. _____ ab eīs parātum est?   _____

   5. _____ (gen. pl.) dōna dēsīderās? _____

E. Supply the correct form of the words in parentheses and translate.

   1. Ūnā hōrā iūdicium ab hoste _____ (dare; plupf. pass.).

      _____

   2. Ā _____ (quis; pl.) illa argūmenta herī _____ (incipere; perf. pass.)?

      _____

   3. Brevī tempore ab iūdice _____ (līberāre; 1st pers. pl. fut. perf. pass.).

      _____

4. _____ (quis; gen. pl.) scelera deinde _____ (dēmōnstrāre; plupf. pass.)?

_____

F.   Translate into Latin; employ standard word order and include macrons.

1.   The old man also had been neglected by his family.

_____

2.   By what new game had they been delighted?

_____

3.   At what time will she have been expected tomorrow?

_____

4.   By what name were you called then?

_____

VĪS VERBŌRUM

A.   Answer these questions on the chapter's vocabulary list.

1.   Many first declension **-ia** nouns produce English derivatives in "-y" (e.g., **glōria** > "glory"); identify the derivatives so formed from the following nouns.

a. familia _____   b. victōria _____
c. philosophia _____   d. memoria _____
e. Italia _____

2.   Give the third declension **-or** and **-iō** nouns derived from the fourth principal part of **līberō,** their literal meanings, and their direct English derivatives.

	Meaning	**Derivative**
a. **-or:** _____	_____	_____
b. **-iō:** _____	_____	_____

3.   Complete the analogy **mortālis:immortālis::gravis:**_____.
a. caecus   b. clārus   c. ingēns   d. levis

4.   Which adverb is nearest in meaning to **iam**?
a. cito   b. cūr   c. nunc   d. ōlim

5. Which conjunction is nearest in meaning to **at**?
   a. aut   b. et   c. nisi   d. sed

B. Complete each statement with an English word that demonstrates your knowledge of the Latin etymology (e.g., "A 'laudatory' speech is full of praise").

   1. A "beneficent person" _____ things _____ for others.

   2. Those who are "prejudiced" _____ others _____ they truly know them.

   3. To "contradict" someone is to _____ _____ him.

LĒCTIŌNĒS

A. First read each sentence aloud twice, and then translate as literally as possible within the limits of sound English idiom.

   1. Iūdex ā quō iūdicium parātum est labōre iam superātur.

   _____

   2. At senem cuius familia servāta erat numquam vīdī.

   _____

   3. Ā cīve quī ad Graeciam missus erat pāx et lībertās laudātae sunt.

   _____

   4. Quid auctōrī dictum est cui ea beneficia data sunt?

   _____

   5. Aquae celerēs ex flūminibus flūxerant et cum marī ingentī mixtae erant.

   _____

   _____

   6. Quae argūmenta certa ā iūdicibus contrā ista scelera gravia crās parāta erunt?

   _____

   _____

7. Nisi familiae nostrae līberātae erunt, nihil nōs dēlectābit.

   _____

8. Quis haec iūdicia parāre coeperat aut quī iūdex ea parāre etiam potuerat?

   _____

   _____

B. Answer these questions on "Catullus Bids Farewell" and "The Aged Playwright."

   1. Cūr est poēta miser?
      a. puella eum nōn amat   b. puella est nimis bella
      c. puella eum semper bāsiat   d. puella obdūrat

   2. In sententiā poētae, cui puella vidēbitur pulchra?
      a. Catullō   b. Lesbiae   c. nēminī   d. omnibus

   3. Quis est auctor huius locī dē senibus?
      a. Cicerō   b. Sophoclēs   c. Oedipus   d. iūdex

   4. Quid senēs sānī in mentibus habent?
      a. memoria   b. scientia   c. sapientia   d. haec omnia

   5. Quid Sophoclēs scrīpsit?
      a. Dē Senectūte   b. tragoediae   c. iūdicia   d. haec omnia

   6. Cūr Sophoclēs familiam neglegere vīsus est?
      a. multa diū scrībēbat   b. in iūdicium vocātus est
      c. propter scelera gravia   d. iūdicibus recitāverat

   7. Quandō "Oedipus Colōnēus" ā Sophoclē scrīptus erat?
      a. nūper   b. ōlim   c. diū   d. herī

   8. Cūr ille auctor ab iūdicibus līberātus est?
      a. propter argūmenta certa
      b. quod familiam nōn neglēxerat
      c. quoniam tragoedia eōs dēlectāvit
      d. quod fuit senex

Sed quis custōdiet ipsōs custōdēs: *But who will guard the guards themselves?*

Juvenal

20

Fourth Declension; Ablatives of Place from Which and Separation

---

INTELLEGENDA

Upon completion of this lesson you should be able to
   1. Recognize, form, and translate fourth declension nouns.
   2. Define, recognize, and translate the "ablative of place from which" and "ablative of separation" constructions, and distinguish between the two.
   3. Recognize and translate certain verbs that commonly take an ablative of separation.

Salvē, discipula aut discipule! Before beginning these exercises, be sure you have thoroughly studied Chapter 20 of *Wheelock's Latin* and memorized both the paradigms and the new vocabulary by repeating them *aloud.* **Sī hoc caput cum cūrā discēs, sapientiā numquam carēbis!**

GRAMMATICA

1. All the endings of fourth declension nouns begin with the letter ____, except the _____ and _____ plural.

2. The gender of most fourth declension nouns is _____, but some are _____ and a very few are _____.

3. The ablative of place from which generally requires a verb indicating _____ from one place to another and one of the prepositions _____, _____, or _____.

4. The ablative of separation may or may not require a _____ and generally is not used with a verb of _____, but simply indicates that one person or thing is _____ from another.

5. Which of the following verbs does not commonly take an ablative of separation?
   a. careō   b. discēdō   c. līberō   d. prohibeō

6. Identify the base and gender of **manus dextra,** *right hand,* decline it fully, and provide the English meanings appropriate to each case.
   base: _____ _____   gender: _____

	Singular **Latin**		**English**
Nom.	manus	dextra	the right hand
Gen.	_____	_____	_____
Dat.	_____	_____	_____
Acc.	_____	_____	_____
Abl.	_____	_____	_____
	Plural		
Nom.	_____	_____	_____
Gen.	_____	_____	_____
Dat.	_____	_____	_____
Acc.	_____	_____	_____
Abl.	_____	_____	_____

7. Identify the base and gender of **genū sinistrum,** *left knee,* and decline it fully.

   base: _____ _____   gender: _____

	Singular		**Plural**	
Nom.	genū	sinistrum	_____	_____
Gen.	_____	_____	_____	_____
Dat.	_____	_____	_____	_____
Acc.	_____	_____	_____	_____
Abl.	_____	_____	_____	_____

8. Choose the correct form of the adjective and then translate the entire phrase.

	Adjective	**Translation**
a. frūctuī (sweet)	_____	_____
b. metuum (serious)	_____	_____
c. senātū (Roman)	_____	_____
d. sēnsūs (gen.; common)	_____	_____
e. spīritum (immortal)	_____	_____
f. versūs (acc.; three)	_____	_____

9. Identify the number, gender, case, and grammatical use of these nouns and pronouns in the chapter's Practice and Review sentences (e.g., **senēs** [sentence 1], plural, masculine, nominative, subject).

	Number	**Gender**	**Case**	**Use**
a. argūmentīs (1)	_____	_____	_____	_____
b. urbe (2)	_____	_____	_____	_____
c. medica (4)	_____	_____	_____	_____
d. manū (4)	_____	_____	_____	_____
e. metū (5)	_____	_____	_____	_____
f. quō (5)	_____	_____	_____	_____
g. Graeciā (8)	_____	_____	_____	_____
h. quibus (9)	_____	_____	_____	_____
i. versūs (10)	_____	_____	_____	_____
j. genua (11)	_____	_____	_____	_____

EXERCITĀTIŌNĒS

A. Translate the following into English or Latin.

1. senātuī _____
2. of the senate _____
3. versū _____
4. for the feeling _____
5. metuum _____
6. the enjoyment (subj.) _____
7. manūs (subj.) _____
8. of the verses _____
9. frūctum _____
10. with the horns _____
11. genibus (abl.) _____
12. of the dread _____
13. sēnsūs (dir. obj.) _____
14. with the hands _____
15. spīrituī _____
16. the knees (subj.) _____
17. cornua _____
18. with spirit _____

B. Supply the correct form of the words in parentheses and translate.

1. Deinde in Graeciā _____ (metus) servitūtis superāvimus.

   _____

2. At neque _____ (frūctus; pl.) pācis neque _____ (metus; sg.) bellī caruistī.

   _____

3. Hae _____ (manus) mīserōrum _____ (servitūs; sg.) līberātae erant.

   _____

4. Iūdicium ab iūdice clārō contrā _____ (senātus) iam prōnūntiātum est.

   _____

C. Transform from singular to plural or plural to singular and translate the new phrase.

1. metus certus

   Transformation: _____

   Translation: _____

2. spīrituum mortālium

    Transformation: _____

    Translation: _____

3. cornibus sinistrīs (abl.)

    Transformation: _____

    Translation: _____

4. Versūs lēctī erant.

    Transformation: _____

    Translation: _____

5. Sēnsus mixtus est.

    Transformation: _____

    Translation: _____

6. Hōc frūctū dēlector.

    Transformation: _____

    Translation: _____

D. Transform one of the nominative nouns to genitive to create a meaning-ful phrase, and then translate (e.g., **puella fortūna** > **fortūna puellae,** *the girl's fortune*).

	Transformation	**Translation**
1. coniūrātī metus	_____	_____
2. beneficium senātus	_____	_____
3. auctor versus	_____	_____
4. lūdus frūctus	_____	_____

E. Translate into Latin, using standard word order and including macrons.

1. The fear of serious crime has terrified our family.

    _____

2. Thousands of verses had been written by that illustrious author.

    _____

3. Those conspirators seem to lack the common friendship of the people.

_____

_____

4. Why can the citizens not defend themselves from the enemy?

_____

VĪS VERBŌRUM

A. Answer these questions on the chapter's vocabulary list.

1. Which noun does not have a related meaning?
    a. genū   b. manus   c. ōs   d. scientia

2. Which noun is synonymous with **metus**?
    a. argūmentum   b. probitās   c. timor   d. vēritās

3. Which verb is an antonym of **prohibeō**?
    a. admittō   b. discēdō   c. moveō   d. parō

4. Identify the third declension **-iō** noun derived from the fourth principal part of **prohibeō,** and then give its direct English derivative and meaning.

    Latin Noun   **Eng. Noun**   **Translation**

    _____   _____   _____

B. Complete each statement with an English word that demonstrates your knowledge of the Latin etymology (e.g., "A 'laudatory' speech is full of praise").

1. A "cornucopia" is literally a _____ of _____.

2. "Fructose" is sugar obtained from _____.

3. To "genuflect" is to bend one's _____.

4. Literally, a "manuscript" is _____ by _____, and to "manufacture" is to _____ by _____.

5. In origin a "senate" was a council of _____.

6. To "conspire" is literally to _____ _____, a "respirator" helps a person to _____ _____, and when the Muses "inspired" an artist they literally _____ _____ him or her.

7. A proofreader's "caret" indicates that a sentence _____ something.

LĒCTIŌNĒS

A. First read each sentence aloud twice, and then translate as literally as possible within the limits of sound English idiom.

1. Dē quibus montibus illud flūmen celere fluit?

_____

2. Nisi eōs sceleribus istīus tyrannī līberābimus, metū gravī semper superābuntur.

_____

_____

3. Ōdī servitūtem, quae hominēs ā frūctibus dulcibus lībertātis prohibet.

_____

_____

4. Fīliī eōrum hōs versūs in lūdō crās prōnūntiābunt.

_____

5. Cūr senātus cīvēs nostrōs ā metū illōrum coniūrātōrum herī nōn dēfendit?

_____

_____

6. Senex miser in genū dextrum cecidit et mortem celerem exspectābat.

_____

B.   Answer these questions on "Cicero Urges Catiline's Departure."

1.   Quem Cicerō in hōc locō appellat? (**Respondē ūnō verbō Latīnō.**) _____

2.   Quid Rōma contrā coniūrātōs eō tempore habuit?
     a. senātūs consultum   b. vīrēs   c. cōnsilium   d. haec omnia

3.   Nisi Catilīna discēdet, quis metū nōn līberābitur? (**Respondē ūnō verbō.**) _____

4.   Ā quō Catilīna diū dēsīderātus est? (**Respondē in tōtā sententiā.**)

_____

5.   Contrā quam cīvitātem Catilīna et coniūrātī bellum gerent? (**Ūnō verbō respondē.**) _____

SPQR, Senātus Populusque Rōmānus: *The Senate and the People of Rome*
Motto of the Roman empire

21

Third and Fourth Conjugations: Passive Voice of the Present System

INTELLEGENDA

Upon completion of this lesson you should be able to

1. Recognize, form, and translate the passive voice of third and fourth conjugation verbs in the present system.

2. Recognize, form, and translate the present passive infinitive of third and fourth conjugation verbs.

3. Provide a "synopsis" of a verb in the indicative mood.

Salvēte iterum, discipulae atque discipulī! Before attempting these exercises, be sure you have thoroughly studied Chapter 21 of *Wheelock's Latin* and memorized both the verb paradigms and the new vocabulary by repeating the words *aloud.* **Valēte iterum!**

GRAMMATICA

1. The pattern of substituting passive endings for active endings in the present system works essentially the same for third and fourth conjugation verbs as for first and second.   T/F

2. The principal irregularity in forming third and fourth conjugation present system passives is in the _____ person singular, _____ tense, for verbs of the _____ conjugation.

3. Conjugate **tangō, tangere,** in the present, future, and imperfect passive indicative.

Present
Singular	**Plural**	**Future** **Singular**	**Plural**
1. _____	_____	_____	_____
2. _____	_____	_____	_____
3. _____	_____	_____	_____

Imperfect
Singular	**Plural**
1. _____	_____
2. _____	_____
3. _____	_____

4. Translate the above conjugation of **tangō, tangere,** in the present, future, and imperfect passive indicative.

Present
Singular	**Plural**	**Future** **Singular**	**Plural**
1. _____	_____	_____	_____
2. _____	_____	_____	_____
3. _____	_____	_____	_____

Imperfect
Singular	**Plural**
1. _____	_____
2. _____	_____
3. _____	_____

5. Conjugate the indicated verbs in the present, future, and imperfect passive indicative.

Present, relinquere
Singular	**Plural**	**Future, scīre** **Singular**	**Plural**
1. _____	_____	_____	_____
2. _____	_____	_____	_____
3. _____	_____	_____	_____

Imperfect, dēfendere

Singular	Plural
1. _____	_____
2. _____	_____
3. _____	_____

6. Identify, in order, the three present system passive third and fourth conjugation verbs in Practice and Review sentences 1–8, give their active equivalents, and translate both the active and passive forms.

Passive	English	Active	English
a. _____	_____	_____	_____
b. _____	_____	_____	_____
c. _____	_____	_____	_____

7. Transform the following active sentence to passive without altering the sense of the action, and then translate both active and passive versions.

	Active	Passive
Latin:	Vīcīnī casam relinquent.	_____
English:	_____	_____

8. Provide the active or passive equivalents of the following infinitives and translate both.

Active	English	Passive	English
a. rapere	_____	_____	_____
b. _____	_____	tangī	_____
c. relinquere	_____	_____	_____
d. _____	_____	scīrī	_____
e. continēre	_____	_____	_____
f. _____	_____	dēlectārī	_____
g. dēfendere	_____	_____	_____
h. _____	_____	iubērī	_____
i. sentīre	_____	_____	_____
j. _____	_____	prōnūntiārī	_____

9. Provide a synopsis of **mittō, mittere, mīsī, missum,** in the second person singular.

Present	**Future**	**Impf.**	**Perfect**	**Fut.Perf.**	**Plupf.**
Active					

_____ _____ _____ _____ _____ _____

Passive

_____ _____ _____ _____ _____ _____

10. Translate the above synopsis of **mittō, mittere, mīsī, missum,** in the second person singular.

Present	**Future**	**Impf.**	**Perfect**	**Fut.Perf.**	**Plupf.**
Active					

_____ _____ _____ _____ _____ _____

Passive

_____ _____ _____ _____ _____ _____

EXERCITĀTIŌNĒS

A. Translate the following into Latin or English.

1. Casae rapientur. _____

2. Causae sciēbantur. _____

3. Ex fenestrā iacitur. _____

4. Nāvēs relinquēbantur. _____

5. Gēns dēfendētur. _____

6. You yourself are being sent. _____

7. Troy was being defended. _____

8. Safety is abandoned. _____

9. The end will be perceived. _____

10. We ourselves are touched. _____

B. Transform the following active sentences to passive without altering the sense of the action, and then translate.

1. Illī nautae asperī nāvēs rapient.

   Transformation: _____

   Translation: _____

2. Cūr māter tua tē in casā relinquit?

   Transformation: _____

   Translation: _____

3. Senātus Rōmānus scelera gravia eius sciēbat.

   Transformation: _____

   Translation: _____

C. Supply the correct form of the words in parentheses and translate.

1. Multae gentēs in fīnibus Graeciae _____ (continēre; impf.).

   _____

2. At illī versūs laudis causā _____ (scrībere; fut.).

   _____

3. Propter beneficia ā familiā, vīcīnīs, atque gente omnī iam bene _____ (scīre; 2nd pers. sg. pres.).

   _____

   _____

4. Vulgus pecūniae causā frūctū lūdōrum _____ (prohibēre; fut.).

   _____

D. Translate into Latin; employ standard word order and include all macrons.

1. This band of conspirators will be ordered to depart for the sake of the people.

   _____

   _____

2. The territory was being seized because of that judge's arguments.

    _____

3. We were again writing a letter about our fears and other feelings.

    _____

4. Slavery ought to be prohibited throughout the entire world.

    _____

VĪS VERBŌRUM

A. Answer these questions on the chapter's vocabulary list.

1. **Fāma:** "fame":: **causa:** _____.

2. **Probus** (*honest*) > **probitās** > "probity"; **vīcīnus** >
    _____ > _____.

3. Which noun does not have a related meaning?
    a. cornū   b. familia   c. gēns   d. populus

4. Which verb is close in meaning to **sciō**?
    a. careō   b. intellegō   c. ōdī   d. scrībō

5. Which adjective has a meaning in common with **asper**?
    a. acerbus   b. certus   c. commūnis   d. sinister

B. Complete each statement with an English word that demonstrates your
    knowledge of the Latin etymology (e.g., "A 'laudatory' speech is full
    of praise").

1. To "defenestrate" someone is literally to throw him or her
    _____ from a _____ (ouch!).

2. One who is "omniscient" _____ _____ things, and
    one who is "prescient" _____ things _____ they
    happen.

3. If our interest in a topic is only "tangential," we will just
    _____ upon it briefly, and something "intact" has
    _____ been _____.

4. A "relic" has been _____ _____ from an earlier age.

5. A "raptorial" bird violently _____ its prey.

LĒCTIŌNĒS

A. First read each sentence aloud twice, and then translate as literally as possible within the limits of sound English idiom.

1. Animus eius pecūniā aut cupiditāte frūctūs tangī nōn poterat.

   _____

2. Amor patriae in omnī spīritū sentiēbātur.

   _____

3. Sapientia et vēritās certa in hominibus stultīs nōn invenientur.

   _____

4. Virtūs etiam multā pecūniā nōn parātur.

   _____

5. Spīritus auctōris quī haec carmina scrīpsit ā deīs deābusque immortālibus saepe tangēbātur.

   _____

   _____

6. Ubi poenīs asperīs iūdiciō rēgis līberātus est, in genū dextrum cecidit et eī iterum grātiās ēgit.

   _____

   _____

7. Quis ex montibus Graeciae in fīnēs Trōiae contrā hostēs asperōs mittētur?

   _____

   _____

8. Salūtis commūnis causā nāvēs illīus gentis rapī iussērunt.

   _____

9. Fuērunt paucae fenestrae in casīs vulgī Rōmānī, quod eō tempore cīvēs miserī pecūniā caruērunt.

   _____

   _____

10. Nisi cum cūrā atque virtūte labōrābis, nihil frūctūs ā tē in hōc mundō post mortem relinquētur.

    _____

    _____

Name: _____ *Section:* _____ *Date:* _____

B. Answer these questions on "Virgil's Messianic Eclogue."

1. Quī poēta hunc locum scrīpsit? _____

2. Quandō aetās nova, dē quā auctor dīcit, veniet?
   a. nunc   b. numquam   c. ōlim   d. nūper

3. Ā quō mundus aetāte novā regētur?
   a. puerō   b. patre puerī   c. Achille   d. mātre puerī

4. Quis ad Trōiam mittētur?
   a. puer   b. pater puerī   c. Achillēs   d. alius Achillēs

5. Quandō erunt nūlla bella atque nūllae cūrae?
   a. ubi puer dē caelō mittētur   b. ubi puer mātrem sciet
   c. ubi puer erit vir   d. ubi pauca mala remanēbunt

Carmina morte carent: *Poetry never dies*
Ovid

22

Fifth Declension; Ablative of Place Where; Summary of Ablative Uses

INTELLEGENDA

Upon completion of this lesson you should be able to
   1. *Recognize, form, and translate fifth declension nouns.*
   2. *Define, recognize, and translate the "ablative of place where" construction.*
   3. *Distinguish among the several uses of the ablative case introduced thus far.*

Iterum salvēte, amīcae ac amīcī! Before beginning these exercises, be sure you have thoroughly studied Chapter 22 of *Wheelock's Latin* and memorized both the paradigms and the new vocabulary by repeating them *aloud.* **Tenēte fidem et semper eritis fēlīcēs!**

GRAMMATICA

1. The vowel ____ characterizes all the endings of fifth declension nouns.
2. Fifth declension nouns are _____ gender, except _____ and its compounds, which are _____.

3. The **-e-** of the fifth declension genitive singular ending is long when preceded by a _____ and short when preceded by a _____.

4. Identify the base and gender of **spēs incerta,** *the uncertain hope,* decline it fully, and provide the English meanings appropriate to each case.

    base: _____ _____   gender: _____

    Singular
	Latin		**English**
Nom.	spēs	incerta	the uncertain hope
Gen.	_____	_____	_____
Dat.	_____	_____	_____
Acc.	_____	_____	_____
Abl.	_____	_____	_____

    Plural
Nom.	_____	_____	_____
Gen.	_____	_____	_____
Dat.	_____	_____	_____
Acc.	_____	_____	_____
Abl.	_____	_____	_____

5. Identify the base and gender of **fidēs commūnis,** *the common trust,* and decline it fully.

    base: _____ _____   gender: _____

	Singular		**Plural**	
Nom.	fidēs	commūnis	_____	_____
Gen.	_____	_____	_____	_____
Dat.	_____	_____	_____	_____
Acc.	_____	_____	_____	_____
Abl.	_____	_____	_____	_____

6. Choose the correct form of the adjective and then translate the entire phrase.

	Adjective	**Translation**
a. diem (lucky)	_____	_____
b. spērum (equal)	_____	_____
c. reī (Latin)	_____	_____
d. fidē (alone)	_____	_____

7. The "place where" construction commonly requires the preposition _____ or _____, followed by a noun (or pronoun) in the _____ case.

8. If the noun in an ablative of manner construction is modified by an adjective, the preposition **cum** may simply be _____ or it may be placed _____ the adjective.

9. Which ablative case use always requires a preposition?
   a. means   b. manner   c. accompaniment   d. all these

10. With which ablative case use is a preposition not optional?
    a. manner   b. separation   c. place where   d. all these

11. Which ablative case use does not require a preposition?
    a. with cardinal numerals   b. time   c. agent   d. place from which

12. Identify the number, gender, case, and grammatical use of these nouns in the chapter's Practice and Review sentences.

	Number	**Gender**	**Case**	**Use**
a. rēbus (6)	_____	_____	_____	_____
b. spē (7)	_____	_____	_____	_____
c. parte (8)	_____	_____	_____	_____
d. spēs (9)	_____	_____	_____	_____
e. fidē (9)	_____	_____	_____	_____

13. Identify the number, gender, case, and grammatical use of these nouns in the chapter's **Sententiae Antīquae.**

	Number	Gender	Case	Use
a. rē pūblicā (4)	_____	_____	_____	_____
b. diē (7)	_____	_____	_____	_____
c. fidē (8)	_____	_____	_____	_____
d. fidē (9)	_____	_____	_____	_____
e. manū (9)	_____	_____	_____	_____

EXERCITĀTIŌNĒS

A. Translate the following into Latin or English.

   1. ferrō ācrī (abl.) _____

   2. tribus diēbus _____

   3. modī incertī (pl.) _____

   4. aequō cum animō _____

   5. ē montibus mediīs _____

   6. in the middle of the house _____

   7. of the powerful fires _____

   8. for the Roman republic (dat.) _____

   9. five of those days _____

   10. with the Latin ships _____

B. Transform from singular to plural or plural to singular and translate
    the new sentence or phrase.

   1. Mē ex igne ēripuit.

       Transformation: _____

       Translation: _____

   2. Spēs nostrās cernunt.

       Transformation: _____

       Translation: _____

3. ultrā aequum modum

   Transformation: _____

   Translation: _____

4. in rēbus incertīs

   Transformation: _____

   Translation: _____

5. post diem fēlīcem

   Transformation: _____

   Translation: _____

6. sub fenestrīs mediīs

   Transformation: _____

   Translation: _____

C. Transform one of the nominative nouns to genitive to create a meaning-ful phrase, and then translate (e.g., **puella fortūna** > **fortūna puellae,** *the girl's fortune*).

	Transformation	Translation
1. diēs fīnis	_____	_____
2. metus ferrum	_____	_____
3. senātus fidēs	_____	_____
4. rēs pūblica salūs	_____	_____
5. spēs coniūrātī	_____	_____

D. Supply the correct form of the words in parentheses and translate.

1. _____ (fidēs) gentium quondam erat fortis.

   _____

2. _____ (spēs) pācis in mundō numquam tollētur.

   _____

3. Ignis spīritūs hūmānī _____ (fidēs) alitur.

   _____

Name: _____ *Section:* _____ *Date:* _____

4. Multī cīvēs _____ (rēs pūblica; gen.) ē manibus coniūrātōrum eripiuntur.

   _____

   _____

5. Numerus _____ (diēs) nostrōrum incertus est.

   _____

E. Translate into Latin, using standard word order and including macrons.

1. Many were rescued from slavery on that day.

   _____

2. They departed from the middle of the city with great hope.

   _____

3. He ordered them to defend the republic from danger.

   _____

VĪS VERBŌRUM

A. Answer these questions on the chapter's vocabulary list.

1. Which noun does not have a related meaning?
   a. annus   b. causa   c. diēs   d. hōra

2. Which adverb has a meaning synonymous with **quondam**?
   a. iam   b. iterum   c. ōlim   d. prōtinus

3. Complete the analogy **dexter : sinister : : fēlīx :**
   a. asper   b. commūnis   c. fortūnātus   d. miser

4. Complete the analogy **amō : ōdī : : tollō :**
   a. rapiō   b. relinquō   c. sciō   d. tangō

5. Which verb does not belong?
   a. dīcit   b. inquit   c. prohibet   d. prōnūntiat

B. Complete each statement with an English word that demonstrates your
   knowledge of the Latin etymology (e.g., "A 'laudatory' speech is full
   of praise").

1. A "bona fide" contract is made in _____ _____, and you might name your pup "Fido" because he is so _____.

2. A criminal's "m.o." or "modus operandi" is his _____ of operating.

3. To approach a task with "equanimity" is to do so with a _____ _____.

4. An "immoderate" person does _____ keep within normal _____.

5. The "Mediterranean" was so named because of its location in the _____ of many _____.

LĒCTIŌNĒS

A. First read each sentence aloud twice, and then translate as literally as possible within the limits of sound English idiom.

1. Rem pūblicam magnā cum spē gessit.

    _____

2. Eō diē vīcīnī eius cum cūrā labōrāvērunt atque multās rēs parāvērunt.

    _____

    _____

3. Paucīs diēbus Cicerō rem pūblicam ē perīculō ēripiet.

    _____

4. Ubi in genua ceciderat, amīcus eum sustulit.

    _____

5. Manum dextram ex igne prōtinus ēripuit, sed tamen omnī sēnsū caruit.

    _____

    _____

Name: _____   Section: _____   Date: _____

6. Vulgus beneficia aut frūctum in versibus illīus auctōris nōn cernit.

_____

7. "Sē dēfendit animal cornibus," pater eius inquit, "ferrō vir."

_____

8. Multa in mundō continentur ex quibus hominēs frūctum trahere possunt.

_____

_____

B. Answer these questions on "The Young Interns" and "Ambition and Literature."

1. Quid est Symmachus?
   a. discipulus   b. medicus   c. poēta   d. amīcus poētae

2. Quōcum discipulī vēnērunt?
   a. poētā   b. Symmachō   c. manibus gelātīs   d. aquilōne

3. Quid virī clārī ex poētīs parāre possunt?
   a. litterās   b. fāmam   c. versūs   d. gentēs

4. Quō omnēs trahuntur?
   a. cupiditāte laudis   b. litterīs Graecīs
   c. versibus Latīnīs   d. pecūniā

5. Ubi litterae Rōmānae leguntur?
   a. in Graeciā   b. in ferē omnibus terrīs
   c. in Italiā   d. in hīs omnibus locīs

Carpe diem: *Seize the day*
Horace

23

Participles

INTELLEGENDA

Upon completion of this lesson you should be able to
   1. Define and explain the basic functions of a "participle."
   2. Recognize, form, and translate the four participles of regular Latin verbs.

Salvē, amīce aut amīca! Before beginning these exercises, be sure you have thoroughly studied Chapter 23 of *Wheelock's Latin* and memorized both the paradigms and the new vocabulary by repeating them *aloud*. **Carpe diem!**

GRAMMATICA

1. A participle is a verbal
    a. adjective   b. adverb   c. noun   d. pronoun

2. Regular transitive verbs have _____ participles.
    a. one   b. two   c. three   d. four

3. Of the three participle tenses, which has both active and passive forms?
    a. present   b. perfect   c. future   d. none of these

4. Which participle has only active forms?
    a. present   b. perfect   c. future   d. none of these

5. Which participle has only passive forms?
    a. present   b. perfect   c. future   d. none of these

6. The _____ active and _____ passive participles are
    formed on the present stem (from the _____ principal part).

7. The _____ active and _____ passive participles are
    formed on the participial stem (from the _____ principal
    part).

8. Present participles are easily recognized because their stem ends with
    the two letters _____, and future active participle forms are
    easily recognized because their stem ends with the two letters _____.

9. Forms of the future passive participle, or "gerundive," are easily rec-
    ognized by their stem ending in the two letters _____, and the
    perfect passive participle is easily recognized as the _____ prin-
    cipal part of most regular transitive verbs.

10. In present participle forms, the stem vowel of all verbs is long before
    -ns in the nominative (and neuter accusative) and _____ be-
    fore _____ in all other forms.

11. In all **-iō** verbs the letters _____ appear before **ns/nt** in the
    present participle.

12. Provide the missing participles.

	Active	**Passive**
Present	ēducāns, ēducantis	
Perfect		_____
Future	_____	_____
Present	_____	
Perfect		contentus, -a, -um
Future	_____	_____
Present	_____	
Perfect		_____
Future	versūrus, -a, -um	_____
Present	_____	
Perfect		_____
Future	_____	ēripiendus, -a, -um

Present _____

Perfect _____   scītus, -a, -um

Future _____   _____

13. Translate the participles of the first two verbs in the preceding
    question (*to educate* and *to contain*).

	Active	**Passive**
Present	_____	
Perfect		_____
Future	_____	_____

Present	_____	
Perfect		_____
Future	_____	_____

14. Which participle is not declined like **magnus, -a, -um**?
    a. present active   b. perfect passive
    c. future active   d. future passive

15. Present participles are declined as **i**-stems, except that the ablative
    singular sometimes ends with the letter ____ when the participle has a
    verbal or substantive function rather than serving purely as an

    _____ _____.

16. The stem of the _____ active participle can only be found
    from the _____ singular ending, but stems for the three other
    participles can be found by dropping **-us/-a/-um** from the nominative.

17. Decline the present participle of **rapiō,** neuter only.

	Singular	**Plural**
Nom.	_____	_____
Gen.	_____	_____
Dat.	_____	_____
Acc.	_____	_____
Abl.	_____, _____	_____

18. As adjectives, participles must agree with the nouns or pronouns they
    modify in
    a. number   b. gender   c. case   d. all these

19. As verbs, participles may
    a. be modified by adverbs   b. take direct objects
    c. take indirect objects   d. all these

20. The time of the action described by a participle is _____ to
    the tense of the _____ _____.

21. Match.

    Participle   **Time of Action**
    ____ present   a. prior to main verb
    ____ perfect   b. same as main verb
    ____ future   c. subsequent to main verb

22. Translate only the participial phrase, first as a phrase, then as a
    clause (e.g., **Māter, fīlium amāns, eum laudāvit,** *loving her son, since
    she loved her son*).

    a. Vir, amīcum in fenestrā vidēns, gaudet.

        Phrase: _____

        Clause: _____

    b. Dux magnanimus, mīlitēs Latīnōs vidēns, eōs prōtinus laudāvit.

        Phrase: _____

        Clause: _____

    c. Mīlitēs, ā duce magnanimō laudātī, quondam fuērunt fēlīcēs.

        Phrase: _____

        Clause: _____

EXERCITĀTIŌNĒS

A. Translate the following into English or Latin in accordance with their
    tense and voice.

    1. pressūrus _____

    2. gaudēns _____

    3. iussūrī _____

    4. labōrātūrōs _____

5. opprimendus _____

6. ostenta _____

7. petendum _____

8. relinquendī _____

9. tāctus _____

10. scientēs _____

11. having been turned _____

12. about to raise _____

13. writing _____

14. (fit) to be seen _____

15. (about) to be given _____

16. (deserving) to be sent _____

17. suppressing _____

18. having been pressed _____

19. going to exhibit _____

20. about to seek _____

B. Supply the correct form of the words in parentheses and translate.

1. Ōrātōrēs, ā duce asperō _____ (opprimere; perf. participle), dīcere nōn poterant.

   _____

   _____

2. Signum ducis _____ (vidēre; pres. participle), mīlitēs ad lītus īnsulae navigāvērunt.

   _____

   _____

3. Sacerdōs dōna _____ (dēsīderāre; perf. participle) ē mediā arce ēripit.

   _____

   _____

4. Equī, per agrōs _____ (currere; fut. act. participle), prōti-
    nus terrēbantur.

    _____

    _____

C. Transform from singular to plural or plural to singular and translate
    the new phrase.

1. mīles, ad īnsulam veniēns

    Transformation: _____

    Translation: _____

2. arcēs, ā vulgīs oppressae

    Transformation: _____

    Translation: _____

3. causae aequae ostentae

    Transformation: _____

    Translation: _____

4. pater, fīlium ēducātūrus

    Transformation: _____

    Translation: _____

5. casae relinquendae

    Transformation: _____

    Translation: _____

6. hastam ā mīlite iactam

    Transformation: _____

    Translation: _____

7. nāvēs lītora petentēs

    Transformation: _____

    Translation: _____

8. vīcīna ex igne ērepta

    Transformation: _____

    Translation: _____

9. sacerdōtī gaudentī

Transformation: _____

Translation: _____

10. ōrātor fidem petēns

Transformation: _____

Translation: _____

D. First translate the sentence, then transform the subordinate clause to a participial phrase with equivalent meaning and translate the participial phrase literally (e.g., **Ubi pater fīliam vīdit, eam laudāvit,** _When the father saw his daughter, he praised her_ > **Pater, fīliam vidēns, eam laudāvit,** _seeing his daughter_).

1. Quandō ab īnsulā vēnērunt, Graecī gaudēbant.

Sentence translation: _____

Transformation: _____

Phrase translation: _____

2. Quod Trōiam amant, ex igne ferrōque eam dēfendunt.

Sentence translation: _____

Transformation: _____

Phrase translation: _____

3. Quoniam ā servitūte asperā eō diē līberātī sunt, hominēs sunt fēlīcēs.

Sentence translation: _____

Transformation: _____

Phrase translation: _____

4. Duae fīliae iterum gaudent, quod mātrem crās vidēbunt.

Sentence translation: _____

Transformation: _____

Phrase translation: _____

E. Translate into Latin; employ standard word order and include all macrons.

1. They were glad about the gifts exhibited.

   _____

2. Shall we ever be happy, desiring only fortune and fame?

   _____

3. They were uncertain about the men to be saved.

   _____

4. The horse, about to come into the city, had been made by the Greeks.

   _____

   _____

VĪS VERBŌRUM

A. Answer these questions on the chapter's vocabulary list.

1. **Discō : discipulus :: dūcō :** _____.

2. **Nūllus : ūllus :: numquam :** _____.

3. Which verb is nearly synonymous with **ostendō**?
   a. cernō   b. dēmōnstrō   c. teneō   d. tollō

4. Identify the third declension **-iō** noun derived from the fourth principal part of each of the following verbs, and then give their direct English derivatives and their meanings.

	Latin Noun	Eng. Noun	Translation
a. petō	_____	_____	_____
b. opprimō	_____	_____	_____
c. dēprimō	_____	_____	_____
d. revertō	_____	_____	_____

B. Complete each statement with an English word that demonstrates your knowledge of the Latin etymology (e.g., "A 'laudatory' speech is full of praise").

1. To "avert" a risk is literally to _____ it _____.

2. Living in "isolation" is like being on an _____.

3. A "hastate" leaf is shaped like the tip of a _____.

4. A "littoral" region is near the _____.

LĒCTIŌNĒS

A. First read each sentence aloud twice, and then translate as literally as possible within the limits of sound English idiom.

1. Ab hostibus captus, dē gente suā nihil dīxit.

   _____

2. Aliquem dōna semper petentem nōn dīligō.

   _____

3. Ad lūdum tuum fīlium meum docendum mīsī.

   _____

4. Hīs īnsidiīs territī, vītam miseram sine spē vīvēmus.

   _____

5. Fidem habentibus nihil est incertum.

   _____

6. Sunt modī certī ac fīnēs in rēbus, ultrā quōs numquam possumus esse fēlīcēs.

   _____

   _____

7. Aliquis diem capiēns bene vīvet.

   _____

8. Sōla dulcia in mundō petentēs, fidē atque probitāte caruimus.

_____

9. "Rēs pūblica," inquit ōrātor magnanimus, "semper est cōnser-
    vanda."

_____

_____

10. Quidquid est in istō equō, timeō Graecōs dōna gerentēs.

_____

B. Answer these questions on "Laocoon Speaks Out."

1. Quam diū Graecī contrā Trōiānōs bellum gerēbant? (**Respondē in
    Latīnā.**)

    _____

2. Quōs Minerva iūvit? (**Respondē in tōtā sententiā.**)

    _____

3. Quī mīlitēs sunt in equō ligneō? (**In tōtā sententiā.**)

    _____

4. Quis scīvit equum esse īnsidiās? _____

5. Quid Lāocoōn in uterum equī iēcit? _____

6. Ad fīnem huius locī quid aut quis tremit?
    a. Lāocoōn   b. equus   c. hasta sacerdōtis   d. manus sacerdōtis

Quidquid bene dictum est ab ūllō, meum est:
Whatever has been said well by anyone is mine
Seneca the Younger

24

Ablative Absolute; Passive Periphrastic; Dative of Agent

INTELLEGENDA

Upon completion of this lesson you should be able to
  1. Define, recognize, and translate the "ablative absolute" construction.
  2. Define, recognize, and translate the "passive periphrastic" construction.
  3. Define, recognize, and translate the "dative of agent" construction.

Salvēte, discipulae discipulīque! Before beginning these exercises, be sure you have thoroughly studied Chapter 24 of *Wheelock's Latin* and memorized both the paradigms and the new vocabulary by repeating them *aloud.* By the way, with participles and the passive periphrastic mastered, you now understand that the **Intellegenda** (the gerundive of **intellegere**) leading off each of these lessons are literally learning objectives that "have to be understood." **Latīna omnibus intellegenda atque amanda est!**

GRAMMATICA

1. The ablative absolute is a type of participial phrase usually consisting of a _____ and a modifying _____ in the _____ case.

2. Only _____ connected with the rest of the sentence, and usually set off by _____, the ablative absolute describes some general _____ under which the action of the sentence occurs.

3. Because the absolute phrase is completely self-contained, it never modifies or refers directly to a _____ or _____ in the rest of the sentence.

4. Two nouns or a noun and an _____ in the ablative case can also constitute an ablative absolute, with the _____ _____ of the verb **sum** (which was lacking in classical Latin) to be understood.

5. While the ablative absolute can be translated literally, it is usually better style to transform the phrase to a clause by supplying a subordinating conjunction (usually _____, _____, or _____), making the ablative _____ the subject, and converting the participle to a regular verb in the appropriate _____ relative to the main verb.

6. Translate each ablative absolute, literally first as a phrase, then as a clause; e.g., **Rōmā vīsā, mīlitēs gaudēbant,** *(With) Rome having been seen* and *when Rome was (had been) seen.*

   a. Fābulā narrātā, servī rīdēbant.

   Phrase: _____

   Clause: _____

   b. Imperātōre imperium accipiente, mīlitēs gaudēbant.

   Phrase: _____

   Clause: _____

   c. Ōrātōre dictūrō, multī cīvēs in senātum veniunt.

   Phrase: _____

   Clause: _____

7. Identify and translate literally the four ablative absolute phrases in **Sententiae Antīquae** 1–8.

   Ablative Absolute   **Literal Translation**

   a. _____   _____

   b. _____   _____

   c. _____   _____

   d. _____   _____

8. Passive periphrastic verbs consist of a _____ _____ _____ (also known as the _____) plus a form of the verb **sum** and indicate _____ or _____ action rather than simple futurity.

9. Also sometimes employed to indicate obligatory action is the verb
   a. cernō   b. dēbeō   c. ostendō   d. petō

10. As in such perfect passive constructions as **fēmina laudāta est,** the participle in a passive periphrastic construction must _____ with the _____ in _____, _____, and _____.

11. To indicate the agent, i.e. the person performing the action, with a passive periphrastic the Roman used
    a. ablative with **ā/ab**
    b. ablative with no preposition
    c. dative with **ā/ab**
    d. dative with no preposition

12. Because a literal translation of a passive periphrastic generally sounds awkward, it is usually best to convert the clause into an _____ construction.

13. Translate each passive periphrastic first literally and then as an active clause (e.g., **Hic liber mihi legendus est,** *This book has to be read by me* > *I have to read this book.*)

    a. Perfugium servō quaerendum est.

       Passive: _____

       Active: _____

    b. Dux mīlitibus expellendus erit.

       Passive: _____

       Active: _____

    c. Carthāgō Rōmae dēlenda erat.

       Passive: _____

       Active: _____

14. Identify and translate literally the two passive periphrastics in Practice and Review sentences 1–8.

    Passive Periphrastic   **Literal Translation**

    a. _____   _____

    b. _____   _____

15. List in order, with the sentence number, and translate literally the two datives of agent in **Sentențiae Antīquae** 1–8.

	Sent. No.	Dative of Agent	Translation
a.	_____	_____	_____
b.	_____	_____	_____

EXERCITĀTIŌNĒS

A. Supply the correct form of the words in parentheses and translate.

1. _____ (servus; capere, perf. pass. participle), ducēs arcem eō diē recēpērunt.

   _____

2. Imperium ducī magnanimō _____ (quaerere; participle expressing necessity) est.

   _____

3. Hominēs malī sacerdōtī ē mediā arce _____ (expellere; participle expressing necessity) erunt.

   _____

4. _____ (spēs; opprimere, perf. pass. participle), quisque prōtinus fūgit.

   _____

B. Transform from singular to plural or plural to singular and translate the new phrase.

1. equō versō

   Transformation: _____

   Translation: _____

2. ferrīs sublātīs

   Transformation: _____

   Translation: _____

3. Fābulae narrandae erant.

   Transformation: _____

   Translation: _____

4. fidēbus ostentīs

   Transformation: _____

   Translation: _____

5. Hasta tibi excipienda est.

   Transformation: _____

   Translation: _____

6. rēbus pūblicīs ēreptīs

   Transformation: _____

   Translation: _____

7. Modī virīs petendī sunt.

   Transformation: _____

   Translation: _____

8. Īnsula videnda erit.

   Transformation: _____

   Translation: _____

9. lītoribus inventīs

   Transformation: _____

   Translation: _____

10. Spēs pellenda est.

    Transformation: _____

    Translation: _____

C. First translate the sentence, then transform the subordinate clause to an ablative absolute with equivalent meaning and translate the ablative absolute literally (e.g., **Ubi pater fīliam vīdit, familia gaudēbat,** *When the father saw his daughter, the family rejoiced* > **Fīliā ā patre vīsā,** *(With) the daughter (having been) seen by her father).*

Name: _____ *Section:* _____ *Date:* _____

1. Ubi equus vīsus erat, omnis Trōia gaudēbat.

    Sentence translation: _____

    Transformation: _____

    Abl. absolute translation: _____

2. Dum illī mīlitēs sōlācium accipiunt, urbs aliīs defendenda est.

    Sentence translation: _____

    Transformation: _____

    Abl. absolute translation: _____

D. Translate into Latin; employ participles, ablative absolutes, and passive periphrastics wherever possible.

1. When these gifts had been received, the general thanked his soldiers.

    _____

    _____

2. After the leader had been banished, the senate had to give command to a new general.

    _____

    _____

3. With the state seeking peace, we should drive out that tyrant.

    _____

4. Whatever frightens you now, afterwards you should fear nothing.

    _____

VĪS VERBŌRUM

A. Answer these questions on the chapter's vocabulary list.

1. **Fābula** > **fābulōsus, -a, -um** > "fabulous" :: **imperium** >
    _____ > _____.

2. Identify the third declension **-iō** noun derived from the fourth principal part of each of the following verbs, and then give their direct English derivatives and their meanings.

	Latin Noun	Eng. Noun	Translation
a. excipiō	_____	_____	_____
b. recipiō	_____	_____	_____
c. repellō	_____	_____	_____
d. expellō	_____	_____	_____
e. dērīdeō	_____	_____	_____

3. Which adverb can not be an antonym of **posteā**?
   a. ante   b. crās   c. ōlim   d. quondam

4. Which verb is the most direct antonym of **expellō**?
   a. accipiō   b. inquit   c. premō   d. revertō

5. Give the third declension **-or** and **-iō** nouns derived from the fourth principal part of **narrō,** their literal meanings, and their direct English derivatives.

	Meaning	Derivative
a. **-or:** _____	_____	_____
b. **-iō:** _____	_____	_____

B. Complete each statement with an English word that demonstrates your knowledge of the Latin etymology (e.g., "A 'laudatory' speech is full of <u>praise</u>").

1. An "imperious" person is always giving _____, and his favorite verb forms are called _____.

2. Achilles was "invulnerable" because he _____ _____ be _____—except in his heel!

3. If you "despise" others, you literally "look down" on them; when you "deride" others, you literally _____ _____ at them.

LĒCTIŌNĒS

A. First read each sentence aloud twice, and then translate as literally as possible within the limits of sound English idiom.

1. Aequīs virīs imperium tenentibus, ut omnēs dīcunt, rēs pūblica valēbit.

   _____

   _____

2. Omnēs cīvēs istum imperātōrem timēbant, quī expellendus erat.

   _____

3. Tyrannō superātō, cīvēs atque servī lībertātem et iūra recēpērunt.

   _____

4. Gentibus Latīnīs victīs, Rōma tōtam Italiam tenēre cupīvit.

   _____

5. Servitūs omnis generis hominibus līberīs per tōtum mundum opprimenda est.

   _____

   _____

6. Vulnere malō receptō, aliquis manum mīlitis ex igne prōtinus excēpit.

   _____

   _____

7. Erimusne umquam fēlīcēs, ultrā fīnēs Italiae vīventēs?

   _____

8. Rēbus incertīs nunc intellēctīs, sōlācium perfugiumque accipere possumus.

   _____

   _____

B. Answer these questions on "**Dē Cupiditāte**" and "The Satirist's **Modus Operandī.**"

1. Quid stultus ante pecūniam dēsīderat?
    a. omnia   b. virtūs   c. probitās   d. nihil

2. Cuius cupiditās nōbīs nōn fugienda est?
    a. pecūniae   b. glōriae   c. lībertātis   d. imperiōrum

3. Quis est "Iste" dē quō Herculēs dīcit?
    a. Plūtus   b. Fortūna   c. lucrum   d. pecūnia

4. Quō modō Horātius saturās scrībet?
    a. modō iūcundō   b. modō gravī
    c. modō fictō   d. hīs omnibus modīs

5. Dē quō (aut quibus) auctor scrībet?
    a. vēritāte   b. culpīs   c. vitiīs   d. hīs omnibus

6. Essentially Horace is telling us that while his subject matter is _____, his approach will be _____.

7. Explain very briefly how Horace involves and even "threatens" his audience in this last passage.

    _____

    _____

    _____

Pelle morās—brevis est magnī fortūna fāvōris:
Banish delay—the fortune of high favor is fleeting
Silius Italicus

25

Infinitives; Indirect Statement

INTELLEGENDA

Upon completion of this lesson you should be able to
 1. *Define and explain the basic functions of an "infinitive."*
 2. *Recognize, form, and translate the six infinitives of regular Latin verbs.*
 3. *Define, recognize, and translate the "indirect statement" construction.*

Salvē, discipula aut discipule! Before beginning these exercises, be sure you have thoroughly studied Chapter 25 of *Wheelock's Latin* and memorized both the paradigms and the new vocabulary by repeating them *aloud.* **Spērō tē linguam Latīnam iam amāre!**

GRAMMATICA

1. An infinitive is a verbal _____; most transitive verbs have six, i.e., both active and passive forms in the _____, _____, and _____ tenses, though the _____ _____ infinitive is rarely used.

2. A verb's present active infinitive is its _____ principal part; the present passive infinitive substitutes the letter _____ for the active infinitive's final **-e,** except in the _____ conjugation where _____ is substituted for _____.

3. The perfect active infinitive is formed by adding the letters _____ to the _____ active stem; the perfect passive infinitive consists of the _____ _____ _____ plus _____ .

4. The future active infinitive consists of the _____ _____ _____ plus the infinitive _____ ; the rare future passive infinitive consists of the _____ in **-um** (identical to the neuter nominative singular of the _____ _____ _____) plus _____ .

5. Provide the missing infinitives.

	Active	Passive
Present	negāre	_____
Perfect	_____	_____
Future	_____	_____
Present	_____	tenērī
Perfect	_____	_____
Future	_____	_____
Present	_____	_____
Perfect	crēdidisse	_____
Future	_____	_____

6. Translate the infinitives of the first two verbs in the preceding question (*to deny* and *to hold*).

	Active	Passive
Present	_____	_____
Perfect	_____	_____
Future	_____	_____
Present	_____	_____
Perfect	_____	_____
Future	_____	_____

7. Match the infinitive usage.
   ___ Ducem discēdere iussit.   a. subject
   ___ Errāre est humānum.   b. object
   ___ Fābulam bene narrāre potest.   c. complementary

8. The subject of an infinitive is in the _____ case.

9. An indirect statement follows a main verb of _____,
   _____ activity, or _____ perception, has its subject in
   the _____ case, and an _____ instead of a finite verb.

10. The participles forming part of the perfect passive and future active
    infinitives function rather like predicate adjectives with **esse** and thus
    must agree with the infinitive's _____ in _____,
    _____, and _____.

11. Which speech verb does not take an indirect statement?
    a. āit   b. inquit   c. negō   d. nūntiō

12. Which verb does not take an indirect statement?
    a. gaudeō   b. nesciō   c. sentiō   d. suscipiō

13. Like participles, the time of the action expressed by an infinitive is
    relative to the tense of the main verb; match.

    Infinitive   **Time of Action**

    ___ present   a. prior to main verb
    ___ perfect   b. same as main verb
    ___ future   c. subsequent to main verb

14. One mode of expressing indirect statement is commoner in Latin, the
    other in English; match.
    ___ We believe her to be brave   a. Latin
    ___ We believe that she is brave b. English

15. In transforming the Latin indirect statement from an infinitive
    phrase to a more idiomatic English subordinate clause, first supply
    the conjunction _____, then translate the accusative subject
    as if it were in the _____ case, and then transform the
    _____ to a regular verb form in the appropriate
    _____, relative to that of the main verb.

16. In Latin indirect statement the subject is always expressed and is
    always in the _____ case; when a pronoun is used, it will be
    a _____ pronoun if the subject is the same as the subject of
    the main verb and a _____ pronoun when the subject is
    different from that of the main verb.

17. Match to indicate the correct infinitive of **amō**.

    ___ Dīcit discipulum Latīnam (loves)   a. amāre

    ___ Dīxit discipulōs Latīnam (loved)   b. amāvisse

    ___ Dīcit sē Latīnam semper (loved)   c. amātūrum, -am esse

    ___ Dīxit sē Latīnam semper (would love)

    ___ Dīcet discipulōs Latīnam (will love)

    ___ Dīxit eum Latīnam (had loved)

18. **Amandum esse** is an example of a _____ _____ infinitive.

19. Translate into idiomatic English.

    a. Sciō servum hoc facere. _____

    b. Sciō ōrātōrēs hoc fēcisse. _____

    c. Scīvī sacerdōtem hoc fēcisse. _____

    d. Scīvistī eum hoc facere. _____

    e. Scit sē hoc factūram esse. _____

    f. Scīvit sē hoc factūrum esse. _____

    g. Sciō hoc mihi faciendum esse. _____

    h. Scīvī hoc ā tē factum esse. _____

EXERCITĀTIŌNĒS

A. Transform from active to passive or passive to active and translate the new form.

	Transformation	Translation
1. accipere	_____	_____
2. ēducātus esse	_____	_____
3. excēpisse	_____	_____
4. expulsum īrī	_____	_____
5. oppressūrus esse	_____	_____
6. revertī	_____	_____
7. recepta esse	_____	_____

Name: _____ *Section:* _____ *Date:* _____

8. premere   _____   _____

9. putāre   _____   _____

10. patefēcisse   _____   _____

B. Translate from singular to plural or plural to singular and then translate the new sentence.

1. Negat sē hastam iēcisse.

   Transformation: _____

   Translation: _____

2. Nūntiās tē īnsulam petere.

   Transformation: _____

   Translation: _____

3. Putō eam rīsūram esse.

   Transformation: _____

   Translation: _____

4. Ostendit eum ibi iacēre.

   Transformation: _____

   Translation: _____

5. Scīmus mīlitēs pulsōs esse.

   Transformation: _____

   Translation: _____

C. Translate the sentence; then transform the first clause into an indirect statement and translate the new sentence (e.g., **Puella est discipula bona; magister id scit.** > *The girl is a good student; the teacher knows it.* > **Magister scit puellam esse discipulam bonam.** > *The teacher knows that the girl is a good student*).

1. Bellum cum virtūte gesserās; imperātor id crēdidit.

   Translation: _____

   Transformation: _____

   _____

   Translation: _____

2. Linguam Latīnam semper amābis; id spērō!

    Translation: _____

    Transformation: _____

    Translation: _____

3. Fēminae eum iuvābant; fēminae mihi id dīxērunt.

    Translation: _____

    Transformation: _____

    _____

    Translation: _____

D. Supply the correct form of the words in parentheses and translate.

1. Dēhinc negāvit adulēscentem _____ (esse; same time)
    fīlium suum.

    _____

2. Nōn crēdō ducem imperium umquam _____ (relinquere;
    time after).

    _____

3. Imperātor nūntiāvit hostēs ā lītore _____ (āvertere, pass.;
    time before).

    _____

4. Servī posteā dīcent sē hīc ultrā fīnēs Italiae _____ (capere,
    pass.; time before).

    _____

E. Translate into Latin, using standard word order and including macrons.

1. The leader announced that he was sending the horses as gifts.

    _____

2. The loyal general denied that he would come into the city.

    _____

3. Many wise men believe that the human soul is immortal.

    _____

Name: _____   Section: _____ Date: _____

4. The wise and loyal priest warned that the horse had been made by the Greeks.

_____

_____

VĪS VERBŌRUM

A. Answer these questions on the chapter's vocabulary list.

1. **Fēlīx** > **fēlīcitās** > "felicity" :: **ferōx** > _____ > _____ :: **fidēlis** > _____ > _____.

2. **Dīcō : negō :: sciō :** _____.

3. Which adverb is synonymous with **dēhinc**?
    a. deinde   b. nunc   c. ultrā   d. umquam

4. **Ille : hic :: ibi :** _____.

B. Complete each statement with an English word that demonstrates your knowledge of the Latin etymology (e.g., "A 'laudatory' speech is full of praise").

1. A "credulous" person tends to _____ everything he hears.

2. When one item is "subjacent" to another, it literally _____ _____ it.

3. To "negate" a statement is to _____ its existence.

4. If a "peninsula" (from **paene**, *almost, nearly,* + **īnsula**) is "almost an island," then the "penultimate" item in a series is _____ (i.e., next to) the _____.

5. If you are "desperate," your _____ have gone _____.

LĒCTIŌNĒS

A. First read each sentence aloud twice, and then translate as literally as possible within the limits of sound English idiom.

1. Quisquis crēdit sē nūlla vitia habēre, is nimis errat.

   _____

2. Dux magnanimus negāvit arcem Carthāginis dēlendam esse.

   _____

3. Servī spērāvērunt sē perfugium atque sōlācium prō vulneribus ultrā montēs inventūrōs esse.

   _____

   _____

4. Graecī ducēs geminī sēnsērunt Trōiam vīdisse diem ultimum.

   _____

5. Hostēs ferōcēs crēdunt omnem rem pūblicam sibi vincendam
   esse.

   _____

   _____

6. Bene sciō mē multa nescīre; nēmō enim, ut aiunt, potest omnia
   scīre.

   _____

   _____

B. Answer these questions on "The Death of Laocoon."

1. Aenēās, dux Trōiānus, hanc fābulam in carmine Vergiliī narrat; dē
   quō sacerdōte dīcit? _____

2. Cuius deī fuit ille sacerdōs? (**Respondē in tōtā sententiā.**)

   _____

3. How is the phrase **linguīs sībilīs** onomatopoetic?

   _____

4. Serpentibus vīsīs, quī cīvēs fugiunt?
   a. Aenēas et Trōiānī   b. Laocoon et fīliī
   c. puerī puellaeque   d. hī omnēs

5. Sacerdōte et fīliīs necātīs, quid serpentēs petunt?
   a. Laocoon   b. fīliī eius   c. taurus   d. arx Minervae

6. Identify the simile in the second paragraph and explain briefly its irony.

_____

_____

_____

Homō sum—hūmānī nil ā mē aliēnum putō:
I am a human being—I consider nothing human to be alien to me
Terence

26

Comparison of Adjectives; Declension of Comparatives; Ablative of Comparison

INTELLEGENDA

Upon completion of this lesson you should be able to

1. Explain what is meant by "comparison of adjectives."

2. Recognize, form, decline, and translate regular adjectives in the comparative and superlative degrees.

*3. Recognize and translate the uses of **quam** with comparative and superlative adjectives.*

4. Define, recognize, and translate the "ablative of comparison" construction.

Salvēte, discipulae discipulīque cārissimī! Be sure you have thoroughly studied Chapter 26 of *Wheelock's Latin* before attempting these exercises—and remember to memorize the paradigms and vocabulary by repeating them *aloud.* **Latīna est lingua quam potentissima!**

GRAMMATICA

1. A _____ degree adjective indicates that a person or thing possesses a particular quality or characteristic.

2. A comparative degree adjective indicates that a person or thing possesses a greater degree of a characteristic than
    a. another person or thing   b. usual   c. desirable   d. all these

3. A _____ degree adjective indicates that a person or thing has the greatest degree of a characteristic in comparison either with _____ or more others or with what is _____ or _____.

4. Regular comparative degree adjectives are formed by adding _____ (m./f.) and _____ (n.) to the _____ of the positive degree; the genitive singular ends in _____.

5. Regular superlative degree adjectives are formed by adding _____ (m.), _____ (f.), and _____ (n.) to the _____ of the positive degree.

6. Comparative degree adjectives are **i**-stem adjectives of the third declension.   T/F

7. Superlatives follow the declension of **magnus, -a, -um.**   T/F

8. Adjectives whose bases end with a vowel often form the comparative and superlative degree with _____ and _____, respectively.

9. Match the possible translations.
    ___ brighter   a. clārior, clārius
    ___ very bright   b. clārissimus, -a, -um
    ___ rather bright
    ___ more bright
    ___ brightest
    ___ too bright
    ___ most bright

10. When **quam** _____ a comparative it means _____; when it precedes a _____ it indicates the greatest _____ degree of a characteristic.

11. When the first noun or pronoun in a comparison was either in the
    _____ or _____ case, _____ was frequently
    omitted, and the second person or thing compared was in the
    _____ case, the so-called _____ of _____.

12. List the four comparatives and six superlatives in Practice and
    Review 1-12.

    Comparatives   **Superlatives**

    _____   _____

    _____   _____

    _____   _____

    _____   _____

                                       _____

                                       _____

13. Identify the base and gender of **lūx clārior,** *the brighter light,* decline
    it fully, and provide the English meanings appropriate to each case.

    base: _____ _____   gender: _____

	Latin		**English**
	Singular		
Nom.	lūx	clārior	the brighter light
Gen.	_____	_____	_____
Dat.	_____	_____	_____
Acc.	_____	_____	_____
Abl.	_____	_____	_____
	Plural		
Nom.	_____	_____	_____
Gen.	_____	_____	_____
Dat.	_____	_____	_____
Acc.	_____	_____	_____
Abl.	_____	_____	_____

14. Identify the base and gender of **bellum brevius,** *the shorter war,* and decline it fully.

base: _____ _____   gender: _____

	Singular		Plural	
Nom.	bellum	brevius	_____	_____
Gen.	_____	_____	_____	_____
Dat.	_____	_____	_____	_____
Acc.	_____	_____	_____	_____
Abl.	_____	_____	_____	_____

15. Choose the correct form of the adjective and then translate the entire phrase.

	Adjective	Translation
a. cēna (very brief)	_____	_____
b. fābulārum (rather sad)	_____	_____
c. in forō (very full)	_____	_____
d. cum fēminā (more modest)	_____	_____
e. ā tyrannō (most arrogant)	_____	_____
f. poētam (rather urbane)	_____	_____
g. animālia (more ferocious)	_____	_____
h. servī (very faithful)	_____	_____

EXERCITĀTIŌNĒS

A. Transform from singular to plural or plural to singular and translate the new phrase.

1. lēgum acerbiōrum

    Transformation: _____

    Translation: _____

2. ab imperātōre superbissimō

    Transformation: _____

    Translation: _____

3. imperia ingentissima

   Transformation: _____

   Translation: _____

4. in linguīs iūcundissimīs

   Transformation: _____

   Translation: _____

5. noctem fortūnātiōrem

   Transformation: _____

   Translation: _____

6. perfugia salviōra

   Transformation: _____

   Translation: _____

7. sōlāciīs dulcissimīs

   Transformation: _____

   Translation: _____

8. ex somnīs longiōribus

   Transformation: _____

   Translation: _____

9. vulnus gravius

   Transformation: _____

   Translation: _____

10. discipulam sapientissimam

   Transformation: _____

   Translation: _____

B. Supply the correct form of the words in parentheses and translate.

   1. Auctor posteā scrīpsit versūs _____ (turpis; superlative).

      _____

   2. Memoria noctis _____ (fēlīx; superlative) diū remānsit.

      _____

3. Crēdō eam esse _____ (fidēlis; comparative) quam eum.

_____

4. Dux Carthāginis ad senātum litterās quam _____ (brevis; superlative) mittet.

_____

_____

C. Make the comparisons.

1. Quis est senior?
   a. fīlius   b. pater

2. Quis est antīquissimus?
   a. Achillēs   b. Cicerō   c. Caesar

3. Quid est brevissimum?
   a. annus   b. diēs   c. hōra

4. Quod tempus est clārius?
   a. diēs   b. nox

5. Quid est celerius?
   a. equus   b. homō

6. Quid est difficilius?
   a. labor   b. ōtium

7. Quid est trīstissimum?
   a. morbus   b. mors   c. vulnus

8. Quis est potentissimus?
   a. imperātor   b. mīles   c. servus

D. Translate into Latin; employ standard word order and include all macrons.

1. The wisest possible leaders should be invited (pass. periphrastic) to this very serious dinner.

_____

_____

2. The teacher announced that the students would read a rather short but very urbane book.

_____

_____

3. Nothing was sadder than that very faithful slave's death.

_____

4. We hope that the memory of this rather disgraceful night will not remain.

_____

_____

VĪS VERBŌRUM

A. Answer these questions on the chapter's vocabulary list.

1. Many Latin adjectives form feminine third declension nouns by adding **-itūdō,** gen. **-itūdinis,** to the adjective's base; these are abstract nouns referring to the quality represented by the adjective. E.g., **fortis, forte,** gives us **fortitūdō, fortitūdinis,** f., and the English derivative "fortitude," meaning *bravery, courage.* Identify the nouns, their meanings, and their direct English derivatives that are similarly derived from the following Latin adjectives.

	Latin Noun	**Derivative**	**Meaning**
a. sōlus, -a, -um	_____	_____	_____
b. turpis, turpe	_____	_____	_____

2. Which noun is nearly synonymous with **lēx?**
    a. forum b. iūs c. lūx d. senātus

3. Which is not a possible meaning of **quam** in its various uses?
    a. how b. than c. then d. which

4. Which has a meaning essentially opposite the others?
    a. ante b. post c. prae d. prō

5. Complete the analogy **sēnsus : mēns :: līmen :** _____.
    a. animus b. caput c. casa d. oculus

6. Which verb has a meaning similar to **invītō?**
    a. iaceō b. patefaciō c. suscipiō d. vocō

B. Complete each statement with an English word that demonstrates your knowledge of the Latin etymology (e.g., "A 'laudatory' speech is full of praise").

Name: _____   *Section:* _____ *Date:* _____

1. A "subliminal" message is transmitted _____ the usual _____ of perception.

2. "Translucent" material allows _____ to pass from one side _____ to another, and to "elucidate" a subject is to shed _____ upon it.

3. On both the vernal and the autumnal "equinox," the length of the _____ is _____ to that of the day.

4. A "somnambulist" walks in his _____.

LĒCTIŌNĒS

A. First read each sentence aloud twice, and then translate as literally as possible within the limits of sound English idiom.

1. Nūntiāvērunt ducem quam fortissimum vēnisse.

   _____

2. Lūce clārissimā ab omnibus vīsā, cōpiae fortissimae contrā hostēs remissae sunt.

   _____

   _____

3. Istō homine turpissimō expulsō, senātus tantum cīvibus fidēliōribus dōna dēhinc dedit.

   _____

   _____

4. Quīdam negāvērunt hunc auctōrem esse clāriōrem illō.

   _____

5. Remedium hōrum vitiōrum ultimōrum vidētur difficilius.

   _____

6. Ille dux putāvit patriam esse sibi cāriōrem quam vītam.

   _____

7. Nescīvit amīcum geminōs frātrēs iūcundissimōs ad cēnam eā nocte invītātūrum esse.

_____

_____

8. Ut in līmine ultimō stetērunt, fābulam trīstissimam narrābant et multa dē urbe novā quaerēbant.

_____

_____

B. Answer these questions on "The Nations of Gaul" and "The Good Life."

1. Quis librum dē bellō Gallicō scrīpsit? _____

2. Gallia ā tribus gentibus incolitur, tantum hīs exceptīs.
   a. Belgae   b. Aquitānī   c. Gallī   d. Matronae

3. Quid Rōmānī Celtās appellant?
   a. Gallia   b. Gallī   c. differunt   d. fortissimī

4. Quae gēns tribus flūminibus ab aliīs dīviditur?
   a. Belgae   b. Aquitānī   c. Gallī   d. nūlla ex hīs

5. Belgae sunt fortiōrēs quam
   a. Aquitānī   b. Gallī   c. hī duo   d. nēmō

6. Quid, ut Martiālis putat, vītam fēlīciōrem nōn facit?
   a. ōtium   b. voluptās labōris
   c. amīcitia   d. pecūnia ā patre parāta

7. Mors, ut poēta āit, nōn
   a. beāta est   b. cūrīs solūta est   c. rīdenda est   d. timenda est

8. Which of Martial's points seems particularly alien to the work-ethic of our democratic society?

_____

_____

Brevis ipsa vīta est, sed malīs fit longior:
Life itself is short, but it becomes longer with misfortunes
Publilius Syrus

Name: _____   Section: _____ Date: _____

27

Special and Irregular Comparison of Adjectives

INTELLEGENDA

Upon completion of this lesson you should be able to
  1. Recognize, form, and translate adjectives with irregular superlatives and other adjectives with irregular comparisons.
  2. Recognize, form, and translate the irregular adjective/noun **plūs.**

Salvēte, optimae discipulae discipulīque! Be sure you have thoroughly studied Chapter 27 of *Wheelock's Latin* before attempting these exercises—and remember to memorize the paradigms and vocabulary by repeating them *aloud.* **Carpite diem, amīcī dīligentissimī!**

GRAMMATICA

1. Six third declension adjectives ending in **-lis** form their superlatives by adding _____, rather than **-issimus, -a, -um,** to the base of the positive; the six adjectives are: _____, _____, _____, _____, _____, and _____.

2. All adjectives with a nominative masculine ending in **-er** form their superlatives by adding _____ directly to this nominative masculine **-er** form, not to the _____.

3. Several Latin adjectives have comparatives and/or superlatives that are irregularly formed and must be memorized. Which of the following is not irregularly compared?
   a. bonus   b. dīligēns   c. magnus   d. malus

4. Which is regularly compared?
   a. multus   b. parvus   c. pudīcus   d. superus

5. Give the Latin comparatives and superlatives from which the following English words are derived, and list the corresponding positive degree of the Latin word.

Positive	Comparative	Superlative
	pejorative	pessimist
_____	_____	_____
	prior	primary
_____	_____	_____
	superiority	summit and supremacy
_____	_____	_____
	minority	minimize
_____	_____	_____
	majority	maximum
_____	_____	_____
	ameliorate	optimist
_____	_____	_____

6. In the singular **plūs** functions as a neuter _____ and is regularly followed by a noun or pronoun in the _____ case.

7. The plural of **plūs** functions as an _____ and has
   a. consonant-stem forms   b. **i**-stem forms   c. both   d. neither

8. List the five irregular comparatives and three irregular superlatives in
    Sententiae Antīquae 1–5.

    Comparatives _____

    _____   **Superlatives**

    _____   _____

    _____   _____

    _____   _____

9. Identify the base and gender of **plūrēs linguae**, *more languages,* and
    plūra fora, *more marketplaces,* and then decline fully.

    base: _____ _____   base: _____ _____

    gender: _____   gender: _____

Nom.	plūrēs	linguae	plūra	fora
Gen.	_____	_____	_____	_____
Dat.	_____	_____	_____	_____
Acc.	_____	_____	_____	_____
Abl.	_____	_____	_____	_____

10. Choose the correct form of the adjective and then translate the entire
    phrase.

	Adjective	**Translation**
a. post cēnam (very good)	_____	_____
b. lēgis (most difficult)	_____	_____
c. prae līmine (very similar)	_____	_____
d. propter lūcēs (smaller)	_____	_____
e. nocte (former)	_____	_____
f. somnum (very easy)	_____	_____
g. sōlis (very beautiful)	_____	_____
h. contrā nepōtēs (worst)	_____	_____
i. dēlectātiōnum (greatest)	_____	_____
j. discipulās (keenest)	_____	_____

k. cum deīs (highest)   _____   _____

l. sub rosā (very slender)   _____   _____

EXERCITĀTIŌNĒS

A.   Transform from comparative to superlative or from superlative to comparative and translate the new phrase.

1.   servī humiliōrēs

   Transformation: _____

   Translation: _____

2.   animālis ferōciōris

   Transformation: _____

   Translation: _____

3.   nepōtem dissimiliōrem

   Transformation: _____

   Translation: _____

4.   cum cīvibus fidēliōribus

   Transformation: _____

   Translation: _____

5.   geminōs similiōrēs

   Transformation: _____

   Translation: _____

6.   cōnsulī prīmō

   Transformation: _____

   Translation: _____

7.   lingua ūtilior

   Transformation: _____

   Translation: _____

Name: _____   *Section:* _____   *Date:* _____

8. sōlis pulchriōris

Transformation: _____

Translation: _____

9. dēlectātiōnem optimam

Transformation: _____

Translation: _____

10. noctēs pessimae

Transformation: _____

Translation: _____

B. Make the comparisons.

1. Quis est dissimillimus aut dissimillima?
   a. adulēscēns   b. puer   c. puella   d. senex

2. Quid est humillimum?
   a. ager   b. caelum   c. mōns   d. nūbēs

3. Quid est summum?
   a. mōns   b. nūbēs   c. sōl   d. terra

4. Quid est melius?
   a. virtūs   b. vitium

5. Quid est peius?
   a. bellum   b. īnsidiae

6. Quid habet plūs aquae?
   a. flūmen   b. mare

7. Quid habet plūrimās dēlectātiōnēs atque voluptātēs?
   a. lingua Latīna   b. lingua Latīna
   c. lingua Latīna   d. lingua Latīna

8. Quid est minimum?
   a. caput   b. manus   c. oculus   d. ōs

C. Supply the correct form of the words in parentheses and translate.

1. Lūx sōlis _____ (magnus; superlative) in caelō est.

2. _____ (celer; superlative) remedium, ut aiunt, nōn semper est _____ (bonus; superlative).

   _____

3. _____ (sapiēns; comparative) virī _____ (parvus; comparative) numerum vitiōrum saepe habent.

   _____

   _____

4. Dēhinc magistra nūntiāvit sē tantum discipulās _____ (dīligēns; superlative) probātūram esse.

   _____

   _____

D. Translate into Latin; employ standard word order and include all macrons.

1. Certain men hope that here they will receive only the best possible gifts.

   _____

   _____

2. They thought that their ancestors had more virtue than their descendants.

   _____

   _____

3. How many students know that the Latin language is very easy?

   _____

4. Our ancestors believed that the sun was a god.

   _____

VĪS VERBŌRUM

A. Answer these questions on the chapter's vocabulary list.

1. Identify the third declension **-tās** nouns derived from the following adjectives, and then give their direct English derivatives and their meanings.

	Latin Noun	Eng. Noun	Translation
a. humilis, -e	_____	_____	_____
b. ūtilis, -e	_____	_____	_____

2. Which noun is close in meaning to **dēlectātiō**?
    a. cēna   b. forum   c. līmen   d. voluptās

3. Identify the third declension **-iō** nouns derived from the fourth principal part of the following verbs, and then give their direct English derivatives and their meanings.

	Latin Noun	Eng. Noun	Translation
a. pōnō	_____	_____	_____
b. probō	_____	_____	_____

4. Which adjective has a meaning essentially opposite that of **prīmus**?
    a. trīstis   b. turpis   c. ultimus   d. urbānus

5. Which verb has a meaning similar to **expōnō**?
    a. iaceō   b. invītō   c. patefaciō   d. suscipiō

B. Complete each statement with an English word that demonstrates your knowledge of the Latin etymology (e.g., "A 'laudatory' speech is full of praise").

1. A work of art with great "verisimilitude" portrays things in a manner _____ to their _____ character.

2. "Nepotism" is the practice of showing favoritism, especially in business or political appointments, to one's _____ or other relatives.

3. A "solarium" is a room or porch exposed to the _____ and used, for example, by recuperating patients.

4. A "proposition" is something _____ _____ for consideration.

LĒCTIŌNĒS

A. First read each sentence aloud twice, and then translate as literally as possible within the limits of sound English idiom.

1. Dēlectātiōnēs facillimae saepe nōn sunt optimae.

   _____

2. Nepōs minor sed dīligentior maius dōnum accēpit.

   _____

3. Plūrēs virī crēdunt hoc bellum esse peius quam prīmum bellum.

   _____

4. Quot maiōra ac ūtilissima nepōtēs nostrī posteā invenient?

   _____

5. Post tempestātem plūrima flūmina gracillima dē montibus currē-bant atque, nūbibus expulsīs, sōl superus agrōs humilēs aluit.

   _____

   _____

6. Caesar nescīvit hās gentēs esse inter sē dissimillimās.

   _____

7. Quot cōnsilia simillima illī ducēs prōpōsuērunt atque probā-vērunt?

   _____

B. Answer these questions on "Alley Cat," "Thanks a Lot," and "An Uncle's Love."

1. Amatne nunc Catullus Lesbiam? (**Respondē in tōtā sententiā.**)

   _____

2. In which verses of "Alley Cat" does Catullus place key words at the end of the line for emphasis? Explain.

   _____

   _____

   _____

Name: _____ *Section:* _____ *Date:* _____

3. Cui (in secundō carmine) Catullus grātiās agit?
   a. Rōmulus   b. Cicerō   c. nepōtēs Rōmulī   d. poēta pessimus

4. Comment on Catullus' use of superlatives in poem 49.

   _____

   _____

   _____

5. Quī frāter in tertiō locō dīcit?
   a. frāter quī in urbe vīxit   b. frāter quī vītam in agrīs ēgit

6. Quot fīliōs agricola habet? (**In tōtā sententiā.**)

   _____

7. Quis est cārissimus aut cārissima frātrī urbānō?
   a. ipse   b. fīlius suus   c. fīlius frātris   d. uxor pudīca

Omnia sōl temperat: *The sun tempers all things*
Carmina Burana

28

Subjunctive Mood; Present Subjunctive; Jussive and Purpose Clauses

INTELLEGENDA

Upon completion of this lesson you should be able to
1. Define the "subjunctive mood," distinguishing it from the indicative and imperative.
2. Recognize, form, and translate the present subjunctive, active and passive, for verbs of all four conjugations.
3. Define, recognize, and translate the subjunctive "jussive clause."
4. Define, recognize, and translate the subjunctive "purpose clause."

Salvēte, discipulae discipulīque dīligentissimī! Be sure you have thoroughly studied Chapter 28 of *Wheelock's Latin* before attempting these exercises— and remember to memorize the paradigms and vocabulary by repeating them *aloud*. **Carpāmus diem, atque Latīnam discāmus ut maximōs auctōrēs Rōmae antīquae legāmus!**

GRAMMATICA

1. "Mood" is the _____ of expressing a verbal action or state of being.

2. The imperative mood _____ someone to undertake an action; the indicative mood _____ that some action is or is not in fact occurring, or that it did or did not, or will or will not, occur; the subjunctive mood, by contrast, often describes actions that are only _____, _____, or _____.

3. The subjunctive is used _____ (more/less) frequently in Latin than in English.

4. Of the six Latin verb tenses, the _____ and _____ _____ do not have subjunctive forms.

5. Subjunctive forms are differentiated from indicative forms in the present tense chiefly through the change or addition of a _____.

6. The sentence _____ _____ _____ _____ is a helpful mnemonic device for remembering the _____ that immediately precede the personal endings in the present subjunctive of the four conjugations.

7. Conjugate the indicated verbs in the present active subjunctive.

    invītāre   **tacēre**
    Singular   **Plural**   **Singular**   **Plural**

    1. _____   _____   _____   _____

    2. _____   _____   _____   _____

    3. _____   _____   _____   _____

    cēdere
    Singular   **Plural**

    1. _____   _____

    2. _____   _____

    3. _____   _____

8. Conjugate the indicated verbs in the present passive subjunctive.

    pōnere   **ēripere**
    Singular   **Plural**   **Singular**   **Plural**

    1. _____   _____   _____   _____

    2. _____   _____   _____   _____

    3. _____   _____   _____   _____

invenīre

Singular	Plural
1. _____	_____
2. _____	_____
3. _____	_____

9. Translate **invītāre** in the present active subjunctive and **invenīre** in the passive (as conjugated above), using "may" as the English auxiliary.

invītāre   **invenīre**

Singular	Plural	Singular	Plural
1. _____	_____	_____	_____
2. _____	_____	_____	_____
3. _____	_____	_____	_____

10. As the term "subjunctive" implies, subjunctive verbs were most commonly employed in _____ clauses; one of the commonest exceptions, and the only one introduced by Wheelock, is the _____ subjunctive, which is used as the main verb in an independent clause expressing a _____.

11. Match.

    Commonly used to express   **Mood**
    ____ 1st person command   a. imperative
    ____ 2nd person command   b. subjunctive
    ____ 3rd person command

12. In translating the jussive subjunctive, supply the auxiliary _____, followed by the _____ (in the objective case if a pronoun, i.e., not *I, we, he, she, it, they,* but _____, _____, _____, _____, _____, _____).

13. A negative jussive clause is introduced by _____.

14. A purpose clause is a _____ clause indicating the _____ of the action in the _____ clause.

15. Purpose clauses are introduced by the conjunction _____, if positive, or _____, if negative.

16. In a purpose clause, **ut/nē** may be translated as *that, so that,* or *in order that (not),* with _____ supplied as the auxiliary for the

present subjunctive verb; sometimes, when the subject of the main clause and the purpose clause are the same, the conjunction can be omitted in translation (or translated *in order*) and the verb translated simply as an _____.

17.   List the five jussive subjunctives in Practice and Review sentences 1–11.

_____ _____ _____ _____ _____

18.   List the six subjunctives used in purpose clauses in **Sententiae Antīquae** 1–12.

_____ _____ _____ _____ _____

_____

EXERCITĀTIŌNĒS

A.   Transform each sentence from singular to plural or plural to singular and then translate the new sentence.

1.   Parēns fīliam amet.

Transformation: _____

Translation: _____

2.   Nē servī cēnīs egeant.

Transformation: _____

Translation: _____

3.   Probem lēgem ūtilem.

Transformation: _____

Translation: _____

4.   Nepōtēs cursūs currant.

Transformation: _____

Translation: _____

5.   Nē dē hōc taceam.

Transformation: _____

Translation: _____

6.   Occāsiōnem praestet.

Transformation: _____

Translation: _____

B.   Transform the second clause into a purpose clause with the verb in the present subjunctive and then translate the new sentence (e.g., **Cum cūrā labōrat; Latīnam bene discet.** > **Cum cūrā labōrat ut Latīnam bene discat.** > *He works with care in order to learn Latin well*).

1.   Librum maximā cum cūrā scrībit; discipulī bene discent.

   Transformation: _____

   Translation: _____

2.   Quīdam beneficia parentibus praestant; ipsī ā fīliīs suīs dīligentur.

   Transformation: _____

   _____

   Translation: _____

   _____

3.   Prīnceps senātūs lēgēs acerbiōrēs nūntiat; coniūrātī nōn remanēbunt.

   Transformation: _____

   _____

   Translation: _____

   _____

C.   Supply the correct form of the verbs in parentheses and translate.

1.   Nē istī turpissimī hostibus arma aut sōlācium _____ (praestāre; subj.).

   _____

2.   Mōrēs maiōrum _____ (cōnservāre; 1st pers. pl. subj.) ut nōs ipsī maiōrem occāsiōnem pācis _____ (habēre).

   _____

   _____

3.   Parentēs istum superbissimum ē līmine casae _____ (expellere; subj.) nē familia trīstis īnsidiās _____ (timēre).

   _____

   _____

4. Maxima beneficia atque plūrimās dēlectātiōnēs amīcitiae
   _____ (laudāre; 1st pers. sg. subj.).

   _____

D. Translate into Latin; employ standard word order and include all macrons.

   1. Let the emperor send us the best possible arms.

      _____

   2. They come to offer us a better opportunity.

      _____

   3. He is again writing similar words in order to help the people.

      _____

   4. Let her read the letter so that she may not fear death.

      _____

VĪS VERBŌRUM

A. Answer these questions on the chapter's vocabulary list.

   1. Complete the analogy **sōl:diēs::lūna:**_____.
      a. forum   b. lūx   c. nox   d. somnus

   2. Quid est clārissimum?
      a. lūna   b. sōl   c. stēlla   d. vesper

   3. Identify three nouns in the new vocabulary that produce English
      derivatives simply by dropping the genitive ending. _____
      _____   _____

   4. Which adjective is nearly synonymous with **prīnceps**?
      a. dissimilis   b. humilis   c. prīmus   d. urbānus

   5. Which is not related to **mortuus**?
      a. immortal   b. moratorium   c. mortuary   d. post mortem

   6. Which verb is synonymous with **egeō**?
      a. careō   b. cēdō   c. expleō   d. probō

B. Complete each statement with an English word that demonstrates your knowledge of the Latin etymology (e.g., "A 'laudatory' speech is full of praise").

1. "Lunatics" are so-called because they were once thought to be possessed by the power of the _____.

2. A "taciturn" person is _____ and reclusive.

3. To "recede" is to _____ _____; an "antecedent" has _____ _____; to "proceed" is to _____ _____; to "intercede" is to _____ _____; and one who is "deceased" has _____ _____.

LĒCTIŌNĒS

A. First read each sentence aloud twice, and then translate as literally as possible within the limits of sound English idiom.

1. Tantum haec verba fēlīcia vōbīs dīcō nē discēdātis.

   _____

2. Mortuōrum causā haec difficillima faciāmus.

   _____

3. Arma parēmus nē lībertās nostra tollātur.

   _____

4. Meliōra et maiōra faciat nē vītam miserrimam agat.

   _____

5. Deīs summīs et animīs parentum nostrōrum arma dēdicēmus ut officium praestēmus.

   _____

   _____

6. Poēta puellae pudīcae plūrimās rosās gracilēs mittat.

   _____

7. Quot vītae āmittendae sunt ut lībertās cōnservētur?

   _____

8. Crēdāmus nōn sōlum virtūtem esse meliōrem quam vitium, sed etiam eam prae omnibus rēbus hūmānīs habendam esse.

_____

_____

B. Answer these questions on "Remove My Name," "One Must Be Friendly," and "The Days of the Week."

1. Cūr poēta Pontiliānō librōs nōn mittit?
    a. nōn librōs habet, tantum libellōs
    b. spērat Pontiliānum librōs suōs missūrum esse
    c. putat Pontiliānum deinde eī libellōs datūrum esse
    d. omnia haec

2. How does Martial use rhyme effectively in Epigram 7.3?

_____

_____

3. How is Martial's positioning of the personal names **Pyladēn** and **Orestēn** stylistically effective?

_____

_____

4. Quem diem Rōmānī ex sōle appellāvērunt?
    a. prīmum   b. secundum   c. tertium   d. quārtum

5. Quid Hebraeī eundem diem appellāvērunt?
    a. sabbatum   b. ūnum diem sabbatī
    c. diem Saturnī   d. diem dominicum

6. Quī diēs (in Anglicā, i.e., *in English*) ā stēllā clārissimā appellābātur?
    a. Friday   b. Saturday   c. Sunday   d. Monday

Praestātur laus virtūtī, sed multō ocius vernō gelū tabēscit: *Praise is offered for virtue, but it disappears much more quickly than a frost in spring*
Livius Andronicus

29

Imperfect Subjunctive; Present and Imperfect Subjunctive of Sum and Possum; Result Clauses

INTELLEGENDA

Upon completion of this lesson you should be able to

1. Recognize, form, and translate the imperfect subjunctive, active and passive, for verbs of all four conjugations.

*2. Recognize and translate the present and imperfect subjunctives of **sum** and **possum**.*

3. Define, recognize, and translate the subjunctive "result clause."

Carpāmus diem, discipulī discipulaeque dignissimae! Be sure you have thoroughly studied Chapter 29 of *Wheelock's Latin* before attempting these exercises—and remember to memorize the paradigms and vocabulary by repeating them *aloud*. **Discite Latīnam tantā cum cūrā ut in mentibus vestrīs semper remaneat!**

GRAMMATICA

1. The imperfect subjunctive for any verb is formed by adding the usual present system endings directly to the _____ _____ _____ (i.e., the _____ principal part) after lengthening the final **-e** (except before **nt** and final **-m, -r,** and **-t**).

2. Conjugate the indicated verbs in the imperfect active subjunctive.

   probāre

Singular	Plural		**egēre** Singular	Plural
1. _____	_____		_____	_____
2. _____	_____		_____	_____
3. _____	_____		_____	_____

   cēdere

Singular	Plural
1. _____	_____
2. _____	_____
3. _____	_____

3. Conjugate the indicated verbs in the imperfect passive subjunctive.

   praestāre

Singular	Plural		**explēre** Singular	Plural
1. _____	_____		_____	_____
2. _____	_____		_____	_____
3. _____	_____		_____	_____

   mollīre

Singular	Plural
1. _____	_____
2. _____	_____
3. _____	_____

4. Translate **probāre**, *to approve,* in the imperfect active subjunctive and **mollīre**, *to calm,* in the passive (as conjugated above), using "might" as the English auxiliary.

probāre, active		**mollīre, passive**	
Singular	**Plural**	**Singular**	**Plural**
1. _____	_____	_____	_____
2. _____	_____	_____	_____
3. _____	_____	_____	_____

5. The present subjunctive of **sum** adds the usual _____ endings to the stem _____ (with the vowel shortened before **-m, -nt, and -t**); for the present subjunctive of **possum,** simply add the prefix _____ to each of these forms.

6. The imperfect subjunctives of both **sum** and **possum** follow the normal rule, i.e., present _____ plus _____ endings.

7. Conjugate **sum** in the present subjunctive, **possum** in the imperfect.

sum, present		**possum, imperfect**	
Singular	**Plural**	**Singular**	**Plural**
1. _____	_____	_____	_____
2. _____	_____	_____	_____
3. _____	_____	_____	_____

8. The imperfect subjunctive is employed in a variety of clause types, ordinarily when the main verb is a _____ tense.

9. The exact translation of the imperfect subjunctive, like that of any subjunctive tense, depends upon the type of _____ in which it is employed; in purpose clauses, the imperfect is commonly translated with the auxiliary _____ (vs. the present tense, where the auxiliary is _____).

10. A result clause is a _____ clause indicating the _____ of the action in the _____ clause.

11. Match.

Used to Express	**Clause Type**
___ a command	a. jussive
___ the consequences of an action	b. purpose
___ the objective of an action	c. result

12. Result clauses are regularly introduced by the conjunction _____; if negative, the clause contains some _____

word (vs. negative purpose clauses, which are introduced by
_____).

13. Whether positive or negative, result clauses can usually be
distinguished from purpose clauses by sense and context and by the
fact that the main clause introducing a result clause usually contains
a word indicating degree, including the adverbs _____,
_____, and _____, meaning *so,* or the adjective
_____, meaning *so much, so great.*

14. In a result clause, **ut** is translated as
a. that   b. so that   c. in order that   d. all these

15. In a result clause the subjunctive verb is ordinarily translated as an
_____, i.e., without an _____; "may" or "might" are
used, however, when the result described is only _____ rather
than actual.

16. List the six subjunctives in Practice and Review sentences 1–11, and
identify the clause type (jussive, purpose, or result) in which each
appears.

Subjunctive   **Clause Type**

_____   _____

_____   _____

_____   _____

_____   _____

_____   _____

_____   _____

EXERCITĀTIŌNĒS

A. Transform from singular to plural or plural to singular and then translate, using "may" as the auxiliary for present subjunctives, "might"
for imperfects.

1. fātum dūrum respondēret

Transformation: _____

Translation: _____

2. nātae dīligentēs taceant

   Transformation: _____

   Translation: _____

3. ingenium eius probētur

   Transformation: _____

   Translation: _____

4. sōlēs surgerent

   Transformation: _____

   Translation: _____

5. parēns ōsculō molliātur

   Transformation: _____

   Translation: _____

6. urbēs similēs conderentur

   Transformation: _____

   Translation: _____

7. in cursibus contendant

   Transformation: _____

   Translation: _____

8. prīmō nepōtī id dēdicet

   Transformation: _____

   Translation: _____

B. Transform the second clause into a result clause with the verb in either the present or imperfect subjunctive, depending on the tense of the main verb, and then translate the new sentence (e.g., **Tantā cum cūrā labōrat; Latīnam bene discit.** > **Tantā cum cūrā labōrat ut Latīnam bene discat.** > *He works with such great care that he is learning Latin well*).

1. Illum librum ūtilissimum tantā cum cūrā scrīpsit; discipulī eius bene discēbant.

   Transformation: _____

   _____

   Translation: _____

   _____

2. Mentēs discipulōrum quidem sunt tam ācrēs; linguam Latīnam bene discere possunt.

    Transformation: _____

    _____

    Translation: _____

    _____

3. Ille prīnceps vērō fuit ita fortis; nēmō contrā eum pugnāre potuit.

    Transformation: _____

    _____

    Translation: _____

    _____

C. Supply the correct form of the verbs in parentheses and translate.

1. Discipulī tantōs librōs lēgērunt ut vēritātem _____ (discere).

    _____

2. Auctor vērō tam bene scrīpsit ut plūrimī librōs eius _____ (legere).

    _____

3. Adulēscēns tam dūrus erat ut nūllōs amīcōs dēnique _____ (habēre).

    _____

4. Tantā cum sapientiā dīxit ut nē ōrātōrēs potentissimī quidem contrā verba eius _____ (pugnāre).

    _____

D. Translate into Latin; employ standard word order and include all macrons.

1. The constellations were so bright that everyone could see them.

    _____

2. He gave them better arms so that the walls might not be overcome.

    _____

3. You have such a quick mind that you can learn very many things without labor.

_____

_____

VĪS VERBŌRUM

A. Answer these questions on the chapter's vocabulary list.

1. **Glōria** > **glōriōsus, -a, -um** > "glorious" :: **ingenium** > _____ > _____ :: **contentum** > _____ > _____.

2. Which adjective has one or more meanings in common with **dūrus**?
   a. acerbus b. dignus c. gracilis d. humilis

3. Which noun is synonymous with **nāta**?
   a. dēlectātiō b. fīlia c. nātūra d. occāsiō

4. Which verb is an antonym of **respondeō**?
   a. condō b. pōnō c. praestō d. quaerō

5. Which is unrelated in meaning?
   a. ita b. quot c. sīc d. tam

6. Complete the analogy **moenia : urbs :: arma :** _____.
   a. corpus b. mīles c. maiōrēs d. fātum

7. Which is a synonym of **ōsculum**?
   a. amīca b. bāsium c. auris d. occāsiō

8. Which does not belong with **sīdus**?
   a. lūna b. sōl c. sōlācium d. stēlla

B. Complete each statement with an English word that demonstrates your knowledge of the Latin etymology (e.g., "A 'laudatory' speech is full of <u>praise</u>").

1. To "dignify" a question is to consider it _____ of a response.

2. To "mollify" an adversary is to make him _____, and an "emollient" medication makes the skin _____.

3. A "pugnacious" bully always wants to _____.

4. Latin's "resurgence" in the curriculum indicates that it is
_____ _____ in interest.

LĒCTIŌNĒS

A. First read each sentence aloud twice, and then translate as literally as possible within the limits of sound English idiom.

1. Illī adulēscentēs quidem erant tam dissimilēs ut nēmō putāret eōs esse frātrēs.

   _____

   _____

2. Lūna atque sīdera supera vērō sunt tam clāra ut perīcula vesperī aut noctis nōn timeāmus.

   _____

   _____

3. Sīc dē maiōribus mortuīs dēnique respondeāmus ut memoria factōrum eōrum resurgat et semper remaneat.

   _____

   _____

4. Catullus ex amīcā ōscula tam multa quam sīdera noctis dēsīderābat.

   _____

   _____

5. Tam diū contendērunt atque tantā cum virtūte pugnāvērunt ut urbis moenia, quae maiōrēs dignissimī ōlim condiderant, numquam vincerentur.

   _____

   _____

   _____

6. Optimī librī discipulīs legendī sunt ut vēritātem et mōrēs bonōs discant.

_____

_____

7. Omnēs cīvēs sē patriae dēdicent nē hostēs lībertātem tollant.

_____

8. Ingenium Caesaris fuit tam ācre ut nē ab hostibus dūrissimīs quidem mollīrī posset.

_____

_____

B. Answer these questions on "A Great Orator," "How Many Kisses," and "You're All Just Wonderful."

1. Quandō fuit Cicerō tam perturbātus?
   a. ubi surrēxit ut respondēret   b. ubi diū responderat
   c. ut omnia timēret   d. sī causam neglēxerat

2. Cicerō putāvit audītōrēs dē _____ eius dictūrōs esse.
   a. ingeniō   b. virtūte   c. officiō   d. hīs omnibus

3. Of the two similes in Catullus 7, one contains a striking personification; explain briefly.

_____

_____

4. Quod ūnum verbum nōbīs dē mente Catullī dīcit? _____

5. Cūr Callistratō nōn omnēs laudandī sunt?
   a. quod tantum dignōs laude   b. quod malōs sōlōs semper
       laudat   laudat
   c. nē laudēs eius vēritāte egeant   d. propter haec omnia

Tanta potentia fōrmae est: *So great is the power of beauty*
Ovid

30

Perfect and Pluperfect Subjunctive; Indirect Questions; Sequence of Tenses

INTELLEGENDA

Upon completion of this lesson you should be able to

1. Recognize, form, and translate the perfect and pluperfect subjunctive, active and passive, for verbs of all four conjugations.

2. Provide a complete synopsis of a verb, in both the indicative and subjunctive moods.

3. Define, recognize, and translate the subjunctive "indirect question."

4. Define, recognize, and translate the "active periphrastic."

5. Explain "sequence of tenses" in sentences containing subjunctive clauses.

Salvē atque carpe diem, amīce aut amīca! Be sure you have thoroughly studied Chapter 30 of *Wheelock's Latin* before attempting these exercises—and remember to memorize the paradigms and vocabulary by repeating them *aloud.* **Disce Latīnam maximā cum cūrā et sciēs quantās dēlectātiōnēs haec lingua tibi dare possit!**

GRAMMATICA

1. The perfect active subjunctive for any verb is formed by adding
_____ plus the personal endings to the _____ stem
(identified from the _____ principal part), with the vowel
_____ shortened before **-m, -t,** and **-nt;** for the perfect passive,
substitute the subjunctive _____ for **sum** in the indicative
form.

2. The pluperfect active subjunctive for any verb is formed by adding
_____ plus the personal endings to the _____ stem,
with the vowel _____ shortened before **-m, -t,** and **-nt;** for the
pluperfect passive, substitute the subjunctive _____ for **eram**
in the indicative form.

3. Conjugate **cognōscō, cognōscere, cognōvī, cognitum,** in the perfect subjunctive, active and passive.

Active		**Passive**	
Singular	**Plural**	**Singular**	**Plural**
1. _____	_____	_____	_____
2. _____	_____	_____	_____
3. _____	_____	_____	_____

4. Translate the above forms of **cognōscere,** *to recognize;* use the
auxiliary "may have."

Active		**Passive**	
Singular	**Plural**	**Singular**	**Plural**
1. _____	_____	_____	_____
2. _____	_____	_____	_____
3. _____	_____	_____	_____

5. Conjugate **amō, amāre, amāvī, amātum,** in the pluperfect subjunctive,
active and passive.

Active		**Passive**	
Singular	**Plural**	**Singular**	**Plural**
1. _____	_____	_____	_____
2. _____	_____	_____	_____
3. _____	_____	_____	_____

6. Translate the above forms of **amāre,** *to love;* use the auxiliary "might have."

Active		Passive	
Singular	**Plural**	**Singular**	**Plural**
1. _____	_____	_____	_____
2. _____	_____	_____	_____
3. _____	_____	_____	_____

7. Provide a complete synopsis of **dēdicō, dēdicāre, dēdicāvī, dēdicātum,** in the third person singular.

INDICATIVE

Present	**Future**	**Impf.**	**Perfect**	**Fut.Perf.**	**Plupf.**

Active

_____ _____ _____ _____ _____ _____

Passive

_____ _____ _____ _____ _____ _____

SUBJUNCTIVE
Active

_____ _____ _____ _____

Passive

_____ _____ _____ _____

8. Translate the above synopsis of **dēdicāre,** *to dedicate;* employ the auxiliaries "may," "might," "may have," and "might have," as usual in a conjugation or synopsis.

INDICATIVE

Present	**Future**	**Impf.**	**Perfect**	**Fut.Perf.**	**Plupf.**

Active

_____ _____ _____ _____ _____ _____

Passive

_____ _____ _____ _____ _____ _____

SUBJUNCTIVE
Active

_____ _____ _____ _____

Passive

_____   _____ _____   _____

9. An indirect question is a _____ clause, introduced by an
    _____ word, which reports some question _____, i.e.,
    not via a direct quotation.

10. Like an indirect statement, an indirect question is usually preceded
    by a verb of _____, _____ _____, or
    _____ _____; but its own verb, instead of being an
    _____ is a finite verb in the _____ mood.

11. An indirect question is easily distinguished from the other
    subjunctive clauses learned thus far, both by sense and context and
    by the fact that it is introduced by an _____ word rather than
    by **ut** or **nē.**

12. In an indirect question the subjunctive verb is usually translated as
    an _____, i.e., without an _____.

13. An active periphrastic consists of the _____ _____
    participle plus a form of the verb _____, and can be used to
    indicate _____ time in a subjunctive clause.

14. Identify the one active periphrastic appearing in the **Lēctiōnēs** below.

    _____

15. List the seven subjunctives in Practice and Review sentences 1–5, and
    identify the clause type (jussive, purpose, result, or indirect question)
    in which each appears.

Subjunctive   **Clause Type**

_____   _____

_____   _____

_____   _____

_____   _____

_____   _____

_____   _____

16. The rule for sequence of tenses addresses the logical progression of
    tenses from a _____ clause to a _____ clause.

17. In general, the primary tenses include the _____ and _____, whereas the historical tenses include all _____ tenses.

18. A primary tense main verb must be followed by a _____ tense verb in a subordinate clause; a secondary tense main verb must be followed by a _____ tense.

19. In a primary tense sequence, a present subjunctive indicates action occurring at the _____ time as the main verb or _____ that of the main verb, and a _____ subjunctive indicates action _____ to the main verb.

20. In a secondary tense sequence, an _____ subjunctive indicates action occurring at the same time as the main verb or after that of the main verb, and a _____ subjunctive indicates action _____ to the main verb.

21. List the subjunctive verbs in the indirect questions in **Sententiae Antīquae** 1–6, identify the sequence (primary or historical), and indicate the time of the action in the subjunctive clause relative to that of the main clause (before, same time, after).

Subjunctive	**Sequence**	**Relative Time**
_____	_____	_____
_____	_____	_____
_____	_____	_____
_____	_____	_____
_____	_____	_____
_____	_____	_____

EXERCITĀTIŌNĒS

A. Transform from singular to plural or plural to singular and then translate, using "may," "might," "may have," and "might have" as the auxiliaries for, respectively, the present, imperfect, perfect, and pluperfect subjunctives (remember, however, that the actual auxiliaries, if any, employed in translating sentences into English depend upon the type of clause in which the subjunctive is used).

1. quid prīnceps bibat

   Transformation: _____

   Translation: _____

2. quantōs honōrēs accēperint

   Transformation: _____

   Translation: _____

3. quantae mēnsae explērentur

   Transformation: _____

   Translation: _____

4. cūr nāta respondisset

   Transformation: _____

   Translation: _____

5. quandō hī rīdiculī rogent

   Transformation: _____

   Translation: _____

6. quae occāsiō cognita sit

   Transformation: _____

   Translation: _____

7. quārē parēns dubitāret

   Transformation: _____

   Translation: _____

8. ā quō comprehēnsus esset

   Transformation: _____

   Translation: _____

9. quae fāta expōnantur

   Transformation: _____

   Translation: _____

10. utrum maneam an discēdam

    Transformation: _____

    Translation: _____

B.   Transform the direct question into an indirect question with the verb in the appropriate tense, depending on the tense of the main verb, and translate the new sentence (e.g., **Vir rogat, "Quid fēcistī?"** > **Vir rogat quid fēcerīs.** > *The man asks what you did*).

1.   Magistra rogābat, "Quid discipulī didicērunt?"

Transformation: _____

Translation: _____

2.   Cēterī quaerunt, "Quandō numerus armōrum minuētur?"

Transformation: _____

Translation: _____

3.   "Quot ōscula cupiō?" Tibi dīcam!

Transformation: _____

Translation: _____

C.   Supply the correct form of the verbs in parentheses and translate.

1.   Prīmō rogāvit ubi tanta arma repente _____ (invenīre; pass., time before).

_____

2.   Mundus quidem quaerit unde malum _____ (venīre; same time).

_____

3.   Pater meus dēnique exposuit ubi māter eō vesperō fūrtim _____ (cēdere; same time).

_____

4.   Mox praestent quantās dīvitiās _____ (cōnsūmere; 3rd pers., pl., time before).

_____

D.   Translate into Latin; employ standard word order and include all macrons.

1.   We learned so much that we arrested the two men.

_____

2.   We will soon learn why the two men have been arrested.

_____

3. The harsh leader asked from what place (whence) the soldiers had come.

_____

_____

4. You know why he is hesitating about that honor.

_____

VĪS VERBŌRUM

A. Answer these questions on the chapter's vocabulary list.

1. Which does not belong?
   a. aqua   b. cēna   c. lūna   d. mēnsa

2. **Rīdiculus** > _____ > "ridiculous."

3. Which is not interrogative?
   a. ita   b. quantus   c. unde   d. utrum . . . an

4. Identify the third declension **-iō** nouns derived from the fourth principal part of the following verbs, and then give their direct English derivatives and their meanings.

	Latin Noun	**Eng. Noun**	**Translation**
a. cognōscō	_____	_____	_____
b. comprehendō	_____	_____	_____
c. cōnsūmō	_____	_____	_____
d. expōnō	_____	_____	_____

5. Which is closest in meaning to **cēterī**?
   a. alius   b. alter   c. certus   d. incertus

6. Complete the analogy **mors : vīta :: mortuus :** _____.

B. Complete each statement with an English word that demonstrates your knowledge of the Latin etymology (e.g., "A 'laudatory' speech is full of praise").

1. A "furtive" glance is one taken _____.

2. A "bibulous" fellow _____ a lot.

3. An "indubitable" fact can _____ be _____.

4. In music, a "diminuendo," like a decrescendo, is a gradual _____ in loudness or force.

5. A "prerogative" is the right to be _____ _____ others what one wishes.

LĒCTIŌNĒS

A. First read each sentence aloud twice, and then translate as literally as possible within the limits of sound English idiom.

1. Ōrātor repente rogāvit cūr cēterī cīvēs ingenium huius virī nōn cognōvissent.

   _____

   _____

2. Nesciō utrum vīvī an mortuī plūs honōris crās acceptūrī sint.

   _____

3. Scīsne quam dignus honōribus ille prīnceps fuerit?

   _____

4. Ille auctor narrābat nōbīs quantā cum cūrā Rōmulus moenia urbis condidisset.

   _____

   _____

5. Post cum frātre pugnāvit, Rōmulus sīc contendit ut vērō moenia Rōmae potentissimae ad summa sīdera mox surgerent.

   _____

   _____

6. Audīvimus coniūrātōs esse tam malōs atque virtūte sīc egēre ut, comprehēnsī atque ā cōnsule rogātī, dē tōtīs īnsidiīs prīmō tacērent.

   _____

   _____

7. Ōrātor audītōrēs verbīs mollīvit nē īrā vincerentur.

   _____

8. Scīsne quam multae stēllae sint in caelō?—tam multa bāsia dēsī-
   derō, mea amīca!

   _____

   _____

B. Answer these questions on "Evidence and Confession" and the three
   selections from Martial.

   1. Unde rēs pūblica ērepta est?
      a. fronte   b. labōribus   c. cōnsiliīs   d. igne

   2. Ā quō ērepta est?
      a. labōribus   b. cōnsiliīs   c. Cicerōne   d. hīs omnibus

   3. Cuius signum in litterīs inventum est?
      a. Catilīnae   b. Cicerōnis   c. Lentulī   d. nēminis

   4. Quis dē īnsidiīs dēnique ac repente dīxit? _____

   5. Quot rīdiculī sunt in prīmō ac secundō carminibus?
      a. ūnus   b. duo   c. trēs   d. quattuor

   6. Comment on the chiasmus in **bonās pōnis, sed pōnis opertās** and
      how it is effective.

      _____

      _____

   7. Quandō Marō dīcit sē Martiālī dōna datūrum esse?
      a. dum vīvet   b. post mortem poētae
      c. post mortem suam   d. numquam

   8. Quid Martiālis dēsīderat?
      a. dōna   b. mortem Marōnis   c. ridēre Marōnem   d. haec omnia

   9. Ut Martiālis putat, quis est dignus maiōre honōre?
      a. Catullus   b. Vergilius   c. uter   d. neuter

   Nunc est bibendum: *Now we must drink*
   Horace

31

Cum Clauses; Ferō

INTELLEGENDA

Upon completion of this lesson you should be able to
 *1. Define, recognize, distinguish among, and translate the four types of
 "cum clauses."*
 2. Recognize, form, and translate the irregular verb ferō.

Salvēte, discipulī dignissimī! Before beginning these exercises, be sure you
have thoroughly studied Chapter 31 of *Wheelock's Latin* and memorized
both the paradigms and the new vocabulary by practicing them *aloud*. **Cum
multum labōrētis, multa discētis!**

GRAMMATICA

1. As a preposition, **cum** means _____ and links a noun or pronoun with some other element in a sentence; as a _____, **cum**
   can be translated _____, _____, or _____, and
   links two clauses.

2. Match.

   Cum Clause Type

   ____ adversative
   ____ causal
   ____ circumstantial
   ____ temporal

   Translation

   a. when (exact time)
   b. when (general)
   c. since
   d. although

3. Match.

Cum Clause Type	Mood
____ adversative	a. indicative
____ causal	b. subjunctive
____ circumstantial	
____ temporal	

4. **Cum** clauses are easily distinguished from the other subjunctive clauses already learned, since they are introduced by _____; the temporal clause is distinguished from the others, since its verb is in the _____ mood; the remaining three types are distinguished by analyzing the relationship between the event described in the **cum** clause and that described in the _____ clause; and the adversative clause is often further recognizable from the fact that the adverb _____ often occurs in the main clause.

5. List the verbs in the three **cum** clauses in Practice and Review sentences 1–10, and then identify the specific clause type.

Verb	Clause Type
_____	_____
_____	_____
_____	_____

6. As can be seen from the examples in Chapter 31, the verb in a **cum** clause is regularly translated as an _____, i.e., without any subjunctive auxiliaries.

7. **Ferō,** *to bear, carry,* is a slightly irregular verb of the _____ conjugation; although the third and fourth principal parts are unusual, all the _____ system tenses are nevertheless regularly formed, and the only irregularities in the present system are a few forms that drop the stem vowel in the _____ tense (indicative, imperative, and infinitive).

8. List the nine irregular present system forms of **ferō.**

Present Indicative		Present Imperative		Present Infinitive	
Active	**Passive**	**Singular**	**Plural**	**Active**	**Passive**
Singular					
_____	_____	_____	_____	_____	_____
_____	_____				
Plural					
_____					

9. Provide a complete synopsis of **ferō, ferre, tulī, lātum,** in the second person singular.

INDICATIVE

Present	Future	Impf.	Perfect	Fut.Perf.	Plupf.

Active

_____ _____ _____ _____ _____ _____

Passive

_____ _____ _____ _____ _____ _____

SUBJUNCTIVE

Active

_____ _____ _____ _____

Passive

_____ _____ _____ _____

10. Translate the above synopsis of **ferō, ferre, tulī, lātum,** *to carry,* in the second person singular; use "may," "might," "may have," and "might have," for the subjunctives (though the actual translation of a subjunctive, of course, depends upon the type of clause in which it is employed).

INDICATIVE

Present	Future	Impf.	Perfect	Fut.Perf.	Plupf.

Active

_____ _____ _____ _____ _____ _____

Passive

_____ _____ _____ _____ _____ _____

SUBJUNCTIVE

Active

_____ _____ _____ _____

Passive

_____ _____ _____ _____

EXERCITĀTIŌNĒS

A. Transform from singular to plural or plural to singular and then translate. Use *when* for **cum,** as always, if the verb is indicative; use *since* if the verb is subjunctive, but remember that the actual translation of **cum** with the subjunctive depends upon the relationship between the actions in the main and subordinate clauses. And remember that no subjunctive auxiliaries are used in translating **cum** clauses.

1. cum elephantus dormīvit

    Transformation: _____

    Translation: _____

2. cum assēs oblātī essent

    Transformation: _____

    Translation: _____

3. cum auxilia adferātis

    Transformation: _____

    Translation: _____

4. cum digitus dolēret

    Transformation: _____

    Translation: _____

5. cum rūmor relātus sit

    Transformation: _____

    Translation: _____

6. cum sōlēs occiderant

    Transformation: _____

    Translation: _____

7. cum vīna ūsque biberent

    Transformation: _____

    Translation: _____

8. cum dē exsiliīs rogābant

    Transformation: _____

    Translation: _____

9. cum quidem nātam ferat

    Transformation: _____

    Translation: _____

10. cum invidiae minuantur

    Transformation: _____

    Translation: _____

B. Transform the ablative absolute or other participial phrase into a **cum** clause with the verb in the appropriate tense, identify the type of **cum** clause, and translate (e.g., **Tantō igne vīso, omnēs repente territī sunt. > Cum tantus ignis vīsus esset, omnēs repente territī sunt;** causal clause. > *Since such a great fire had been seen, all were suddenly frightened*).

1. Ex Italiā dēnique missus, cōnsul tamen exsilium dūrum bene fert.

    Transformation: _____

    _____

    Clause type: _____

    Translation: _____

    _____

2. Mēnsā expositā, istī rīdiculī numquam dubitābant tantum vīnum bibere quantum invenīre poterant.

    Transformation: _____

    _____

    Clause type: _____

    Translation: _____

    _____

3. Hostibus semel collātis, eō tempore ipsō verbīs dūrīs respondē-runt atque repente pugnāre coepērunt.

Transformation: _____

_____

Clause type: _____

Translation: _____

_____

C. Supply the correct form of the verbs in parentheses, and translate.

1. Cum iste _____ (esse; same time) vir ingeniī mediocris, tamen eum semper ferēbāmus.

_____

_____

2. Cum cōnsul in exsilium _____ (mittere; exact same time), nūllum auxilium tum oblātum est.

_____

_____

3. Cum ā hostibus _____ (cognōscere; 3rd pers. pl., time before), amīcī sē ad vōs nāve fūrtim contulērunt.

_____

_____

4. Cum auxilium _____ (ferre; 3rd pers. pl., time before), ūnō annō haec moenia condere potuimus.

_____

_____

D. Translate into Latin; employ standard word order and include all macrons.

1. When they compared the rumors, they saw that they lacked any truth.

_____

_____

2. Although they brought help back to their friends, they could not save them.

_____

_____

3. Since those men are envious, many good men are grieving.

_____

4. At that very hour, when the soldiers were sleeping, they brought us aid.

_____

_____

VĪS VERBŌRUM

A. Answer these questions on the chapter's vocabulary list.

1. Which three nouns in the list have produced English derivatives identical to their bases? _____ _____

_____

2. **Invidia** > _____ > "invidious."

3. Which word has a meaning in common with the conjunction **cum**?
   a. sīc b. ubi c. unde d. utrum . . . an

4. Which noun has a meaning in common with **rūmor**?
   a. as b. fāma c. fātum d. ōsculum

5. Which verb is an antonym of **occidō**?
   a. cōnsūmō b. contendō c. molliō d. surgō

6. Which adverb has a meaning in common with **ūsque**?
   a. ita b. mox c. semper d. vērō

B. Complete each statement with an English word that demonstrates your knowledge of the Latin etymology (e.g., "A 'laudatory' speech is full of <u>praise</u>").

1. At a "conference" we _____ _____ persons with similar interests.

2. An "aquifer" is an underground layer of porous rock that
   _____ _____.

3. An "oblation" is a ritual _____ of sacrifice or thanks-
   giving.

4. To "collate" various manuscripts involves _____ them
   _____ for comparison.

LĒCTIŌNĒS

A. First read each sentence aloud twice, and then translate as literally as
possible within the limits of sound English idiom.

1. Cum hoc semel dīxissēmus, illī respondērunt sē pācem aequam
   oblātūrōs esse.

   _____

   _____

2. Cum sē in exsilium contulisset, tamen amīcōs novōs mox invēnit.

   _____

3. Cum amīcitiam nōbīs offerant, eīs auxilium mox offerēmus.

   _____

4. Cum exposuisset quid peteret, negāvistī tantum auxilium posse
   offerrī.

   _____

   _____

5. Cum cōnsilia tua dēnique comprehendāmus, dolēmus ac īnsidiās
   tuās nōn ferēmus.

   _____

   _____

6. Cum tantum auxilium populō obtulerim, comprehendisne cūr
   cēterī mihi invideant?

   _____

   _____

7. Vīnum quod iste apud sē obtulit fuit tam mediocre ut id bibere prīmō nōn possēmus.

_____

_____

8. Cum cognōverīs memoriam familiae esse perpetuam, scīs nōs ūsque amātūrōs esse parentēs utrum vīvōs an mortuōs.

_____

_____

9. Cum parvus fīlius eā nocte dormiēbat, pater eī ōsculum dedit, eum digitō tetigit, atque trēs assēs in mēnsā eius posuit.

_____

_____

10. Cum ultimus sōl noster occiderit, in morte ūsque dormiēmus.

_____

B.   Answer these questions on "A Thousand Kisses," "Ringo," and "Witticisms."

1. In hōc quīntō carmine Catullī, poēta dīcit vītam esse nihil sine

_____.

2. Rūmōrēs senum dē vītā atque amōre sunt dignī ūnō _____.

3. Poēta confert sōlem et lūcem cum _____ atque noctem cum _____.

4. Cum lūx vītae occiderit, quam diū erit nox nostra? _____

5. Comment briefly on the contrast between "one" and "many" in Catullus 5 and on what the contrast may symbolize.

_____

_____

_____

6. Cum Charīnus dormiat, anulī sunt in _____.

7. Quot anulōs hic in duōbus manibus fert?
   a. sex   b. trīgintā   c. sexāgintā   d. mīlia multa

8. Cum dīcit Damasippō, "Bene aetātem fert," Cicerō vērō putat
   a. hoc vīnum nōn esse quadrāgintā annōrum
   b. hoc vīnum esse optimum
   c. hoc vīnum esse antīquum
   d. sē plūs huius vīnī apud Damasippum ūsque cupitūrum esse

Aurea mediocritās: *The golden mean*
Horace

32

Formation and Comparison of Adverbs; Volō, Mālō, Nōlō; Proviso Clauses

INTELLEGENDA

Upon completion of this lesson you should be able to
 1. Recognize, form, compare, and translate regular adverbs.
 2. Recognize, form, and translate adverbs with irregular superlatives and other adverbs with irregular comparisons.
 3. Recognize and translate the uses of **quam** *with comparative and superlative adverbs.*
 4. Recognize, form, and translate the irregular verbs **volō, nōlō,** *and* **mālō***.*
 5. Recognize and translate the uses of **nōlō** *in "negative commands."*
 6. Define, recognize, and translate the subjunctive "proviso clause."

Salvē, discipula aut discipule! Before beginning these exercises, be sure you have thoroughly studied Chapter 32 of *Wheelock's Latin* and memorized both the paradigms and the new vocabulary by practicing them *aloud.* **Dummodo linguam Latīnam magnopere amēs, eris ūsque fēlīx!**

GRAMMATICA

1. While many adverbs have their own peculiar forms, often without comparatives and superlatives or any English derivatives, and must simply be memorized, many others can be compared and have positive degree forms composed either from first/second declension adjectives, with the letter _____ added to the adjective's _____, or from third declension adjectives with _____ added to the _____.

2. Adverbs regularly formed from third declension adjectives with a base in **-nt-** add only _____ to form the positive degree.

3. Provide the positive degree adverb forms and translate.

Adjective	Adverb	English	Adjective	Adverb	English
a. acerbus	_____	_____	b. certus	_____	_____
c. brevis	_____	_____	d. dīligēns	_____	_____
e. similis	_____	_____	f. miser	_____	_____
g. potēns	_____	_____	h. sānus	_____	_____
i. pār	_____	_____	j. fidēlis	_____	_____

4. For most adverbs that can be compared, the comparative degree adds _____ to the base and is thus identical to the neuter nominative singular of the comparative _____.

5. Superlative adverbs usually add the letter _____ to the base of the corresponding superlative _____.

6. While some adverbs have their own peculiar forms in the comparative or superlative and must simply be memorized, those derived from irregular _____ usually have similar irregularities, but with adverbial endings.

7. Match.

Translation	Degree
____ very bravely	a. positive
____ rather bravely	b. comparative
____ most bravely	c. superlative
____ bravely	
____ too bravely	

8. Provide the missing adverb forms and translate.

		Positive	Comparative	Superlative
a.	**Latin**	asperē	_____	_____
	English	roughly	_____	_____
b.	**Latin**	_____	_____	minimē
	English	_____	_____	least
c.	**Latin**	rīdiculē	_____	_____
	English	ridiculously	_____	_____
d.	**Latin**	_____	gravius	_____
	English	_____	more seriously	_____
e.	**Latin**	fēlīciter	_____	_____
	English	happily	_____	_____

9. **Quam** is used with adverbs in essentially the same ways as with _____; after comparatives the translation is _____, and _____ superlatives the translation is *as -ly as possible.*

10. Identify the degree of these adverbs from the Practice and Review sentences.

Adverb	Degree	Adverb	Degree
a. Prīmō (sent. 1)	_____	b. fortiter (1)	_____
c. Maximē (2)	_____	d. celerrimē (3)	_____
e. melius (5)	_____	f. certē (10)	_____

11. **Volō,** *to wish, want,* is an irregular verb of the _____ conjugation; answer these questions on its irregularities.

a. It lacks _____ voice forms entirely.

b. The _____ system is entirely regular.

c. The only irregular present system forms are in the _____ tense indicative, subjunctive, and infinitive.

d. The imperfect subjunctive follows the usual rule, adding the _____ _____ to the present _____.

e. _____ is the base for present system indicatives, _____ for present system subjunctives.

12. Provide a complete synopsis of **volō, velle, voluī,** in the second person singular.

    INDICATIVE

Present	Future	Impf.	Perfect	Fut.Perf.	Plupf.
_____	_____	_____	_____	_____	_____

    SUBJUNCTIVE

_____	_____	_____	_____

13. Translate the above synopsis of **volō,** *to wish,* in the second person singular; use "may," "might," etc., for the subjunctives (though the actual translation of a subjunctive, of course, depends upon the type of clause in which it is employed).

    INDICATIVE

Present	Future	Impf.	Perfect	Fut.Perf.	Plupf.
_____	_____	_____	_____	_____	_____

    SUBJUNCTIVE

_____	_____	_____	_____

14. The compounds **nōlō** and **mālō** follow **volō** closely, but have _____ vowels in their _____ and have a few other striking peculiarities, which (as seen in the Appendix to *Wheelock's Latin*) are limited to the _____ tense.

15. Provide a complete synopsis of **nōlō, nōlle, nōluī,** *to be unwilling,* in the second person plural.

    INDICATIVE

Present	Future	Impf.	Perfect	Fut.Perf.	Plupf.
_____	_____	_____	_____	_____	_____

    SUBJUNCTIVE

_____	_____	_____	_____

16. Provide a complete synopsis of **mālō, mālle, māluī,** *to prefer,* in the third person plural.

    INDICATIVE

Present	Future	Impf.	Perfect	Fut.Perf.	Plupf.
_____	_____	_____	_____	_____	_____

SUBJUNCTIVE

_____   _____ _____   _____

17. Both **volō** and **mālō** lack imperatives, but **nōlō** has the singular imperative _____ and the plural imperative _____, both of which were commonly used with a _____ infinitive to express _____ commands.

18. A proviso clause is a _____ clause introduced by _____ or some other word (plus _____, if negative) and indicating a provisional circumstance on which the action in the main clause is contingent; the verb in such a clause is regularly in the _____ mood.

19. As seen from the examples in the text, the verb in a proviso clause is ordinarily translated into the _____ mood in English, without any subjunctive auxiliaries.

EXERCITĀTIŌNĒS

A. Transform from singular to plural or plural to singular and then translate.

1. Custōdiam celeriter vult.

   Transformation: _____

   Translation: _____

2. Exercitus maximē nōlet.

   Transformation: _____

   Translation: _____

3. dummodo id vērē velīs

   Transformation: _____

   Translation: _____

4. Dīvitēs certē nōlunt.

   Transformation: _____

   Translation: _____

5. Pauper hoc māluerat.

   Transformation: _____

   Translation: _____

6. Dōna līberius praebēbunt.

   Transformation: _____

   Translation: _____

7. Parem honōrem prōmīsit.

   Transformation: _____

   Translation: _____

8. Invidiae clārē patent.

   Transformation: _____

   Translation: _____

9. Digitī ācriter dolēbant.

   Transformation: _____

   Translation: _____

10. Exsilium male tulit.

    Transformation: _____

    Translation: _____

B. Supply the correct form of the words in parentheses and translate.

1. Dummodo ex paupertāte magnopere nē _____ (dolēre; 2nd pers. sg. pres.), apud Rōmānōs beātē vīvere poteris.

   _____

   _____

2. Lēgēs quam aequissimās habēre _____ (sapiēns; superlative adverb) māluistis.

   _____

   _____

3. Cum vīnum optimum in mēnsā exposuisset, amīcī tamen bibere
    prīmō _____ (nōlere; perf.).

    _____

    _____

4. Cum exercitus auxilium ad pauperēs repente adferre _____
    (volō; same time), cēterī omnibus mīlitibus grātiās agere
    _____ (volō; impf.).

    _____

    _____

5. _____ (nōlō; sg. imper.) offerre auxilium mediocre illīs
    pauperibus, cum tam maiōra beneficia praebēre vērē possīs.

    _____

    _____

C. Translate into Latin; employ standard word order and include all ma-
    crons.

1. Our students can learn more quickly now, provided that they are
    willing.

    _____

    _____

2. The army hesitated to promise more guards.

    _____

3. When the conspirators have been arrested, we will soon learn
    what leader they preferred.

    _____

    _____

VĪS VERBŌRUM

A. Answer these questions on the chapter's vocabulary list.

1. **Glōria:** "glory" :: **custōdia:** _____.

    2.   Which verb is close in meaning to **praebeō**?
        a. cōnferō b. cōnsūmō c. offerō d. referō

    3.   Which verb has a meaning in common with **volō**?
        a. cupiō b. dormiō c. invideō d. minuō

B.   Complete each statement with an English word that demonstrates your knowledge of the Latin etymology (e.g., "A 'laudatory' speech is full of praise").

    1.   If a defendant's guilt is "patent," it is _____ to everyone.

    2.   A plea of "nolo contendere" indicates that the defendant is _____ _____ to contest the charges against him.

    3.   An artist who is "peerless" is without _____.

    4.   To act on one's own "volition" is to do what one is _____ to do.

LĒCTIŌNĒS

A.   First read each sentence aloud twice, and then translate as literally as possible within the limits of sound English idiom.

    1.   Hī dīvitiās celerrimē invēnērunt; illī diūtissimē erunt pauperēs.

        _____

        _____

    2.   Iste plūrimōs honōrēs quam facillimē accipere vult.

        _____

    3.   Tyrannus cīvēs suōs ita male opprimēbat ut ūsque vellent līberī esse.

        _____

        _____

    4.   Semel rogāvit mīlitēs utrum prō patriā fortiter occidere vellent an nōllent.

        _____

        _____

5. Paucīs elephantīs vīvīs, exercitum tamen trāns montēs in Italiam dūcere voluit.

_____

_____

6. Vult scīre unde fūrtim veniant atque quantum auxilium ferant.

_____

7. Nōlīte ūsque rogāre quid prōmissūrī sīmus.

_____

8. Dummodo haec facere vērē mālīs, tibi parem occāsiōnem praebēbō.

_____

_____

B. Answer these questions on "The Character of Cimon," "A Vacation," and "Please . . . Don't."

1. Quid Cimon nōn habuit?
   a. līberālitās in pauperēs   b. auctōritās apud mīlitēs
   c. custōdiae in hortibus   d. mors omnibus acerba

2. Cum Cimon occidisset, quid cīvēs ēgērunt?
   a. diū fuērunt trīstēs   b. memoriam eius neglēxērunt
   c. fāmam eius dēlēvērunt   d. facta eius culpāvērunt

3. Cūr Martiālis ex urbe discēdit?
   a. ut in agrīs labōret   b. ut Nōmentum videat
   c. nē Linum videat   d. ut cum Linō sit

4. Quid Martiālis ex Māmercō vult?
   a. quidquid Māmercus vult   b. audīre nihil
   c. plūrima carmina   d. esse audītor eius

Citius, altius, fortius: *Swifter, higher, stronger*
Motto of the modern Olympic games

33

Conditions

INTELLEGENDA

Upon completion of this lesson you should be able to
1. Define "conditional sentence."
2. Recognize, distinguish among, and translate the six basic types of Latin conditional sentences.

Salvē, discipule discipulave! Before beginning these exercises, be sure you have thoroughly studied Chapter 33 of *Wheelock's Latin* and memorized the new vocabulary by practicing *aloud*. **Sī Latīnam maximē amābis, diūtissimē eris fēlīx!**

GRAMMATICA

1. A condition is a very common sentence type, consisting of two clauses: 1) a condition or _____, a subordinate clause usually introduced by _____ (meaning _____) or, if negative, by _____ (meaning _____ _____ or _____), and stating a hypothetical action or circumstance, and 2) a conclusion or _____, the main clause, which expresses the anticipated outcome if the premise should turn out to be true.

2. There are a total of _____ basic conditional sentence types, _____ with their verbs in the indicative mood and _____ with their verbs in the subjunctive.

3. Conditions in the _____ mood are more likely to be realized; _____ conditions are either less likely to be realized or even contrary to the actual facts of a situation.

4. Although the Romans did sometimes use "mixed conditions" with different tenses or moods in the protasis and apodosis, the basic types of conditions employed the same tense and mood in both clauses; match.

   Condition Type
   ____ simple fact present
   ____ simple fact past
   ____ simple fact future
   ("future more vivid")
   ____ contrary to fact, present
   ____ contrary to fact, past
   ____ future less vivid
   ("should-would")

   Tenses
   a. present subjunctive
   b. present indicative
   c. perfect or imperfect indicative
   d. pluperfect subjunctive
   e. future (or fut. perf.) indicative
   f. imperfect subjunctive

5. In the simple fact conditions, the verbs in both protasis and apodosis are translated quite straightforwardly as indicatives; the following pairs of auxiliaries are employed, however, in the protasis and apodosis of the contrary to fact and less vivid conditions.

   Condition Type
   ____ contrary to fact, present
   ____ contrary to fact, past
   ____ future less vivid

   English Auxiliaries
   a. should . . . would
   b. were . . . would
   c. had . . . would have

6. In the simple fact future condition, the verb of the protasis is usually translated in the _____ tense, even though in Latin the tense is

   _____.

7. Identify the type of the 11 "further examples" presented in the chapter's discussion of conditions.

   1. _____   2. _____

   3. _____   4. _____

   5. _____   6. _____

   7. _____   8. _____

   9. _____   10. _____

   11. _____

8. Give the sentence number and identify the specific type of all six conditions in Practice and Review sentences 1–11.

Sent. No.   **Condition Type**

_____   _____

_____   _____

_____   _____

_____   _____

_____   _____

EXERCITĀTIŌNĒS

A. Transform from singular to plural or plural to singular and then translate, with careful attention to verb tenses and the correct auxiliaries.

1. sī dīves recūsāvisset

   Transformation: _____

   Translation: _____

2. nisi pauperēs trāderent

   Transformation: _____

   Translation: _____

3. sī paria auxilia praebent

   Transformation: _____

   Translation: _____

4. nisi vīna mera biberent

   Transformation: _____

   Translation: _____

5. sī custōdia stultē dormit

   Transformation: _____

   Translation: _____

6. sī plēbēs vērē nōluissent

    Transformation: _____

    Translation: _____

7. sī philosophī mālint

    Transformation: _____

    Translation: _____

8. nisi elephantus'occidet

    Transformation: _____

    Translation: _____

9. sī digitī male doluērunt

    Transformation: _____

    Translation: _____

10. sī opēs diūtius offerant

    Transformation: _____

    Translation: _____

B. Supply the correct form of the words in parentheses and translate.

1. Sī exercitus ad plēbēs opem _____ (adferre; future less vivid), pauperēs certissimē nōn _____ (recūsāre).

    _____

    _____

2. Nisi philosophus sē in exsilium _____ (cōnferre; contrary to fact, past), is atque amīcī celeriter _____ (occidere).

    _____

    _____

3. Nisi tū ipse ūsque _____ (invidēre; contrary to fact, present), nōn _____ (esse) tanta invidia atque rūmōrēs malī contrā tē.

    _____

    _____

4. Nisi opem prōmittere _____ (volō; future more vivid), plūs plēbis, heu, _____ (dolēre) atque paupertās per urbem _____ (patēre).

_____

_____

C. Translate into Latin; employ standard word order and include all macrons.

1. If you refuse that help, you will surrender your freedom.

_____

2. If you should refuse that help, you would surrender your freedom.

_____

3. If you had refused that help, you would have surrendered your freedom.

_____

_____

4. If you were refusing that help, you would be surrendering your freedom.

_____

_____

5. Since you refused that help, you are surrendering your freedom.

_____

6. Provided that you do not refuse that help, you will not surrender your freedom.

_____

_____

VĪS VERBŌRUM

A. Answer these questions on the chapter's vocabulary list.

1. An antonym of **initium** is
   a. fīnis   b. invidia   c. sāl   d. speculum

2. **Suāvis** > _____ > "suavity," which means _____.

3. Which adverb is synonymous with **subitō**?
   a. postea   b. repente   c. semel   d. ūsque

Name: _____ _Section:_ _____ _Date:_ _____

4. Complete the analogy **-que:et::-ve:**_____ .

5. Which noun has a meaning related to **plēbs**?
   a. exercitus   b. mīles   c. populus   d. senātus

6. Which verb is an antonym of **recūsō**?
   a. accipiō   b. doleō   c. invideō   d. referō

7. Which adjective does not have a related meaning?
   a. bellus   b. candidus   c. merus   d. pulcher

B. Complete each statement with an English word that demonstrates your knowledge of the Latin etymology (e.g., "A 'laudatory' speech is full of praise").

1. Those who live in "opulence" have great _____ .

2. A "salinometer" measures the amount of _____ in a chemical solution.

3. Something "traditional" has been _____ _____ from one generation to the next.

LĒCTIŌNĒS

A. First read each sentence aloud twice, and then translate as literally as possible within the limits of sound English idiom.

1. Ō turpissime, sī tē in speculō semel videās, heu, vēritās mōrum tuōrum pateat!

   _____

   _____

2. Apud mē iterum optimē cēnābis, mī amīce, sī vīnum suāvissimum et merissimum, cēnam candidam, atque plūrima verba fēlicia tēcum referēs—nam verba iūcunda certē sunt sāl vērum et cēnae et vītae!

   _____

   _____

   _____

   _____

3. Nisi tam mediocrēs librōs in adulēscentiā lēgissēs, ab initiō
scrīptor melior fuissēs.

_____

_____

4. Sī quis auxilium opēsve offerret, plēbs esset beātior.

_____

5. Sī Latīnam nunc amās, nēmo esse fortūnātior potest!

_____

B. Answer these questions on "B.Y.O.B.," "The Rich Get Richer," "Aris-
totle," and "Your Loss."

1. Quem Catullus ad cēnam invītat? (**Respondē in tōtā sententiā.**)

_____

2. Amīcus Catullī bene cēnābit, dummodo cēnam _____.
a. amet   b. condat   c. ferat   d. cōnsūmat

3. Catullus habet plūs
a. arāneārum   b. cēnae   c. salis   d. pecūniae

4. Quid Fabullus esse volet?
a. amīcus Catullī   b. amōrēs merī   c. unguentum   d. nāsus

5. Cūr?
a. ut sit suāvior   b. ut unguentum olfaciat
c. nē sit sine cēnā   d. ut cēnam olfaciat

6. Quis, in carmine Martiālis, plūs dīvitiārum recipiet?
a. pauper   b. Aemilianus   c. Martiālis   d. dīves

7. Quae studia, ut Quīntiliānus narrat, rēx Philippus maximē
dīlēxit?
a. prīma initia studiōrum   b. summa studia philosophiae
c. summa studia litterārum   d. studia in senectūte

8. Quis, ut Cicerō āit, Tarentum prīmō cēpit? _____

9. Quis urbem dēnique vīcit? _____

10. Uter plūs salis habuit? _____

Rēgem nōn faciunt opēs: *Riches do not make a king*
Seneca the Younger

Name: _____ Section: _____ Date: _____

34

Deponent Verbs; Ablative with Special Deponents

INTELLEGENDA

Upon completion of this lesson you should be able to
1. *Define, recognize, form, and translate "deponent verbs."*
2. *Recognize, form, and translate deponent imperatives.*
3. *Define, recognize, form, and translate "semi-deponent verbs."*
4. *Define, recognize, and translate the "ablative with special deponents"*
construction.

Salvēte, discipulae discipulīque! Before beginning these exercises, be sure you have thoroughly studied Chapter 34 of *Wheelock's Latin* and memorized both the paradigms and the new vocabulary by practicing them *aloud*. **Nisi prīmō rem bene gerētis, cōnāminī, iterum cōnāminī!** *(If at first you don't succeed. . . .)*

GRAMMATICA

1. Deponent verbs have chiefly _____ forms with _____ meanings and only _____ principal parts.

2. Deponents have the same four participles as regular verbs; while the perfect passive participle usually follows the above rule, the other participles involve the following exceptions:

Participle	Form (Act./Pass.)	Meaning (Act./Pass.)
a. present active participle	_____	_____
b. future active participle	_____	_____
c. fut. pass. participle (gerundive)	_____	_____

3. Deponents have only three infinitives, one for each time frame, past, present, future; while the _____ and _____ infinitives follow the above rule for forms vs. meanings, the _____ infinitive has _____ forms with _____ meanings.

4. Passive imperative forms exist only for _____ verbs; the singular imperative is identical to the alternate _____ person singular form of the _____ indicative tense, and the plural is identical to the _____ person _____ form of the _____ indicative tense.

5. A deponent verb's singular imperative also resembles its (non-existent) present active _____, with which it should not be confused in translation.

6. Provide a complete synopsis of **cōnor, cōnārī, cōnātus sum**, *to try,* in the third person singular.

INDICATIVE

Present	Future	Impf.	Perfect	Fut.Perf.	Plupf.
_____	_____	_____	_____	_____	_____

SUBJUNCTIVE

_____	_____	_____

7. Translate the above synopsis of **cōnor, cōnārī, cōnātus sum**, *to try,* in the third person singular; use "may," "might," etc., for the subjunctives (though the actual translation of a subjunctive, of course, depends upon the clause type).

INDICATIVE

Present	Future	Impf.	Perfect	Fut.Perf.	Plupf.
_____	_____	_____	_____	_____	_____

SUBJUNCTIVE

_____	_____	_____

8. Give the participles of **patior, patī, passus sum,** *to endure,* and translate.

	Active	Passive
Latin		
Present	_____	
Perfect		_____
Future	_____	_____
English		
Present	_____	
Perfect		_____
Future	_____	_____

9. Give the infinitives and imperatives of **loquor, loquī, locūtus sum,** *to speak,* and their English translations.

	Infinitives		Imperatives	
	Latin	English	Latin	English
Present	_____	_____	Sg. _____	_____
Perfect	_____	_____	Pl. _____	_____
Future	_____	_____		

10. Semi-deponent verbs are regular in the _____ system but deponent in the _____ system.

11. List and translate all the deponent and semi-deponent verbs in Practice and Review sentences 1–6.

Latin	English	Latin	English
_____	_____	_____	_____
_____	_____	_____	_____
_____	_____	_____	_____
_____	_____	_____	_____

12. The five special deponent verbs that take an ablative "object" (actually an ablative of means) are, in alphabetical order: _____, _____, _____, _____, and _____.

13. Give the sentence number and identify the four ablatives with special deponents in **Sententiae Antīquae** 1–14.

    Sent. No.   **Ablative with Special Deponent**

    _____   _____

    _____   _____

    _____   _____

    _____   _____

EXERCITĀTIŌNĒS

A. Transform from singular to plural or plural to singular and then translate, with careful attention to verb tenses and the correct auxiliaries.

   1. anima ē corpore ēgrediātur

      Transformation: _____

      Translation: _____

   2. Dē remissiōne arbitrātur.

      Transformation: _____

      Translation: _____

   3. Vocibus clārīs locūtī sunt.

      Transformation: _____

      Translation: _____

   4. Exercitus proficīscēbātur.

      Transformation: _____

      Translation: _____

   5. Custōdiae (dat.) fatētur.

      Transformation: _____

      Translation: _____

   6. Nātī sunt līberī.

      Transformation: _____

      Translation: _____

Name: _____ *Section:* _____ *Date:* _____

7. Dīves rūsticābitur.

   Transformation: _____

   Translation: _____

8. pauper tē sequerētur

   Transformation: _____

   Translation: _____

9. vīnīs merīs ūsī sint

   Transformation: _____

   Translation: _____

10. Pār cōnsilium mōlītur.

    Transformation: _____

    Translation: _____

B. Supply the correct form for the verbs in parentheses and translate.

   1. Exercitus ad īnsulam mox _____ (proficīscī; fut.).

      _____

   2. Cum vīnō suāvī, autem, aquā _____ (ūtī; 1st pers. pl. perf.).

      _____

   3. Pauperēs sedēre _____ (hortārī; 1st pers. sg. perf.), sed re-
      cūsāvērunt.

      _____

   4. Remissiōnis causā ex urbe discessimus et _____ (rūsticārī;
      impf.).

      _____

C. Translate into Latin; employ standard word order and include all macrons.

   1. About to die, he dared to speak freely.

      _____

   2. Having started from the city, they suddenly followed the enemy.

      _____

3. They will enjoy both the water and the wine.

_____

4. His son was born while they were living in the country.

_____

VĪS VERBŌRUM

A. Answer these questions on the chapter's vocabulary list.

1. Complete the analogy **vōx:loquor::mēns:**_____.
   a. arbitror   b. crēscō   c. trādō   d. sequor

2. Which verb is synonymous with **ēgredior**?
   a. discēdō   b. fateor   c. mōlior   d. spectō

3. Which noun is an antonym of **morior**?
   a. mōlior   b. nāscor   c. occidō   d. recūsō

B. Complete each statement with an English word that demonstrates your knowledge of the Latin etymology (e.g., "A 'laudatory' speech is full of praise").

1. When a disease is in "remission," it has _____ its hold on the patient.

2. "Post-natal" care is provided by a physician _____ _____, whereas "pre-natal" care is administered _____ _____.

3. A **cum** "adversative" clause describes an action _____ to what you would expect, in view of the action in the main clause.

4. An "animated" cheerleader has lots of team _____.

5. The "conative" sense of the imperfect tense implies an action _____ in the past.

6. An "excrescense" has _____ abnormally _____ the surface of a plant or an animal's body.

7. A "loquacious" person _____ a lot; in a "soliloquy" he _____ _____.

LĒCTIŌNĒS

A. First read each sentence aloud twice, and then translate as literally as possible within the limits of sound English idiom.

1. Arbitrātur mala paupertātis adversae nōn patienda esse.

   _____

2. Tālia verba vocibus trīstibus locūtī, profectī sumus nē in eō locō miserō morerēmur.

   _____

   _____

3. Omnibus opibus nostrīs ūtāmur ut patria nostra quam celerrimē servētur.

   _____

   _____

4. Istī miserī, quī in tālī paupertāte nātī sunt, nunc quoque—heu— in eādem paupertāte moriuntur!

   _____

   _____

5. Dīvitiae tuae certē crēscent, dummodo pecūniam bonā fidē cōn- servāre cōnēris.

   _____

   _____

6. Ut ego arbitror, liber bonus est remissiō animae.

   _____

7. Nisi morī vīs—vae tibi—nunc fatēre omnia vitia culpāsve!

   _____

8. Rōmānī urbem candidissimam magnō cum labōre mōlītī sunt.

B. Answer these questions on the readings from Martial, Seneca, and Catullus.

1. Explain how word order gives the Zoilus epigram the sort of surprise ending that is typical of Martial.

_____

_____

2. Quis Fabullam maximē laudat? _____

3. "Polysyndeton" is the use of more conjunctions than usual, to achieve some sort of emphasis; how is this device effectively employed in Martial 1.64?

_____

_____

4. Dē quō prīncipe Seneca in hōc locō scrīpsit? _____

5. Cum prīnceps comoedōs audīret, quid fēcit?
   a. mortuus est　　　　　　b. ultimum verbum locūtus est
   c. sē concacāvit　　　　　　d. haec omnia

6. In hōc carmine Catullī, quis est similis deō?
   a. Lesbia ipsa　　　　　　b. vir quī cum Lesbiā sedet
   c. Catullus ipse　　　　　　d. rēx beātus

7. Cum Catullus Lesbiam spectat auditque, cūr loquī nōn potest?
   a. lingua torpet　　　　　　b. igne cōnsūmitur
   c. aurēs tintinant　　　　　　d. ea vidētur pār deō

8. What is actually happening to the speaker in 11–12 and how is the metaphor in **geminā . . . nocte** especially effective?

_____

_____

Et mihi rēs, nōn mē rēbus, subiungere cōnor:
And I try to subordinate life to myself, not myself to life
Horace

35

Dative with Adjectives; Dative with Special Verbs; Dative with Compounds

INTELLEGENDA

Upon completion of this lesson you should be able to
 1. *Explain the basic function of the dative case.*
 2. *Define, recognize, and translate the "dative with adjectives" construction.*
 3. *Define, recognize, and translate the "dative with special verbs" construction.*
 4. *Define, recognize, and translate the "dative with compounds" construction.*

Salvēte, discipulae discipulīque! Before beginning these exercises, be sure you have thoroughly studied Chapter 35 of *Wheelock's Latin* and memorized both the list of special verbs governing the dative case and all the new vocabulary by practicing them *aloud.* **Crēdite mihi—studēte Latīnae et semper sapiētis!**

GRAMMATICA

1. The dative case is in general employed to indicate the person or thing that some action or circumstance applies to or refers to _____, as opposed to the accusative which indicates the direct object of an action.

2. An adjective indicating attitude, relation, or quality may take a noun or pronoun in the dative case to indicate, literally or figuratively, the _____ in which the adjective applies; such adjectives in English are usually followed by the words _____, _____, or _____.

3. Which adjective is least likely to take a dative?
    a. alius   b. cārus   c. fidēlis   d. similis

4. Several special Latin verbs, most of them indicating attitude or relationship, take a noun or pronoun in the dative case, where in English we would expect a _____ object; these Latin verbs, however, are generally intransitive and their dative "objects" actually indicate the person (or thing) to whom (or which) the attitude _____.

5. Many compound verbs take a noun or pronoun in the dative case, especially when the meaning of the compound verb is significantly _____ from that of its simple form; often the dative appears to function as a sort of object of the prepositional _____, though the preposition would take a different case if separate from the verb. If the simple verb is transitive, the compound sometimes takes, in addition to the dative, an _____ case noun or pronoun as direct object of the root verb.

6. List the five uses of the dative case learned thus far.

    _____   _____

    _____   _____

    _____

7. Give the sentence number and identify the 11 dative nouns and pronouns and their specific uses in Practice and Review sentences 1–11.

Sent. No.	Dative	Dative Case Use
_____	_____	_____
_____	_____	_____
_____	_____	_____
_____	_____	_____
_____	_____	_____
_____	_____	_____
_____	_____	_____
_____	_____	_____
_____	_____	_____
_____	_____	_____

EXERCITĀTIŌNĒS

A. Transform from singular to plural or plural to singular and then translate, with careful attention to verb tenses and the correct auxiliaries.

1. Tālī praemiō studēbat.

   Transformation: _____

   Translation: _____

2. Nātae meae virīs nūbent.

   Transformation: _____

   Translation: _____

3. Huic illum antepōnit.

   Transformation: _____

   Translation: _____

4. Ignōsce amīcō īrātō.

   Transformation: _____

   Translation: _____

5. Nōlī imperāre mihi!

   Transformation: _____

   Translation: _____

6. heu, vōbīs noceant

   Transformation: _____

   Translation: _____

7. hostibus parcerēmus

   Transformation: _____

   Translation: _____

8. imperātōrī pāruissem

   Transformation: _____

   Translation: _____

9. Audītōribus persuādēmus.

   Transformation: _____

   Translation: _____

10. Nātae candidae subrīdet.

    Transformation: _____

    Translation: _____

B. Supply the correct form of the words in parentheses and translate.

   1. Sī quis tantum _____ (pecūnia) serviet—vae miserum!—
      pectus numquam erit līberum.

      _____

      _____

   2. Aestās est tempus nōbīs iūcundum quod _____ (discipu-
      lus; pl.) atque _____ (magister; pl.) eōrum placet.

      _____

      _____

3. Sī salvēre ac sapere vultis, fovēte animās atque nōlīte _____ (corpus; pl.) nocēre.

_____

_____

4. Mīror tē _____ (amīcitia; sg.) dīvitiās semper antepōnere.

C. Translate into Latin; employ standard word order and include all macrons.

1. Let us first obey our hearts.

_____

2. The more faithful guards served him well.

_____

3. The very angry father suddenly forgave his son.

_____

4. That student always studies Latin with the greatest care.

_____

VĪS VERBŌRUM

A. Answer these questions on the chapter's vocabulary list.

1. Complete the analogy **casa : iānua :: urbs :** _____.
   a. fenestra   b. porta   c. remissiō   d. via

2. Which verb is synonymous with **imperō**?
   a. arbitror   b. crēscō   c. iubeō   d. ēgredior

3. Which verb is an antonym of **noceō**?
   a. iuvō   b. mōlior   c. patior   d. trādō

B. Complete each statement with an English word that demonstrates your knowledge of the Latin etymology (e.g., "A 'laudatory' speech is full of praise").

1. True "students" (like you!!) are _____ for learning.

2. A "janitor" literally watches the _____, and "January" is the _____ into the new year.

3. A "pectoral" is armor or an ornament worn over the _____.

4. An "innocuous" remark is _____ intended to do any _____.

5. A "nubile" young lady is ready for _____.

6. An "implacable" tyrant can _____ be _____.

7. A bear hibernates in the winter; some animals "estivate" in the _____.

LĒCTIŌNĒS

A. First read each sentence aloud twice, and then translate as literally as possible within the limits of sound English idiom.

1. Cum familia nostra aestāte rūsticārētur, sub sōle candidō iacēbāmus et mare cum voluptāte spectābāmus.

   _____

   _____

2. Audītōrēs magnā vōce hortātus est, sed eum sequī proficīscīve ex urbe recūsāvērunt.

   _____

   _____

3. Sedeāmus loquāmurque dē hāc occāsiōne optimā, atque diē ūtāmur!

   _____

   _____

4. Ille prīnceps nātus est temporibus adversīs sed fēlīcissimā aetāte mortuus est.

   _____

   _____

5. Fatētur sē plūrimīs nocuisse, sed nunc cēterīs parcere et nōbīs omnibus placēre vult.

    _____

    _____

6. Ille servus, quī semper fuit mihi cārus, fīliō meō servīvit et eum servāre cōnātus est.

    _____

    _____

7. Sī quis hunc labōrem suscēpisset, multīs pepercisset.

    _____

8. Sī Deum nōbīs ignōscere volumus, nōs dēbēmus aliīs hominibus ignōscere.

    _____

    _____

9. Mihi nunc nōn crēdunt, neque umquam nātae meae crēdere volent.

    _____

    _____

10. Huic ducī pāreāmus ut nōbīs parcat et urbem quam celerrimē servet.

    _____

    _____

B. Answer these questions on the readings from Ovid, Cicero, and Martial.

    1. Ovidius loquitur dē fōrmīs mūtātīs ab _____ ad tempora sua.
        a. animō   b. initiō mundī   c. mundō   d. carmine suō

    2. Quae ā deīs mūtāta sunt?
        a. multae fōrmae   b. nova corpora
        c. coepta poētae   d. haec omnia

    3. In locō ā Cicerōne scrīptō, quis est "eum" (line 2)? _____

4. Quis est "illam"? _____

5. Quid est "id"? _____

6. Cum Nāsīca ad casam eius advēnit, ubi fuit poēta Ennius?
    (**Respondē in tōtā sententiā.**) _____

    _____

7. Quis in hāc fābulā plūs salis habet—Ennius Nāsīcave?
    _____

8. In prīmīs duōbus carminibus ā Martiāle scrīptīs, quī
    mātrimōnium petunt? _____ _____

9. In hīs duōbus carminibus, quī sapiunt? _____ _____
    _____ Quis mox moriētur? _____

10. Identify the polysyndeton in Martial 1.10 and comment on its
    effect (see the **Lēctiōnēs,** Chapter 34, if you do not remember the
    term).

    _____

    _____

11. In tertiō carmine Martiālis, quī sunt "turba"?
    a. ludī   b. magistrī   c. puerī puellaeque   d. discipulī

> **Virtūs praemium est optimum:** *Virtue is the best reward*
> Plautus

36

Jussive Noun Clauses; Fīō

INTELLEGENDA

Upon completion of this lesson you should be able to
1. *Define, recognize, and translate the subjunctive "jussive noun clause."*
2. *Recognize, form, and translate the irregular verb* **fīō**.

Salvēte, lēctōrēs lēctrīcēsque cārissimae! Before beginning these exercises, be sure you have thoroughly studied Chapter 36 of *Wheelock's Latin* and memorized both the paradigms and the new vocabulary by practicing them *aloud*. **Hortor vōs ut labōrem cum studiō accēdātis: sī id faciētis, fīētis sapientissimī atque fēlīcissimī!**

GRAMMATICA

1. A jussive noun clause is a kind of _____ command, a subordinate clause introduced by _____ or, if negative, _____, and with its verb in the _____ mood. Such a clause reports _____, not in a direct quotation, what someone has commanded, requested, advised, etc.

2. As an indirectly reported command, the jussive noun clause may be compared conceptually with an indirect statement, which, however, has _____ introductory word and requires an _____ verb, and with an indirect question, which also takes a verb in the _____ mood, but which is introduced by an _____ word.

3. The verb in the main clause that introduces a jussive noun clause either commands, requests, advises, or otherwise expresses the wish of its subject. Circle the eight verbs in the following list that commonly introduce a jussive noun clause.

arbitror	moneō	quaerō
foveō	nūbō	rogō
hortor	ōrō	sequor
imperō	persuādeō	subrīdeō
mōlior	petō	ūtor

4. **Volō, nōlō,** and **mālō** usually take an _____, but sometimes take a jussive noun clause; **iubeō** nearly always takes an _____.

5. Jussive noun clauses are sometimes confused with _____ clauses, since they are identical in appearance; the jussive noun clause, however, always has the sort of introductory verb indicated above and serves as the noun object of that verb, answering the question _____, rather than serving adverbially and answering the question _____.

6. Jussive noun clauses are easily distinguished from simple jussive clauses (Chapter 28), since the latter are _____ clauses that give direct commands rather than _____ clauses in which commands are reported _____.

7. Though sometimes translated as an English noun clause introduced by "that," the Latin jussive noun clause is usually translated with no _____ word (except "not," if the clause is negative) and with the verb transformed to an _____.

8. Give the sentence number and identify the 10 subjunctive verbs and their specific types in Practice and Review sentences 1–9.

Sent. No.	Subjunctive	Clause Type
_____	_____	_____
_____	_____	_____
_____	_____	_____
_____	_____	_____
_____	_____	_____
_____	_____	_____
_____	_____	_____

Name: _____ Section: _____ Date: _____

_____   _____   _____

_____   _____   _____

_____   _____   _____

9. **Fīō,** an irregular verb meaning *to occur, happen, become,* was commonly used by the Romans in place of the passive of the present system of the verb _____, and so also has the passive meanings _____ _____, _____ _____, even though it is _____ in form; answer these questions on its irregularities.

   a. The _____ system of **fīō** is supplied by the perfect passive system of _____.

   b. The _____ system is irregular and must be memorized.

   c. The stem vowel _____ is long in all present system forms except _____, _____, and the _____ subjunctive.

10. Provide a complete synopsis of **fīō, fierī, factus sum,** in the third person singular.

INDICATIVE

Present	Future	Impf.	Perfect	Fut.Perf.	Plupf.
_____	_____	_____	_____	_____	_____

SUBJUNCTIVE

_____   _____ _____   _____

11. Translate the above synopsis of **fīō,** using the meaning *to become,* in the third person singular; use "may," "might," etc., for the subjunctives (though the actual translation of a subjunctive, of course, depends upon the type of clause in which it is employed).

INDICATIVE

Present	Future	Impf.	Perfect	Fut.Perf.	Plupf.
_____	_____	_____	_____	_____	_____

SUBJUNCTIVE

_____   _____ _____   _____

EXERCITĀTIŌNĒS

A. Transform from singular to plural or plural to singular and then translate. For all the jussive noun clauses except number 10 (where you must use "that" as the introductory word), you can use the rule outlined above, i.e., translate the verb as an infinitive, with no introductory word except, for a negative clause, "not." Note that one of these does not contain a jussive noun clause—do you know which one and why?

1. Hortābor tē nē accēdās.

    Transformation: _____

    Translation: _____

2. Cūrāte ut diēs carpātis.

    Transformation: _____

    Translation: _____

3. Ōrō eum ut fīat vir melior.

    Transformation: _____

    Translation: _____

4. Monuit tē ut hostem contunderēs.

    Transformation: _____

    Translation: _____

5. Rogō eum ut librum exigat.

    Transformation: _____

    Translation: _____

6. Petit ā tē nē illum cōgās.

    Transformation: _____

    Translation: _____

7. Quaerēbās ab eō ut cōnārētur.

    Transformation: _____

    Translation: _____

8.   Iussī eum requīrere tē.

     Transformation: _____

     Translation: _____

9.   Moneō eam ut sē recreet.

     Transformation: _____

     Translation: _____

10. Dēcernunt ut ēgrediāminī.

     Transformation: _____

     Translation: _____

B.   Supply the correct form for the verbs in parentheses and translate.

1.   Eīs persuāsimus nē eī _____ (nocēre; 3rd pers. pl.).

     _____

2.   Lēctōrēs hortor ut magnā vōce _____ (loquī; 3rd pers. pl.).

     _____

3.   Ab eā quaesīveram ut mihi _____ (ignōscere; 3rd pers. sg.).

     _____

4.   Imperāvit eī nē potentior _____ (fierī; 3rd pers. sg.).

     _____

5.   Monēsne mē ut tibi _____ (pārēre; 1st pers. sg.)?

     _____

C.   Translate into Latin; employ standard word order and include all macrons.

1.   Persuade her to become your friend.

     _____

2.   Warn him not to despise our leaders.

     _____

3. They ordered (imperō) him to spare those soldiers.

_____

4. The woman begged him to cheer up their daughter.

_____

5. We urged them to confess the plot without fear.

_____

VĪS VERBŌRUM

A. Answer these questions on the chapter's vocabulary list.

1. Which adverb does not belong?
   a. cōtīdiē   b. numquam   c. saepe   d. semper

2. A synonym of **cupīdō** is
   a. anima   b. cupiditās   c. pectus   d. remissiō

3. An antonym of **fortasse** is
   a. certē   b. heu   c. semel   d. vae

4. An antonym of **accēdō** is
   a. antepōnō   b. crēscō   c. ēgredior   d. rūsticor

5. A synonym of **oblectō** is
   a. mīror   b. nāscor   c. placeō   d. studeō

6. Identify the third declension **-iō** nouns derived from the fourth principal part of the following verbs, and then give their direct English derivatives and their literal meanings.

	Latin Noun	Eng. Noun	Translation
a. contundō	_____	_____	_____
b. ōrō	_____	_____	_____
c. recreō	_____	_____	_____
d. requīrō	_____	_____	_____

7. Identify the third declension **-or** nouns derived from the fourth principal part of the following verbs, and then give their direct English derivatives and their literal meanings.

	Latin Noun	Eng. Noun	Translation
a. cūrō	_____	_____	_____
b. ōrō	_____	_____	_____

B. Complete each statement with an English word that demonstrates your knowledge of the Latin etymology (e.g., "A 'laudatory' speech is full of praise").

   1. An "excerpt," metaphorically, is something _____ _____ a crop.

   2. A "lectern" is literally a stand used for _____ .

   3. A "cogent" argument is persuasive because it _____ _____ all the evidence in a compelling manner.

   4. An evening "serenade" should _____ your emotions and thus make you feel "serene."

LĒCTIŌNĒS

A. First read each sentence aloud twice, and then translate as literally as possible within the limits of sound English idiom.

   1. Petīvit ab amīcō īrātō nē eōs miserrimōs in vinculīs servitūtis tenērent.

   _____

   _____

   2. Hortor tē ut sapiās ac eā aestāte remissiōnis causā ex urbe proficīscāris.

   _____

   _____

   3. Imperāvit servō ut ad iānuam adversam cōtīdiē sedēret et casam spectāret.

   _____

   _____

4. Nōlī patī eōs, quī tibi tam male servīvērunt, tālia praemia accipere.

    _____

    _____

5. Carmina illīus lēctrīcis audītōrēs semper oblectant atque pectora serēnant recreantque.

    _____

    _____

6. Tē ōrō ut fīās discipulus quam sapientissimus, cupīdinēs stultās contemnās, atque omnem diem carpās.

    _____

    _____

7. Senex hortātus est Rōmānōs ut ferōcēs cōgerent, eōs ex Italiā exigerent, et superbōs contunderent, sed omnibus cēterīs parcerent.

    _____

    _____

    _____

8. Deus dēcrēvit ut lūx fieret, atque lūx candida facta est.

9. Cūrā ut cōtīdiē fīās sapientior et beātior et amīcīs iūcundior.

    _____

10. Sī fortasse requīris quid faciam, accēde et tibi dīcam.

    _____

B. Answer these questions on the selections from Martial, Catullus, Horace, and Cicero.

    1. In prīmō carmine, quid Avītus in librō Martiālis inveniet?
        a. bona   b. mediocria   c. mala   d. haec omnia

    2. In carmine secundō, quid Martiālis cum libellīs suīs cōnfert?
        _____

    3. Quōcum cocus cōnfertur? _____

4. In tertiō carmine, quot verba (*verbs*) sunt? (**Respondē in Latīnā.**)
   _____

5. List all the verbs in Catullus 85 in two groups, those that suggest feeling/passion/suffering and those that suggest knowing/reason/doing.
   Feeling/suffering: _____
   Knowing/doing: _____
   Comment on the arrangement of these two categories of verbs within the poem and on the effect of the contrast.

   _____

   _____

   _____

6. In quārtō carmine, quid Celer maximē vult?
   a. audīre carmina Martiālis   b. recitāre carmina Martiālis
   c. recitāre carmina sua   d. Martiālem recitāre carmina eius

7. Explain briefly what Horace means by a man who is **in sē ipsō tōtus.**

   _____

   _____

8. Quī sunt trēs coniūrātī in ōrātiōne Cicerōnis?
   _____ _____ _____

9. Quibus Lentulus imperāvit ut equitātum in Italiam mitterent?
   _____

10. Cui imperāvit ut ad urbem mīlitēs dūceret? _____

Labōrāre est ōrāre: *To work is to pray*
Motto of the Benedictine Monks

37

Conjugation of Eō; Constructions of Place and Time

INTELLEGENDA

Upon completion of this lesson you should be able to
  1. *Recognize, form, and translate the irregular verb **eō**.*
  2. *Define, recognize, and translate the various place and time constructions discussed in the chapter, including "place where," "place to which," "place from which," the "ablative of time when or within which," and the "accusative of duration of time."*
  3. *Define, recognize, form, and translate the "locative case."*
  4. *Explain the special rules for place constructions involving the names of cities, towns, small islands, and the three nouns **domus, humus,** and **rūs**.*

Salvēte, lēctrīcēs lēctōrēsque iūcundissimī! Before beginning these exercises, be sure you have thoroughly studied Chapter 37 of *Wheelock's Latin* and memorized both the paradigms and the new vocabulary by practicing them *aloud.* **Spērō vōs ā studiō ac amōre linguae Latīnae numquam abitūrōs esse!**

GRAMMATICA

1. **Eō, īre,** *to go,* is an irregular verb of the _____ conjugation; answer these questions on its irregularities.

   a. The _____ voice is relatively uncommon, except in transitive _____, and so is not presented in our text.

   b. The normal present stem _____ changes to _____ before the vowels ___, ___, and ___ throughout the present system as well as in the gerund and all forms of the present participle except the singular of the _____ case.

   c. The future tense has the endings of a _____ or _____ conjugation verb.

   d. The _____ system is formed regularly, except that the vowel combination _____ before **s** usually contracts to _____.

2. Provide a complete synopsis of **eō, īre, iī, itum,** in the third person singular.

   INDICATIVE

Present	Future	Impf.	Perfect	Fut.Perf.	Plupf.
_____	_____	_____	_____	_____	_____

   SUBJUNCTIVE

_____	_____	_____	_____

3. Translate the above synopsis of **eō,** *to go,* in the third person singular; use "may," "might," etc., for the subjunctives (though the actual translation of a subjunctive, of course, depends upon the type of clause in which it is employed).

   INDICATIVE

Present	Future	Impf.	Perfect	Fut.Perf.	Plupf.
_____	_____	_____	_____	_____	_____

   SUBJUNCTIVE

_____	_____	_____	_____

4. Provide the indicated information for regular Latin place constructions.

Construction	Case	Prepositions
a. from which	_____	_____
b. to which	_____	_____
c. where	_____	_____

5. To indicate place where, the Romans used the locative case with the names of _____, _____, and _____ _____, as well as with the three nouns _____, _____, and _____.

6. For the singular of _____ and _____ declension nouns, the locative is identical to the _____ case; elsewhere it is usually identical to the _____.

7. Provide the indicated information for Latin place constructions involving the place names and special nouns discussed in the text.

Construction	Case	Prepositions
a. from which	_____	_____
b. to which	_____	_____
c. where	_____	_____

8. **Domus** is a slightly irregular noun with some endings of the _____ declension and some of the _____. List the forms most commonly used for the following place constructions.

Construction	Form of *Domus*
a. from which	_____
b. to which	_____
c. where	_____

9. The locative singular of **rūs** is either _____ or _____.

10. For time when or within which, as we have already learned, the _____ case is used, with _____ preposition; and the prepositions _____, _____, _____, or _____ are commonly employed in English translation.

11. To indicate duration of time, i.e., how long a period of time an action occurs, the _____ case is employed, with _____ preposition; in English translation the preposition _____ is sometimes employed, sometimes omitted.

12. The duration of time construction was often employed with the Latin word _____ to indicate a person's _____.

EXERCITĀTIŌNĒS

A. Translate these brief sentences.

Translation

1. Athēnās fortasse iit.   _____

2. Forīs abīre tibi licet.   _____

3. Humī ūnam hōram sedēbat.   _____

4. Eō tempore rūre rediērunt.   _____

5. Domī ūnō diē periit.   _____

6. Nātus decem annōs, mortem obiit.   _____

7. Domō īrātē exībāmus.   _____

8. Athēnīs exierant et Rōmae vīxit.   _____

9. Rūre requiēscere solēs.   _____

10. Domum paucīs hōrīs adībis.   _____

11. Syrācūsīs eō diē interfectus est.   _____

12. Rōmam cōtīdiē inībātis.   _____

13. Multōs diēs peregrīnābāmur.   _____

14. In itinere grātō abeāmus!   _____

15. Servus ē vinculīs exiit.   _____

B. Supply the correct form of the word in parentheses and translate.

1. Frāter meus _____ (Athēnae) abiit et _____ (Rōma) accēdit.

2. _____ (Rōma) adit ut domum idōneum requīrat.

_____

3. _____ (domus) abierat, cum parentēs essent absentēs.

_____

4. Deinde _____ (Athēnae) rediit et libellum exēgit.

_____

5. Dēnique aut _____ (domus) aut _____ (rūs)
   pereāmus.

_____

C. Translate into Latin; employ standard word order and include all macrons.

   1. My friends left home within three hours.

   _____

   2. They will remain in Rome for a few days.

   _____

   3. Let us return to Athens in one year.

   _____

   4. He will go to Syracuse for seven days.

   _____

   5. One may travel abroad for many years.

   _____

VĪS VERBŌRUM

A. Answer these questions on the chapter's vocabulary list.

   1. A synonym of **domus** is
      a. casa   b. cupīdō   c. iānua   d. lēctrīx

   2. Which noun has a meaning related to **humus**?
      a. aestās   b. pectus   c. praemium   d. terra

3. Which verb has a meaning related to **eō**?
   a. antepōnō   b. carpō   c. cēdō   d. cōgō

4. Which verb is nearly synonymous with **abeō**?
   a. contemnō   b. contundō   c. dēcernō   d. discēdō

5. Which is a synonym of **exeō**?
   a. cūrō   b. ēgredior   c. foveō   d. mīror

6. Which is a synonym of **pereō**?
   a. imperō   b. occidō   c. parcō   d. pāreō

7. Which is a synonym of **interficiō**?
   a. fīō   b. ignōscō   c. necō   d. noceō

8. Which is a synonym of **adeō**?
   a. accēdō   b. nūbō   c. serēnō   d. subrīdeō

9. Which has a meaning in common with **peregrīno**
   a. sapiō   b. recreō   c. oblectō   d. errō

10. Which has a meaning in common with **rede**
    a. studeō   b. serviō   c. reveniō   d. ōrō

B. Complete each statement with an Engl~~~~~ that demonstrates your
   kn~~~~~ 'laudatory' speech is full

1. An "itinerary" provides details of a traveler's _____.

2. An "insolent" person does _____ behave in the
   _____ manner.

3. "Illicit" behavior is _____ _____.

4. To "exhume" a corpse is to remove it _____ the
   _____.

5. A "requiem" is sung to bring _____ to the souls of the
   dead.

LĒCTIŌNĒS

A. First read each sentence aloud twice, and then translate as literally as possible within the limits of sound English idiom.

1. Cōnābātur persuādēre eīs ut Rōmā paucīs hōrīs exīrent, sed plū-rimōs diēs erant immōtī.

   _____

   _____

2. Cēna illīs amīcīs grātissimīs ita placet ut domum redīre nōlint.

   _____

3. Cum fīlius fīliaque rūrī paucōs diēs peregrīnārentur, ad multa loca parentibus absentibus idōnea adiērunt.

   _____

   _____

4. Dummodo in exsilium ā prīncipe nē missus sit, licet eī Rōmam inīre.

   _____

5. Nisi domum īre potes, apud mē requiēscere tibi licet.

   _____

6. Tōtam aestātem Athēnīs esse solitī sumus.

   _____

7. Corpus illīus mīlitis interfectī, quī vīgintī annōs nātus mortem obiit et humī nunc iacet, sub humō mox in pāce requiēscat.

   _____

   _____

8. Frāter fuit eīs tam grātus ut, cum Rōmā abīsset, nihil eōs serēnāre posset.

   _____

   _____

B. Answer these questions on the readings from Martial, Petronius, and Cicero.

1. Cum Martiālis carmina sua recitat, cuius carmina Caeciliānus recitat? (**Respondē in tōtā sententiā.**)

   _____

2. Cuius carmina Martiālis hortātur eum ut recitet?
   a. Martiālis   b. Marsī   c. Catullī   d. sua

3. Cuius īnscrīptiō ā Trimalchiōne legitur?
   a. Pompeiī Magnī   b. Fortūnātae   c. uxoris suae   d. sua

4. Quis dē īnscrīptiōne prīmō flēbat?
   a. Trimalchiō   b. Fortūnāta   c. Habinnas   d. familia

5. Estne locus trīstis aut rīdiculus? Cūr? (**Respondē Anglicē,** i.e., _in English._)

   _____

   _____

6. In litterīs Cicerōnis, unde Licinius fūgit? _____

7. Ad quem urbem prīmō adit? _____

8. Quis Licinium comprehendit? _____

9. Quid Cicerō ex frātre vult? (**Anglicē.**)

   _____

Exeat aulā quī vult esse pius—virtūs et summa potestās nōn coeunt:
Let him depart from the imperial palace who wishes to be pious
—virtue and supreme power do not go together
Lucan

38

Relative Clauses of Characteristic; Dative of Reference; Supines

INTELLEGENDA

Upon completion of this lesson you should be able to
   1. Define, recognize, and translate the subjunctive "relative clause of characteristic."
   2. Define, recognize, and translate the "dative of reference" construction.
   3. Define, recognize, form, and translate "supines."

Salvē, lēctor aut lēctrīx fidēlis! Before beginning these exercises, be sure you have thoroughly studied Chapter 38 of *Wheelock's Latin* and memorized both the paradigms and the new vocabulary by practicing them *aloud*. **Ut fīnem huius librī accēdis—mīrābile dictū—scientia tua linguae Latīnae cōtīdiē fit sublīmior!**

GRAMMATICA

1. The type of relative clause introduced in Chapter 17 provides some factual description of its antecedent, an actual person or thing. By

contrast, the relative clause of characteristic, a subordinate clause introduced by a _____ _____, describes some _____ quality of an antecedent that is itself either _____, _____, _____, or _____ and which, accordingly, has its verb in the _____ mood.

2. In translating the verb in a relative clause of characteristic, the auxiliary _____ is frequently (but not always) employed, and some phrase like _____ _____ _____ or _____ _____ _____ should often be supplied before the relative pronoun to make it clear that its antecedent is indefinite.

3. Give the sentence number and identify the 14 subjunctive verbs and their specific clause types in Practice and Review sentences 1–13.

Sent. No.	Subjunctive	Clause Type
_____	_____	_____
_____	_____	_____
_____	_____	_____
_____	_____	_____
_____	_____	_____
_____	_____	_____
_____	_____	_____
_____	_____	_____
_____	_____	_____
_____	_____	_____
_____	_____	_____
_____	_____	_____
_____	_____	_____
_____	_____	_____

4. A dative of reference or interest is a noun or pronoun in the dative case which indicates a person (or a thing) to whom some statement _____, or from whose _____ it is true, or to whom it is of special _____.

5. The dative of reference can sometimes be translated simply with the

words _____ or _____, but often the context requires a phrase such as "in my opinion," "from your point of view," "in his own heart," "as far as they are concerned," etc.

6. Give the sentence number and identify the eight dative nouns and pronouns and their specific uses in **Sententiae Antīquae** 1–14.

Sent. No.	Dative	Case Use
_____	_____	_____
_____	_____	_____
_____	_____	_____
_____	_____	_____
_____	_____	_____
_____	_____	_____
_____	_____	_____
_____	_____	_____

7. The supine is a defective verbal _____ of the _____ declension, formed on the same stem as the _____ _____ _____ and having only two forms in common use, the _____ and _____ singular.

8. The ablative supine is used with the _____ of certain adjectives to indicate in what _____ a particular quality is applicable.

9. The accusative supine (which must be carefully distinguished from the _____ _____ _____) is used with verbs of _____ to indicate _____.

10. Identify the two supines in the chapter's Practice and Review sentences. _____ _____

EXERCITĀTIŌNĒS

A. Transform from singular to plural or plural to singular and then translate.

1. Is est quī multum querātur.

   Transformation: _____

   Translation: _____

2. Fuit nūllus quī eum recognōsceret.

Transformation: _____

Translation: _____

3. Eae sunt quae nihil metuant.

Transformation: _____

Translation: _____

4. Est quī omne vēndat.

Transformation: _____

Translation: _____

5. Hī nōn sunt quī nōs impediant.

Transformation: _____

Translation: _____

6. Hoc est opus quod eum oblectet.

Transformation: _____

Translation: _____

7. Dolor est quem nōn ferre possim.

Transformation: _____

Translation: _____

8. Hae sunt domūs quās requīrātis.

Transformation: _____

Translation: _____

9. Quī sunt quī nōn redeant?

Transformation: _____

Translation: _____

10. Illa erant itinera quae amārent.

Transformation: _____

Translation: _____

B. Supply the correct form of the verb in parentheses and translate.

   1. Sōla est—mīrābile dictū!—quae tāle odium _____
(metuō; pres. subj.).

     _____

   2. Quis est cuius mēns _____ (esse; pres.) immōta?

     _____

   3. Puella grāta quae hoc opus _____ (exigō; perf.) rūrī pere-
grīnātur.

     _____

     _____

   4. Tibi nēmō erat quī odiō ergā cīvitātem _____ (cōgere;
impf. pass.).

     _____

C. Translate into Latin; employ standard word order and include all macrons.

   1. There are many who do not hesitate to complain.

     _____

   2. There are few who do not dread pain.

     _____

   3. Who is there who does not esteem dignity?

     _____

   4. There was no one who was willing to go either to Athens or to
Syracuse.

     _____

     _____

VĪS VERBŌRUM

A.   Answer these questions on the chapter's vocabulary list.

1.   **Odium** > _____ > "odious."

2.   **Mīror** > **mīrābilis**, *remarkable* :: **amō** > _____,
     _____.

3.   Which adjective has a meaning in common with **pristinus**?
     a. absēns   b. antīquus   c. idōneus   d. īnfīrmus

4.   Which is a synonym of **metuō**?
     a. adeō   b. cūrō   c. soleō   d. timeō

5.   Which verb is an antonym of **impediō**?
     a. abeō   b. interficiō   c. iuvō   d. recreō

6.   Which is an antonym of **queror**?
     a. serēnō   b. requiēscō   c. obeō   d. gaudeō

7.   Which verb has a meaning related to **recognōscō**?
     a. accēdō   b. fīō   c. intellegō   d. pereō

8.   Complete the analogy **oculus : videō :: pēs :** _____.
     a. currō   b. carpō   c. contemnō   d. dēcernō

9.   **Contundō : contūsiō :: ōrō :** _____.

10. **Humilis : humus :: sublīmis :** _____.
     a. aqua   b. caelum   c. cupīdō   d. sator

B.   Complete each statement with an English word that demonstrates your knowledge of the Latin etymology (e.g., "A 'laudatory' speech is full of praise").

1.   An "arboretum" is a garden where _____ are grown for display or study.

2.   A "querulous" person is always _____.

3.   One who sends his heartfelt "condolences" actually suffers _____ along _____ the bereaved.

4.   In a "cooperative" relationship one person _____ _____ another.

5.   "Quadrupeds" have _____ _____.

LĒCTIŌNĒS

A. First read each sentence aloud twice, and then translate as literally as possible within the limits of sound English idiom.

1. Domum inīre tibi nōn licet, etsī vīsum amīcam tuam īs.

   _____

2. Exī forīs, puer stulte: fīlia mea domī nōn adest!

   _____

3. Recognōscisne tibi dolōrem, quem odium ergā hōs cīvēs fortasse creet?

   _____

   _____

4. Illī sunt quī dīvitiīs dignitātem libenter antepōnant.

   _____

5. Cōtīdiē mihi metuēbam—difficile dictū, heu—mortem patris īnfīrmissimī.

   _____

   _____

6. Fuit multōs annōs Rōmae nēmō quī opus nostrum suspendere aut etiam impedīre posset.

   _____

   _____

7. Agricolae pristinī frūctūs dē arboribus carpēbant et Rōmae vēndēbant.

   _____

   _____

8. Iste, mihi vir pessimus, dē vinculīs in pedibus querēbātur.

   _____

9. Iuppiter, sator hominum deōrumque, nātae ē caelō sublīmī subrīsit—mīrābile dictū—atque eam verbīs fīrmīs serēnāvit.

10. In ōrātiōne Cicerō locūtus est nihil metuendum esse quod animō nocēre nōn posset.

B. Answer these questions on the readings from Martial, Cicero, Pompey, Caesar, and Catullus.

1. In carmine Martiālis, quid bibliopola putat?
    a. Martiālem esse poētam   b. Martiālem esse poētam malum
    c. Lūcānum nōn esse poētam   d. Lūcānum esse poētam

2. Cūr iste amīcus, in prīmā fābulā Cicerōnis, dē fīcū surculōs vult?
    a. quod fīcūs amat   b. ut amīcum querentem impediat
    c. ut uxōrem suspendat   d. quod uxor arborēs amat

3. In secundā fābulā Cicerōnis, ea ōrātiō
    a. fuit digna misericordiā   b. vēram misericordiam mōvit
    c. misericordiam movēre vīsa est   d. haec omnia

4. Ā quibus hae epistulae ad Cicerōnem scrīptae sunt?

        _____ _____

5. Quid prīmus scrīptor Cicerōnem facere vult?
    a. exercitum ad eum dūcere   b. cōnsulēs ad Apuliam mittere
    c. Brundisium adīre   d. cum Caesare sē iungere

6. Quid auctor secundārum litterārum ā Cicerōne petit?
    a. exercitum   b. pecūniam   c. cōnsilium   d. arma

7. Characterize Catullus' attitude toward Caesar in his poem 93.
    a. zealous   b. indifferent   c. obsequious   d. timid

Fīnis corōnat opus: *The end crowns the work*
Ovid

39

Gerund and Gerundive

INTELLEGENDA

Upon completion of this lesson you should be able to
1. *Define, recognize, form, and translate "gerunds."*
2. *Distinguish gerunds from gerundives and gerund phrases from gerundive phrases.*
3. *Recognize and translate gerund and gerundive phrases and supines, as they are employed to indicate purpose.*

Salvē, discipula aut discipule līberālissime! Before beginning these exercises, be sure you have thoroughly studied Chapter 39 of *Wheelock's Latin* and memorized both the paradigms and the new vocabulary by practicing them *aloud.* **Hunc libellum diūtissimē lēgistī Latīnae discendae causā, et ad fīnem fēlīciter mox adveniēs: carpe diem!**

GRAMMATICA

1. As you learned in Chapters 23 and 24, the _____ _____ participle, also called the gerundive, is a fully declin-able verbal _____; commonly employed in the _____ _____ conjugation with a dative of agent, the gerundive has a variety of other uses discussed in this chapter.

2. By contrast, the gerund is a neuter verbal _____ with meanings in the _____ voice and declined only in the singular of the _____, _____, _____, and _____ cases.

3. These four forms of the gerund are _____ to the corresponding neuter forms of the _____.

4. Corresponding to the English gerund in "-ing" ("running," "reading," "living," etc.), the Latin gerund can be modified like a verb ("living well") and take an object, etc. ("reading books"), while as a noun it can be employed in a number of the various case uses; as a noun, however, the gerund cannot be employed as a _____ _____, nor, since it lacks a _____ case, as a _____, two functions that are served by another verbal noun, the _____.

5. Match, to indicate some of the differences between gerunds and gerundives.

    ____ verbal adjective   a. gerund
    ____ verbal noun   b. gerundive
    ____ four forms only
    ____ fully declinable
    ____ three genders
    ____ neuter only
    ____ active meanings
    ____ passive meanings

6. Give the basic English translation of the gerundive of **ōrnō, ōrnāre,** *to adorn,* and then decline fully in Latin.

    ENGLISH: _____ _____ _____

	Masculine	**Feminine**	**Neuter**
Singular			
Nom.	_____	_____	_____
Gen.	_____	_____	_____
Dat.	_____	_____	_____
Acc.	_____	_____	_____
Abl.	_____	_____	_____

Plural

Nom. _____ _____ _____

Gen. _____ _____ _____

Dat. _____ _____ _____

Acc. _____ _____ _____

Abl. _____ _____ _____

7. Decline the gerund of **ōrnō,** *to adorn,* in Latin and English.

     Latin   **English**

Gen. _____ _____

Dat. _____ _____

Acc. _____ _____

Abl. _____ _____

8. While a gerund plus direct object phrase is sometimes used in Latin (**habuit magnum amōrem discendī Latīnam,** *he had a great love of learning Latin*), the Romans commonly preferred to put the noun object in the case in which the gerund would otherwise have appeared and then to modify this noun with a _____ (**habuit magnum amōrem Latīnae discendae**); the translation is the same no matter which construction is used, since English idiom requires the gerund construction rather than the unidiomatic _____ (*he had a great love of Latin to be learned*).

9. Translate the two sentences, indicate which contains the gerund, which the gerundive, and circle the sentence that is in the form preferred by the Romans.

   a. Discimus legendō librōs cum cūrā.
   Gerund ____ Gerundive ____ (Check one)

   _____

   b. Discimus librīs legendīs cum cūrā.
   Gerund ____ Gerundive ____ (Check one)

   _____

10. Commonly used to express purpose were phrases consisting either of _____ plus the _____ case of the gerundive (or gerund) or of _____ plus the _____ case of the gerundive (or gerund).

11. List the five gerundives in Practice and Review sentences 1–12; also identify the nouns they modify and the specific use of each gerundive phrase (e.g., object of preposition, purpose, etc.).

Sent. No.	Gerundive	Noun Modified	Use
_____	_____	_____	_____
_____	_____	_____	_____
_____	_____	_____	_____
_____	_____	_____	_____
_____	_____	_____	_____

12. List the eight gerunds in **Sententiae Antīquae** 1–14 and identify the specific case use of each.

Sent. No.	Gerund	Case Use
_____	_____	_____
_____	_____	_____
_____	_____	_____
_____	_____	_____
_____	_____	_____
_____	_____	_____
_____	_____	_____
_____	_____	_____

13. You have now learned six ways to express purpose in Latin: **ut/nē** with the subjunctive; the supine (with verbs of motion); **ad** with the accusative of the gerund (plus object, etc.); **ad** with the accusative of a noun and gerundive; **causā** with the genitive of the gerund (plus object, etc.); **causā** plus the genitive of a noun and gerundive. Using **veniō, oppugnō,** and **aedificium,** translate into Latin "They are coming to assault the buildings" in these six different ways.

Subjunctive: _____

Supine: _____

Ad + gerund: _____

Ad + **gerundive:** _____

Causā + **gerund:** _____

Causā + **gerundive:** _____

EXERCITĀTIŌNĒS

A. Translate the following brief sentences into idiomatic English

1. Athēnās moeniīs oppugnandīs capiāmus.

   _____

2. Mulier frūctuum vēndendōrum causā ad urbem ambulat.

   _____

3. Ad iniūriam cūrandam ad medicum adiit.

   _____

4. Rōmā abībunt ad peregrīnandum Syrācūsās.

   _____

5. Pernoctandī causā domum ineunt.

   _____

6. Experiendō discimus.

   _____

7. Vīnō lībandō deābus placuimus.

   _____

8. Rōmam flūmine trānseundō redīre potes.

   _____

9. Magistra discendō sē dēdicāvit.

   _____

10. Magnum amōrem currendī habeō.

    _____

B. Supply the correct form of the verbs in parentheses and translate.

1. Aedificiī mīrābilis _____ (vidēre; gerundive) in trānsitū cu-
    pidī erāmus.

    _____

    _____

2. Ars pristina _____ (scrībere; gerund) laudābātur.

    _____

3. Cōnsulēs veterēs ad pācem _____ (petere; gerundive) liben-
    ter ībunt.

    _____

    _____

4. Athēnīs exeāmus et in trānsitū _____ (requiēscere) causā
    rūs peregrīnēmur.

    _____

    _____

C. Translate, using either a gerund or a gerundive in each sentence, in
    accordance with the preferred Latin idiom.

1. We went to Rome for the sake of hearing your oration.

    _____

2. By reading we become wiser.

    _____

3. He spoke in favor of (prō) freeing the city.

    _____

4. We learned much about writing well.

    _____

VĪS VERBŌRUM

A. Answer these questions on the chapter's vocabulary list.

1. **Iniūria** > _____ > "injurious."

2. **Ventum** > _____, meaning _full of wind, windy._

3. Synonymous with **mulier** is
    a. arbor   b. fēmina   c. humus   d. pēs

4. **Trānseō** > **trānsitus, -ūs, m.** > "transit" :: **exeō** >
    _____ > _____.

5. **Mortālis, -e** > **mortālitās, -tātis, f.** > "mortality" ::
    līberālis, -e > _____ > _____ ::
    cupidus, -a, -um > _____ > _____.

6. **Ventus : navigāre :: pēs :** _____.
    a. ambulāre   b. impedīre   c. interficere   d. suspendere

7. A synonym of **vetus** is
    a. absēns   b. fīrmus   c. īnfīrmus   d. senex

8. Closest in meaning to **necesse** is
    a. certus   b. grātus   c. idōneus   d. immōtus

9. **Experior** has a meaning in common with
    a. recognōscō   b. queror   c. obeō   d. cōnor

B. Complete each statement with an English word that demonstrates your knowledge of the Latin etymology (e.g., "A 'laudatory' speech is full of praise").

1. To "edify" someone is to _____ up his moral or spiritual character.

2. A "quasi-legal" measure only appears _____ _____ it were lawful.

3. The true purpose of the "liberal arts" is to _____ one's mind from the mundane.

4. An urban "transit" system is supposed to help you _____ _____ town efficiently.

Name: _____ _Section:_ _____ _Date:_ _____

LĒCTIŌNĒS

A. First read each sentence aloud twice, and then translate as literally as possible within the limits of sound English idiom.

1. Etsī es īnfīrmus, mī fīlī, forīs īre licet ad amīcōs videndōs.

   _____

2. Illī deō sublīmī, satōrī omnium hominum deōrumque, vīnum optimum lībāre oportet.

   _____

   _____

3. Nisi magnum dolōrem ferre aut perīre vīs, tē armīs quam celerrimē ōrnāre et hostēs oppugnāre necesse est.

   _____

   _____

4. Amīcus vetus in tālibus operibus exigendīs multōs diēs labōrāre solēbat.

   _____

   _____

5. Post iter longissimum, quod forīs dormīre metuit, flūmen trānsiit et domum nostrum ad pernoctandum ambulāvit.

   _____

   _____

6. Omnēs mulierēs ex illō aedificiō iniūriae vītandae causā exiērunt.

   _____

   _____

7. Propter dignitātem ac pectus līberāle, imperātor vetus odium ergā nēminem habuit.

   _____

   _____

8. Cupidī ad Italiam navigandī, amīcī meī, ventōs navibus iterum experiāmur!

    _____

    _____

B. Answer these questions on the selections from Catullus, Martial, and Nepos.

1. Comment briefly on Catullus' use of the word **dīcit** in his poem 70 and on how it relates to the metaphors in verse 4.

    _____

    _____

    _____

2. Martiālis trēs virtūtēs in Arriā, uxōre Paetī, in carmine suō dēmōnstrat—quae sunt? (**Respondē Anglicē.**) _____ _____

3. Quis hanc vītam Hannibalis scrīpsit? (**Anglicē.**) _____

4. Cuius odium ergā Rōmānōs Hannibal cōnservāvit? (Answer this and the following questions with just one or two Latin words, as indicated, using the correct case and any necessary prepositions.) _____

5. Ā quō eī imperium datum est? _____ _____

6. Cum Hannibal in Italiam inīret, quis fuit dux exercitūs Carthāginis in Hispāniā? _____ _____

7. Quis exercitum trāns Alpēs ante Hannibalem dūxerat? _____

8. Cum in Italiam inīsset, quō oculō, sinistrō dextrōve, Hannibal bene ūtī poterat? _____

9. Quot imperātōrēs ac mīlitēs Rōmānōs superāvit? _____

Omnia tempus habent . . . tempus nāscendī et tempus moriendī:
To everything there is a season . . . a time to be born and a time to die
Ecclesiastes 3.2

40

-Ne, Num, and Nōnne in Direct Questions; Fear Clauses; Genitive and Ablative of Description

INTELLEGENDA

Upon completion of this lesson you should be able to
1. Recognize and translate the uses of -ne, num, and nōnne in direct questions.
2. Define, recognize, and translate the subjunctive "fear clause."
3. Define, recognize, and translate the "genitive of description" and "ablative of description" constructions.

Salvēte postrēmum, lēctrīcēs et lēctōrēs magnae sapientiae! Before beginning these exercises, be sure you have thoroughly studied Chapter 40 of *Wheelock's Latin* and memorized the new vocabulary by practicing *aloud*. **Dēnique ad fīnem accessistis: nōn iam discipulae discipulīque estis, sed dominae dominīque illīus maximae linguae, Latīnae!**

GRAMMATICA

1. Direct questions may be introduced by an _____ pronoun, by other _____ words such as **ubi** or **cūr**, or by suffixing _____ to the first word of the sentence (often the verb, or some other word on which the question hinges).

2. The suffix _____ introduces a question to which the answer may be either "yes" or "no"; the word _____, however, introduces a question expecting "yes" as an answer and the word _____ introduces a question to which a negative reply is anticipated.

3. A main clause containing a verb of fear or apprehension often precedes a subordinate clause introduced by the conjunction _____, meaning _____, or by _____, meaning _____ _____; the introductory conjunctions are just the opposite of what might be expected, because these subordinate fear clauses were in origin essentially independent _____ clauses.

4. The verb in a fear clause is in the _____ mood and is often translated, as seen from the examples in the text, with the auxiliaries "will" or "would," "may" or "might."

5. Give the sentence number and list the subjunctive verbs in the five fear clauses in Practice and Review sentences 1–12 and the **Sententiae Antīquae.**

Sent. No.	Subjunctive	Sent. No.	Subjunctive
_____	_____	_____	_____
_____	_____	_____	_____
_____	_____		

6. A noun in either the _____ case or the _____ case, when itself modified by an _____, may be employed to modify another noun; the _____ of description was especially common in describing _____ traits; and both types of descriptive phrases, like adjectives, are usually positioned _____ the noun that is being modified.

7. Give the sentence number and list the eight instances of the ablative of description and the four instances of the genitive of description in Practice and Review sentences 1–12 and **Sententiae Antīquae** 1–17;

include both the noun and the modifying adjective that make up the phrase (note that in one of the sentences the same adjective modifies two different descriptive nouns—list them separately).

Sent. No.	Abl. of Description		Sent. No.	Gen. of Description	
_____	_____		_____	_____	_____
_____	_____		_____	_____	_____
_____	_____		_____	_____	_____
_____	_____		_____	_____	_____
_____	_____				
_____	_____				
_____	_____				
_____	_____				

EXERCITĀTIŌNĒS

A. Transform from singular to plural or plural to singular and then translate.

1. Nōnne verēris dominum veterem?

    Transformation: _____

    Translation: _____

2. Metuō ut mētam omnīnō adeam.

    Transformation: _____

    Translation: _____

3. Num mulierēs monumenta repperērunt?

    Transformation: _____

    Translation: _____

4. Fābiturne postrēmum dē hōc opere?

    Transformation: _____

    Translation: _____

5. Nōnne dominī equōs īnfīrmōs fatīgābant?

   Transformation: _____

   Translation: _____

6. Timeō nē hoc saxum cadat.

   Transformation: _____

   Translation: _____

7. Num lacrimam in vultū eius vīdistī?

   Transformation: _____

   Translation: _____

8. Metuēbāmus ut magistrae illōs librōs explicārent.

   Transformation: _____

   Translation: _____

B. Translate.

   1. monumentum aere dūrō _____

   2. mulierēs dignitātis mīrābilis _____

   3. animal pede īnfīrmō _____

   4. iniūria magnō dolōre _____

   5. fēmina mentis līberālis _____

   6. dux mōrum pristinōrum _____

   7. mīles pectoris fīrmī _____

   8. aedificium fōrmā pulchrā _____

C. Supply the correct form of the words in parentheses and translate.

   1. Vereor nē istī hostibus auxilium _____ (ferō; pres.)

      _____

   2. Rōmae fuērunt tot virī iūstī ac fēminae _____
      _____ (magna probitās; gen.).

      _____

3. Num timēs ut domum ambulāre _____ (possum; 2nd pers. sg. pres.)?

_____

4. _____ (answer "yes" is anticipated) humī sub arbore sedē-bant et loquēbantur?

_____

D. Translate into Latin, using standard word order and including all macrons.

1. You did discover those monuments, didn't you?

_____

2. We feared that we would see tears on our mother's face.

_____

3. The slave fears that his master may not be just.

_____

4. You did not suppose, did you, that we would find so many men of great wisdom?

_____

_____

VĪS VERBŌRUM

A. Answer these questions on the chapter's vocabulary list.

1. Which verb has a meaning related to **for**?
   a. experior   b. impediō   c. lībō   d. loquor

2. Which verb has a meaning related to **opīnor**?
   a. oportet   b. oppugnō   c. putō   d. queror

3. Which has a meaning related to **reperiō**?
   a. ōrnō   b. pernoctō   c. recognōscō   d. suspendō

4. Which has a meaning related to **vereor**?
   a. suspendō   b. timeō   c. trānseō   d. vēndō

5. Which does not belong?
   a. aes   b. arma   c. ferrum   d. sator

6. Arrange left to right, from "head to toe": **manus, oculus, nāsus, pēs.**

   _____ _____ _____ _____

7. Which is sometimes a synonym of **vultus**?
   a. odium   b. ōs   c. trānsitus   d. ventus

8. Which has a meaning in common with **postrēmum**?
   a. deinde   b. dēnique   c. libenter   d. quasi

9. Which has a meaning in common with **quīn**?
   a. etsī   b. ergā   c. praeter   d. quidem

10. Which has a meaning in common with **iūstus**?
    a. aequus   b. cupidus   c. necesse   d. sublīmis

11. **Avārus** > **avāritia** > "avarice":: **iūstus** > _____
    > _____.

12. **Tantus:quantus::tot:** _____.

B. Complete each statement with an English word that demonstrates your knowledge of the Latin etymology (e.g., "A 'laudatory' speech is full of praise").

1. "Lacrimal" ducts produce _____.

2. A "saxifrage" is an herb that grows in the cracks in _____.

3. An "inexplicable" phenomenon can _____ be _____, and an "indefatigable" worker can _____ be _____ out.

4. An "infant" is, strictly speaking, a child who can _____ yet _____.

LĒCTIŌNĒS

A. First read each sentence aloud twice, and then translate as literally as possible within the limits of sound English idiom.

1. Nōnne ille poēta monumentum aere perpetuō creāvit?—quīn, ut opīnor, monumentum eius fuit etiam dūrius aere!

   _____

   _____

2. Num scīs utrum aes an saxum sit dūrius?

_____

3. Timeō nē dominus tibi paucās lacrimās habeat.

_____

4. Nōnne mihi dē hīs fāberis, mī pater iūstissime atque sator hominum deōrumque, et postrēmum explicābis omnia quae dē fīliō
   meō repperistī?

_____

_____

_____

5. Verita sum ut fīlius ad mētam omnīnō accēderet.

_____

6. Amīca illīus poētae erat, ut opīnātus est, fēmina oculīs bellīs,
   nāsō gracilī, atque omnīnō pulcherrimō vultū.

_____

_____

7. Timēbam nē audītōrēs ōrātiōne, quae tot argūmenta difficilia con-
   tinēbat, fatīgāret.

_____

_____

8. Ille magister, vir magnae virtūtis quī multa praemia alia docendī
   causā trānsiit, nihil praeter mortem sine honōre timuit.

_____

_____

B. Answer these questions on our final reading selections, from Virgil, Cicero, and Horace, using one or more Latin or English words, as indicated.

   1. Quod nōmen aliud Cytherēa habet? _____ **(Anglicē.)**

   2. Quandō Iuppiter "Cernēs urbem" inquit, in carmine Vergiliī, dē
      quā urbe fātur? _____ **(Latīnē.)**

   3. Quis bellum in Italiā geret? _____ **(Latīnē.)**

4. Quis Rōmam condet? _____ (**Latīnē.**)

5. Quis cum Iove Rōmam fovēbit? _____ (**Latīnē.**)

6. In Cicero's estimation, literature provides a holiday for the human _____ . (**Anglicē.**)

7. Quās aetātēs, ut Cicerō opīnātur, litterae adiuvant?
    a. adulēscentiam   b. senectūtem
    c. tempora adversa   d. omnia tempora

8. Quid litterae nōbīs temporibus malīs dant? (**Latīnē.**)

    _____ _____ _____

9. Quid, ut opīnāris, est illud monumentum dē quō Horātius dīcit? (**Anglicē.**)

    _____

> **Haec studia adulēscentiam alunt, senectūtem oblectant:**
> *These studies nourish our youth and delight our old age*
> Cicero, on the value of literature and the humanities

Well, **discipulae discipulīque,** we hope that your own studies have both nourished your minds and delighted your hearts, and that your affection for Latin will prove to be, in Horace's words, **aere perennius;** and so, **rīdēte, gaudēte, carpite omnēs diēs vestrōs, atque postrēmum, lēctōrēs et lēctrīcēs, valēte!**

Name: _____ Section: _____ Date: _____

ABOUT THE AUTHOR

Paul T. Comeau studied Latin, Classical Greek, and French for more than four years at Joliette Seminary in Quebec. Part of a long military career, from which he retired in 1975, was spent teaching French and serving as the advisor for the Humanities and Social Sciences at the U.S. Air Force Academy. He received a B.A. in Liberal Arts from Assumption College, an M.A. in French Language and Literature and a Ph.D. in Romance Languages and Literatures, both from Princeton University. From 1975 to 1989, as Professor of French and Head of the Department of Foreign Languages at New Mexico State University, he established a two-year Latin program and taught that language for nine years, along with courses in French language, literature, and culture. A number of his articles have appeared in French literary journals, and his publications include a book of literary history, *Diehards and Innovators, the French Romantic Struggle: 1800–1830* (1988). He has received research grants from the National Endowment for the Humanities and the Canadian Embassy. Now retired as Professor Emeritus of French, he is past President of the New Mexico Chapter of the American Association of Teachers of French and a Life Member of the Modern Language Association of America.

ABOUT THE REVISION EDITOR

Richard A. LaFleur received the B.A. and M.A. in Latin from the University of Virginia and the Ph.D. in Classical Studies from Duke University. He has taught since 1972 at the University of Georgia, where he is currently Franklin Professor and (since 1980) Head of one of the largest Classics programs in North America. He has numerous publications in the fields of Latin language, literature, pedagogy, and teacher-preparation, including five recent books, *The Teaching of Latin in American Schools: A Profession in Crisis, Latin Poetry for the Beginning Student, Love and Transformation: An Ovid Reader, Latin for the 21st Century: From Concept to Classroom,* and the new, revised edition of *Wheelock's Latin,* by Frederic Wheelock. Professor LaFleur is also editor of *The Classical Outlook* (since 1979) and a past President of the American Classical League (1984–1986). He has been recipient of nearly half a million dollars in grants from the National Endowment for the Humanities and other agencies and of state, regional, and national awards for teaching and professional service, including, in 1984, the American Philological Association's award for Excellence in the Teaching of Classics.

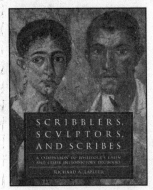

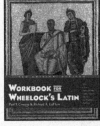